Moral Reasoning

moral reasoning

A Psychological-Philosophical Integration

William D. Boyce *and*
Larry Cyril Jensen

University of Nebraska Press

Lincoln and London

Library of Congress Cataloging in Publication Data

Boyce, William D   , 1952–
  Moral reasoning.

  Includes bibliographical references and index.
  1. Ethics.   2. Moral development.   I.   Jensen, Larry C., joint author.   II.   Title.
BJ45.B74   170   78–5935
ISBN 0–8032–0982–7

Thanks are due the following for permission to reprint copyrighted
material:

Lawrence Kohlberg and the Academic Press, Inc. for Kohlberg's Table 1: Definition of
Moral Stages, in Theodore Mischel, ed., *Cognitive Development and Epistemology* (New
York: Academic Press, Inc., 1971), pp. 164–65. Copyright 1971 by Academic Press, Inc.

William K. Frankena, *Ethics*, 2nd edition, © 1973, pp. 10–11. Adapted by permission of
Prentice-Hall, Inc., Englewood Cliffs, New Jersey.

From pp. 20, 21, 26–28, 30 and 40 in *Political Freedom* by Alexander Meiklejohn.
Copyright © 1948, 1960 by Harper & Row, Publishers, Inc. Reprinted by permission of
the publisher.

Table 17.1 "Parallel Structured Relations between Social Role-Taking and Moral Judg-
ment Stages," from *Social Cognitive Understanding: A Guide to Educational and Clinical
Practice* by Robert L. Selman in *Moral Development and Behavior: Theory, Research, and
Social Issues*, edited by Thomas Lickona. Copyright © 1976 by Holt, Rinehart and
Winston. Reprinted by permission of Holt, Rinehart and Winston.

Table 2.1 "The Six Moral Stages," from *Moral Stages and Moralization: The Cognitive-
Developmental Approach* by Lawrence Kohlberg, in *Moral Development and Behavior:
Theory, Research, and Social Issues*, edited by Thomas Lickona. Copyright © 1976 by
Holt, Rinehart and Winston. Reprinted by permission of Holt, Rinehart and Winston.

Excerpts from *The Grapes of Wrath* by John Steinbeck. Copyright 1939, renewed © 1967
by John Steinbeck. Reprinted by permission of The Viking Press and William Heine-
mann Ltd.

To our brothers, Sheldon and Julian

Contents

Preface

An author may have one of several goals in mind as he begins to write a book. He may attempt a purely scholarly treatise, intended exclusively for professionals in his field; he may write an applied book, directed primarily toward parents and educators; he may write a basic textbook which contains little new information for the professional but which comprises a good overview and introduction for beginners; or he may attempt to make a solid contribution to the professionals in his field and yet organize and write the book in such a way that it provides an introduction to some field (or fields) for relative beginners as well. It is this final goal we have had in mind. Our aim has been to contribute to the professional psychologist's study of moral development and at the same time to present the material in a way that will introduce the nonprofessional to a variety of issues surrounding the study of human morality.

In general, our goal is simply to show psychologists the relevance of moral philosophy to the study of moral development. It is an oddity of the psychological literature on children's moral development that so little reference is made to the contributions of moral philosophers. Surely, those who have been studying and debating issues of morality for over two thousand years have something to offer those of us who have been discussing related issues for about twenty. Yet to date no systematic attempt has been made to integrate the two disciplines and to show how psychologists stand to benefit from such an integration. The specific purpose of this book, therefore, is to document at least one area in which the contribution of moral philosophy to moral psychology can be particularly significant—the area concerning the issue of content and structure in moral thought. While this integration offers a solution to this particular problem in psychological research, it should also stimulate investigation into other ways that such an integration may be useful. That it should do so has been our primary hope in writing this book.

This psychological-philosophical integration lends itself to a broad discussion which makes the book appropriate for the nonprofessional as well as for the professional. The first part, an introduction to moral philosophy, will probably be as new to the psychologist as it will be to the undergraduate and graduate student. The second part presents an overview of the psychological literature on moral development; along with providing a fairly comprehensive introduction for the nonprofessional reader, it discusses several issues important to the professional psychologist and is arranged in a way that should be useful to him. The third part integrates the two disciplines, resulting in a proposed solution to the content-structure problem currently plaguing psychological research. The third part also presents many examples of moral reasoning from literature and law which should be interesting and useful to both the professional and nonprofessional reader. In view of this potentially wide audience, we have been very sensitive to the distinction between completeness and overkill. Particularly in the philosophy section we have attempted to achieve a balance between offending philosophers by omissions and numbing other readers with detail.

We owe a debt of gratitude to many for their assistance in the completion of this book: To Lilly Endowment, Inc. for funds which helped greatly in the preparation of the manuscript; to Blaine R. Porter, Dean of the College of Family Living at Brigham Young University, also for providing greatly appreciated funds; to Professors Robert Stahmann, Trevor McKee, and Terry Olson who directed the senior author's doctoral program (to which this work is related) in the Department of Child Development and Family Relationships at Brigham Young University; to Diane Morita and Sandra Longenecker who supervised the typing of various versions of the manuscript; to Nancy Jensen who offered expert editorial assistance; and to our families for providing support and encouragement throughout the project.

WILLIAM D. BOYCE
LARRY CYRIL JENSEN

· _Brigham Young University_

Moral Reasoning

Introduction:
Thinking About
Moral Problems

You are trapped. Six hundred feet underground in a mine shaft, you and three others are trapped with no food, no blankets, and no communication with the outside. A little water is available, but there is only a limited amount of precious air. The seriousness of the situation is immediately obvious. The time required for rescue operations would be at least seven days, and the available air supply would last all four men only four or five days. Two men would, however, survive on the available air for the time required to be rescued. However, the chances for two men to be rescued diminish each day that all four continue to breathe. If two men are to survive, two must immediately die.

You know, however, that this is not the full story, because many rescue operations take up to two weeks, some even longer. So even if the two survivors have enough air and water, what about food? With that realization, the thought that should never enter the mind of a civilized person enters yours! Will you be "civilized" when faced with the prospect of starvation?

To alter this situation somewhat, suppose that four men are confined in this underground prison: one is a thirty-five-year-old bachelor; another is a conscientious citizen with a wife and three children; the third is a twenty-three-year-old Nazi party member who is single; and the fourth is a moderately retarded middle-aged man with no family. The issue comes up for a vote: Do you decide to dispose of two men in order that two might live, or do you resolve that you will all die together? If you decide the former, which two shall die? What prospect faces the two survivors if the rescue

1

operation is not complete before starvation sets in? Are they justified in committing cannibalism to maintain life?

Such hypothetical moral dilemmas are disturbing. They force us not only to place ourselves in ugly situations but also to examine our thinking, and that can often be an anxiety-arousing experience. Moral dilemmas, perhaps better than anything else, force us to analyze ourselves—what we believe, what we desire, in short, what we are. Such situations also force us to make difficult decisions; they force us to ask, "Why? Why one decision rather than another? Why do I think that way? Is my moral reasoning justifiable? Am I really moral?"

The following dialogues concerning the dilemma of the trapped men illustrate this kind of searching:

A. I think that two of the men should be disposed of to allow at least two to survive.

B. Why? Isn't it wrong to kill?

A. Yes, but it's better that only two die rather than all four.

B. Why?

A. Because this way, at least two men will be able to go on and enjoy life and be happy. The other way, none of them will be able to.

B. Does that make it right to kill two people?

A. Under the circumstances, yes. That way, at least, some good and happiness will result. The other way, none will.

B. Does the rightness of happiness outweigh the wrongness of killing?

A. Yes.

B. Why do you believe that's true?

A. I don't know exactly. It just seems right. It's got to be right!

B. Okay, two members must be killed. Which two?

A. The Nazi and the mentally retarded man.

B. Why?

A. Because the Nazi is really a detriment to society and to the whole world, and the mentally retarded guy is of no particular use. He really has nothing to live for. The bachelor might get married and have children and live a happy life. The married man already has a family. He, of them all, has the greatest right to live. The mentally retarded one isn't capable of enjoying life like the others; he would miss life the least. Besides, he is of the least potential use to society.

B. You're concerned about happiness and the good of society? And the family man and the bachelor are the most capable of experiencing and causing happiness?

A. Yes. The people who will cause the greatest amount of happiness in the world, at least potentially, should be preserved.

B. Why?

A. Because happiness is the thing we should all be striving for. Happiness is what really counts in life.

B. What makes you think that?

A. It's self-evident. It's obvious.

B. What about cannibalism, if it came to that? Would you approve?

A. Under these circumstances, yes. The greatest happiness would result if those two men live. Whatever it takes for them to survive, then, is right.

A second conversation:

X. They all ought to die together.

Y. Why?

X. It's wrong to kill. If I were one of the ones to live, *I* couldn't kill the other two. I'd rather die myself. It's just wrong to kill.

Y. Suppose you were the man with the wife and three children. Wouldn't you want to live for the sake of your family?

X. Yes, but not enough to kill someone else. It's better that four men die than that two men kill the others. It's just wrong to kill.

Y. Why?

X. God has commanded "Thou shalt not kill." It would be breaking a commandment of God for two of the men to take the lives of the other two. If all four die, it is just an accident of nature, but there is no intent on the part of anyone to harm another. But, if two of the men purposely kill the other two to save their own necks, then that is murder, and it is wrong and immoral.

Y. Suppose that two members of the group are killed anyway. Is cannibalism justified as a means of keeping the two survivors alive?

X. No. That is a heathen practice and God would not allow it. It is wrong. I would rather die myself than to do such a thing.

These speakers not only provide different solutions to the dilemma in question but, more important, they illustrate contradictory types of thinking and even different types of justification for their thinking. The first person's concern is with the consequences of the action; if killing two members of the group produces the greatest amount of happiness, then it ought to be done, it is right. The second person reasons by considering the act itself, rather than its consequences. "Sure," he says, "happiness will result if two of the men are permitted to live, but that doesn't change the fact that it's wrong to kill. Regardless of the consequences, it's wrong to kill; it shouldn't be done."

The characters in these dialogues differ in their solutions because they differ, first, in what they believe to be morally good or important. One believes that happiness and productivity are ultimately important, while the other believes it is the wrongness of killing and the rightness of keeping of God's commandments that are most important. Obviously, such differences in moral opinions have a crucial affect on moral reasoning. Second, the characters disagree in their manner of justification, that is, in the way they justify what they think is important. How does one prove that what one believes *is* important and correct? The character in the first dialogue, when asked why he believes happiness is the ultimate end, answers that it is obvious. It is natural to believe that happiness is a good thing and should, therefore, be sought. The second character's answer differs considerably; when asked why it is wrong to kill, he replies that killing is forbidden by God and is therefore wrong. His thinking is that morality proceeds from a divine being whose commandments constitute the definition of morality; therefore, actions that fulfill those requirements are moral and those that do not are immoral. Killing contradicts those divine requirements and is thus immoral. This character, then, appeals to the dictates of a supernatural force or being as justification for his thinking, whereas the first appealed to his own intuition. Their methods of reasoning and justifying their ethical decisions differ, as do their ultimate decisions. As will be seen presently, the study of such points of discussion, reasoning and justification, characterizes the discipline of moral or ethical philosophy.[1] And it is to promote both an understanding and a particular use of the discipline of moral philosophy that this book has been written.

WHY STUDY MORAL PHILOSOPHY?

The question often arises, Why study moral theory? The very existence of this book implies that some people think it is important, but what is the explicit rationale for this book? Why is an understanding or a particular use of moral philosophy important? Two points, at least, must be made in response to these queries.

The Moral Nature of Human Situations

Taking the term *moral* to mean "pertaining to morality" and as opposed to the term *nonmoral* rather than to the term *immoral*, one must speak of all humans as moral beings. It is difficult to think of any sense in which the human situation can be considered separately from a moral situation; indeed, most would agree that the human situation *is* moral and that no line, logical or practical, can be drawn between the two.

But this has an important consequence. Anyone who sees his life in moral terms and who recognizes the moral implications of his behavior will certainly wish to be correct in his judgments and attitudes. Since he cannot avoid making moral choices, he should try to make sure that his moral choices are justifiable. This means that he must know the moral assumptions that underlie his specific choices and judgments.

For example, one may contend that pornography lies outside the realm of legislation and legal debate because one can freely choose whether or not to participate. One is not forced to enter a pornographic bookstore or to buy pornographic material; those who do not wish to do so can simply avoid such places. One may contend that, although indulging in pornography may be immoral, interfering with another's free choice to do so would be just as immoral or perhaps even more immoral.

The individual who employs this line of reasoning may believe that his moral assumption is that freedom of choice is good and ought to be preserved over all else. But suppose that we consider not pornography but gladiatorial contests. Suppose that an independent firm has opened a coliseum in your city and that every Saturday afternoon two men don the garb of gladiators and fight to the death. Now suppose that the two men participate only because they want to—there is a huge cash prize for the winner—and clearly that people attend only if they want to. One is completely free to avoid the spectacle altogether. Again, the issue is one of free choice, but in this case is it morally wrong to subject the issue to legislation and legal debate? Many who say yes when pornography is at issue say no when the issue is gladiatorial combat. Suddenly other moral concerns become important. Some contend that in the case of gladiatorial combat freedom from debasing environmental influence is crucial. Others contend that some people must be protected from themselves; when human life is in danger there is simply too much at stake to justify inaction in the name of freedom of choice. But those who advance such arguments must see how they complicate their previous position on pornography—for similar arguments can be advanced there: e.g., easily accessible pornography also creates a debasing, harmful environment,[2] and although pornography does not kill it causes harm of a different, but perhaps just as serious, nature to the individual who indulges. Should we not, then, legislate against pornography as well as against gladiatorial combat? Suddenly, it is seen that freedom of choice is not the all-encompassing moral assumption it was first thought to be. To justify subjecting one issue and not the other to legislation one must employ other moral assumptions which one holds—freedom of choice alone will not suffice. This is not to say that the individual will be forced to change his mind. But it is to say that he will often be forced to confess that he acted hastily and that the issue is, indeed, more complicated than he first thought. The point is clear: if one wishes to insure the acceptability of specific moral judgments and choices, then he must be quite aware of all the moral assumptions that underlie them, and, insofar as possible, be assured of their correctness as well. Because the study of moral reasoning assists in this process, it can be extremely useful to the person who is willing to undertake it.

Content and Structure of Moral Thought

The primary rationale for the study of moral philosophy presented in this book arises out of a need in psychology. In recent psychological research on moral development a distinction has been drawn between the *content* and the *structure* of moral thought. Briefly, content refers to what an individual believes while structure refers to the cognitive basis of those attitudes and beliefs. While this is a useful and, as will be shown in a later chapter, even crucial distinction, most psychological research to date has focused on the structure of moral thought to the exclusion of the content. However, it is important for the explanatory and predictive purposes of psychological research and theory that the content of individuals' moral beliefs be studied as well. The primary purpose of this book, therefore, is to apply the ideas of moral philosophy about content to the psychological study of moral development. The resulting schema should be used in conjunction with those psychological methods (especially Kohlberg's) that have been designed to explain structure. The results, we hope, will be more and better research on the content of moral reasoning, and a better understanding of the entire process of moral thought.

THE PLAN OF THE BOOK

The first section of this book examines moral philosophy, or the contribution that philosophers have made to the study of moral reasoning. The second section will present the psychological approach to this subject. Finally, the third section will illustrate how the achievements of philosophers and psychologists can be combined to make a contribution to psychological research. Such an interdisciplinary approach will help achieve two goals of the book. First, a greater general understanding of moral reasoning will be reached if both, rather than just one, of these disciplines are used. Second, one can then see how the two disciplines can be integrated, making possible new contributions to the study of moral reasoning.

NORMATIVE AND METAETHICS

A brief overview of ethics, or moral philosophy, will help to introduce the chapters that follow.

The discipline of ethics is conveniently divided into two major categories: normative ethics and metaethics. Normative ethics refers to those moral assumptions or statements that are evaluative; they are one's basic, underlying assumptions about what is good, bad, right, and wrong. Usually, these judgments are implicit and can be explicitly exposed only by logical extension. This logic begins with a specific evaluation, proceeds to a more general maxim, and finally reaches a normative statement (1). For example:

(a) *Specific act:* We really ought to do away with Mom. (She's in so much pain.)

(b) *Maxim:* People who are in great pain ought to be done away with. Life is not worth living when one is always in pain.

(c) *Normative statement:* Pain is bad and ought to be avoided; pleasure is good and ought to be sought.

The final statement above, (c), is the moral assumption upon which the person's more specific judgments are based, his underlying normative moral stance. Likewise, the normative statements for the dialogues above are, respectively: "Happiness is the thing we should all be striving for—happiness is what really counts in life," and "It is wrong to break God's commandments." The specific evaluations each character made were built on the basis of these first principles, or moral assumptions, which constitute the essential feature of what is meant by "moral reasoning."

Metaethics is concerned with the justification of one's basic moral assumptions or normative stance. Metaethics is not a prescriptive system or code of rules like normative ethics; it is essentially analytical and epistemological. Here the questions asked are: How does one justify what he thinks is important or right? How does one know what *is* right? The metaethical issue is raised as soon as a first principle is challenged. The initial series of "whys" in our dialogues serve only to reach a person's normative first principles. After these are explicitly stated, the next "why" is a metaethical one—this query asks for justification of the normative principles. In the first dialogue, intuition or instinct is the metaethical basis for the normative judgment that happiness is the goal of existence; the speaker appeals to his intuition to justify that belief. On the other hand, the second character uses the concept of a supernatural being to justify his normative judgment that killing is wrong. Thus, the characters not only disagree in their normative stands but also in the way they justify them.

Another important concern of metaethics is linguistic or conceptual; that is, exactly what is meant by the terms *good, bad, right*, and *wrong*? What *is* a moral judgment? Although both of these questions, epistemological and linguistic, are important, for present purposes it is the question of justification that is primary, and conceptual definition is important primarily as a means for understanding justifications.[3]

Not all authors clearly distinguish between normative and metaethics because, in practice, they are quite closely related. The reason for distinguishing between them here, however, is that if these two elements are so intimately related, should we not ask *how* they are related? To determine this, we must first distinguish between them, and then, understanding both normative ethics and metaethics in their component parts, we can understand their influence on each other and still better understand the entire process of moral reasoning. This will lay a foundation for the discussion of the psychological literature that follows.

NOTES

1. Common usage will be followed for the terms morality and ethics and their derivatives. The terms will often be used interchangeably in the sense that they both refer to right conduct, but we will use morality as the broader and stronger term. Context will determine when ethics is used simply as reference to the academic discipline of the study of morals.

2. See p. 256 of this book where Alexander Bickel makes this kind of argument.

3. A third category called "descriptive ethics" could also be added to these two main divisions. It refers exclusively to the specific judgments, decisions, and actions of individuals in relation to particular events (e.g., the judgment "pornography is bad"). These particular value judgments and decisions are indicative of the underlying normative ethics, although this underlying value system is often only implicit. For instance, in the example cited in the discussion of normative ethics, item (*a*), "We really ought to do away with Mom," is a descriptive statement. Descriptive ethics is assumed in the preceding discussion and usually is considered not only to be congruent with the normative ethics but also the most effective means of discovering the normative base of a person's ethics. Wilfrid Sellars comments: "The best way of finding out what people's attitudes really are is to watch what they do and say in concrete situations, and by using the 'hypothetico-deductive method,' determine what small number of abstract principles would lead to the concrete evaluations actually made and acted on in the culture in question. . ." (1, p. 3).

I

THE PHILOSOPHER
AND MORAL REASONING

1 / Normative Ethics I: Theories of Value and Egoism

In normative ethics, a distinction is made between statements of value and statements of obligation; the first deal with "good" and the second with "right." That is, in some moral judgments we speak of good acts, evil motives, corrupt politicians, and so forth. In others we speak of our duty, what we ought to do, what actions are right, and so on. The former (usually concerning persons, characteristics, motives, intentions, etc.) are judgments of moral value, and the latter (usually concerning acts) are judgments of moral obligation (5). (To further clarify this distinction, refer to table 1.)

This chapter will introduce the main theories of value and one theory of obligation, namely, egoism. Chapters two and three will describe the remaining theories of obligation. The various criticisms that have been directed against normative theories are not discussed because the purpose of this book is to explain the various ethical positions, not to evaluate them. A reasonably complete understanding of the various theories will facilitate an understanding of the entire process of moral reasoning.

NORMATIVE VALUE—THE GOOD

The broadest division in normative value theory is between those who speak of intrinsic goodness and those who deny such goodness, claiming that anything good is only instrumentally good.

13

TABLE 1. NORMATIVE ETHICS: JUDGMENTS OF VALUE AND OBLIGATION

A. Judgments of moral *value* (good and bad)
  1. Particular
      a) My grandfather was a good man.
      b) Xavier was a saint.
      c) Her character is admirable.
      d) His was a good motive.
  2. General
      a) Benevolence is a virtue.
      b) Jealousy is an ignoble motive.
      c) The ideally good man does not drink or smoke.
B. Judgments of moral *obligation* (right and wrong)
  1. Particular
      a) I ought not to escape from prison now.
      b) You should become a missionary.
      c) What he did was wrong.
  2. General
      a) We ought to keep our agreements.
      b) Love is the fulfillment of moral law.
      c) All men have a right to freedom.

Source: Adapted from 5, pp. 10–11.

Instrumental Value

Those who reject the existence of intrinsic goodness usually argue that there is no real distinction between ends and means. An end, it is said, would necessarily have to be intrinsically good—good in and of itself—to be considered an end, but there can be nothing intrinsically good; there are only various instrumental goods which lead to *perceived* ends. These perceived ends, then, in reality turn out to be means to other perceived ends, and on and on ad infinitum. There is no intrinsically good thing and no ultimate end. John Dewey makes this argument.

Means are means; they are intermediates, middle terms. To grasp this fact is to have done with the ordinary dualism of means and ends. The "end" is merely a series of acts viewed at a remote stage; and a means is merely the series viewed at an earlier one.

Means and ends are two names for the same reality. The terms denote not a division in reality but a distinction in judgment. The first or earliest means is the most important end to discover. . . .

Not the end—in the singular—justifies the means; for there is no such thing as the single all-important end. [4, pp. 34–35, 229; quoted in 6, pp. 129–30]

Dewey is arguing that, because an end is really only a remote means, there is no ultimate end and no intrinsically good thing.

Intrinsic Value

More common among moral philosophers than instrumentalism is the view that traits or experiences can be good in and of themselves; their goodness is not related to consequences or to any other values— separately and singly, apart from everything else, they are good. In arguing for happiness as the only intrinsically good thing, Aristotle supplies the conditions to be fulfilled by anything said to be intrinsically good.

The final good is thought to be self-sufficient. . . . the self-sufficient we now define as that which when isolated makes life desirable and lacking in nothing; and such we think happiness to be; and further we think it most desirable of all things, without being counted as one good among others—if it were so counted it would clearly be made more desirable by the addition of even the least of goods. . . . Happiness, then, is something final and self-sufficient, and is the end of action. [1, p. 942]

Aristotle's observations require that anything said to be intrinsically good must be final and self-sufficient; that is, it must be good even if it were the only thing that existed, it must be good irrespective of any consequences it may have, and it must not be able to be improved upon by the addition of any other experiences, qualities, or goods. Anything that laid claim to intrinsic goodness would fulfill these conditions.

Monism

Philosophical thought about the nature of such intrinsic goodness falls into two categories, monism and pluralism. The monist asserts that only one thing is intrinsically good, and the pluralist asserts that two or more things are intrinsically good. Clearly, in claiming that happiness is the only ultimate intrinsic good, Aristotle is a monist. For him happiness is entirely self-sufficient and "lacking in nothing." Immanuel Kant claimed the same status for "good will" (9), which he defines as a good motive strenuously and seriously applied toward accomplishment; it is the only thing good in itself or "good without qualification."

Historically, the most popular form of monism is hedonism, or pleasure seeking. This approach can be best identified by stating its two main propositions:

(*a*) Pleasure is intrinsically good.

(*b*) Nothing other than pleasure is intrinsically good.

Over the centuries philosophers have offered widely varying opinions about how pleasure is to be used in the solution of moral questions. For instance, in the third century B.C., the philosopher Epicurus became the champion of hedonistic ethics. Though he based his philosophy on pleasure, he taught that some pleasures, such as intellect and imagination, are higher than others, such as physical sensation. In the early nineteenth century, however, the English political philosopher Jeremy Bentham rejected the distinction between higher and lower pleasures. He emphasized quantity of pleasure alone, disregarding the kind of pleasure. John Stuart Mill, in the later nineteenth century, returned to an essentially Epicurean philosophy that distinguished between kinds or qualities of pleasure.

A convenient distinction in moral philosophy, therefore, is made between "quantitative" and "qualitative" hedonists. Bentham (3) is the best example of a quantitative hedonist. He is frequently quoted as saying, "Quantity of pleasure being equal, pushpin is as good as poetry" (5, p. 84), and although this quotation is not perfectly accurate (see 17, p. 29) the impression it creates is. For Bentham pleasure is all of one kind, so measures of quantity are all that are available in determining the value of a given pleasure. The quantitative measures Bentham proposes are (*a*) intensity, (*b*) duration (*c*) certainty, (*d*) propinquity, (*e*) fecundity, or the chance of being followed by sensations of the same kind, (*f*) purity, or the chance of not being followed by sensations of the opposite kind, and (*g*) extent, or the number of people to whom the pleasure extends. These seven measures constitute the so-called hedonistic calculus and are used to estimate the value of a given pleasure or pain. It will be noticed that no measure of kind or quality of pleasure (or pain) is included in Bentham's calculus; all measures are quantitative.

As already mentioned, John Stuart Mill (10, 11), although a disciple of Bentham, offers a contrasting conception of hedonism. He points out that Bentham's conception recognizes no differences between a human being and a lower animal; in whichever state one experiences the greater pleasure, the greater preference is to be found. Thus, to be a happy pig would be preferable to being a miserable human being. In rejecting this conclusion, and the rationale behind it, Mill argues:

Few human creatures would consent to be changed into any of the lower animals for a promise of the fullest allowance of a beast's pleasures. . . . It is better to be a human being dissatisfied than a pig satisfied; better to be Socrates dissatisfied than a fool satisfied.

. . . There is no known Epicurean theory of life which does not assign to the pleasures of the intellect, of the feelings and imagination, and of the moral sentiments, a much higher value of pleasures than to those of mere sensation. [11, pp. 19–20, 18][1]

Because Mill returns to this Epicurean philosophy of hedonism, in which clear emphasis is placed upon quality rather than mere quantity of pleasure, he and those like him may be spoken of as qualitative hedonists.

In order to solve the problem of how quality is to be measured Mill introduces the concept of the "hedonic expert"—one who is acquainted with both (or all) types of pleasures in question and can thus judge their quality and decide between (or among) them. In stating his general philosophy, as well as that of the hedonic expert, Mill observes:

The only true or definite rule of conduct or standard of morality is the greatest happiness [pleasure], but there is needed first a philosophical estimate of happiness. Quality as well as quantity of happiness is to be considered, less of a higher kind is preferable to more of a lower. The test of quality is the preference given by those who are acquainted with both. Socrates would rather choose to be Socrates dissatisfied than to be a pig satisfied. The pig probably would not, but then the pig knows only one side of the question; Socrates knows both. [10, p. 343]

In this way Mill attempts to establish qualitative hedonism as a practical, as well as a theoretical, alternative to Bentham's quantitative hedonism.

In its emphasis on quantity, quantitative hedonism has become most closely associated with pursuit of physical pleasures (presumably because it is in this realm that quantity is most easily increased or multiplied), while qualitative hedonism has become most closely associated with pursuit of mental or spiritual pleasures (presumably because of their inherently higher quality). This difference is generally the most helpful distinguishing feature between the two hedonistic theories.

Pluralism

Although these two hedonistic theories differ in their accounts of pleasure, they are both monistic inasmuch as they both claim pleasure to be the only intrinsically good thing. Opposed to both of these theories are pluralistic theories—those that affirm the existence of more than one intrinsic good. Pluralists contend that the very condition of intrinsicalness precludes fulfillment by only one thing. For although Aristotle proclaims that happiness is the only intrinsic good, is it not improved upon by some additions, perhaps, for instance, knowledge? If so, then happiness does not fulfill the condition of singular intrinsic goodness, for it can be improved upon by the addition of something else. The pluralist will insist this is always the case; there is no single good which cannot be improved upon by the addition of something else. Therefore, the task is to compile a comprehensive list of goods which, when combined, make up "the good."

Several philosophers have attempted this, among them Plato. Plato argues in the *Philebus* (19) that the good life is a "mixed" life—it is balanced among several elements, all of which are necessary to make up the good. In order, Plato lists these elements:

(*a*) Measure, moderation, fitness (that which is "in place")
(*b*) Proportion, beauty, completeness
(*c*) Intelligence and wisdom
(*d*) Sciences, arts, and true opinion (or true convictions)
(*e*) Pure pleasures of the soul

It will be noticed that Plato includes a form of qualitative hedonism in his prescription, but it is by no means the only element of the good life. Indeed it is placed last among those elements considered necessary for the good life. Clearly, Plato was neither a monist nor much of a hedonist.

A more recent example of pluralism is the theory proposed by W. D. Ross. Ross (16) affirms the intrinsic goodness of four things: (*a*) virtuous disposition and action, (*b*) knowledge, (*c*) pleasure, and (*d*) the just apportionment of pleasure to the virtuous. Ross's arguments for these points are ultimately based on their self-evidence (a meta-ethical issue to be discussed in chapter four). For instance, he argues for the goodness of virtuous disposition and action by saying, essentially, that it is simply self-evident that a universe with all virtuous people is preferable to a world with all vicious people—it follows that virtue is an intrinsic good. It is something which, when added to some other good, makes that other good even better or more desirable. By arguing in this way, Ross settles on his four basic elements which, when combined, make up the total good.

To summarize: while monists assert the intrinsic goodness of only one thing—only one thing is final and self-sufficient and cannot be improved upon—pluralists assert there must be more than one intrinsically good thing and that these things combined constitute that good which is entirely self-sufficient. Historically, the most important form monism has taken is that of hedonism, qualitative or quantitative, whereas pluralism has taken many forms. Generally, the forms are guided by the question: what ingredients, when added to a given state of affairs, will make that state better or more desirable?

Nonhedonism

A final category of intrinsic value, and one that cuts across the distinction between monism and pluralism, is the category of non-hedonism. Hedonism proposes that pleasure and only pleasure is intrinsically good; nonhedonism simply denies this concept. If pleasure is an intrinsic good, it is not the *only* intrinsic good. Clearly, this definition gives nonhedonism wide latitude, for one may mean that:

(*a*) pleasure is not intrinsically good, but some one other thing is,
(*b*) pleasure is not intrinsically good, but some other things are, or
(*c*) pleasure is intrinsically good, but it is not the only intrinsic good.

Thus, a nonhedonist may be a monist as in (*b*), or he may be a pluralist as in (*b*) and (*c*).

Clearly, all pluralists are nonhedonists. Philosophers such as Plato and Ross are, by virtue of their pluralism, also nonhedonists.

Similarly, however, many monists are also nonhedonists. Aristotle (1) is a monist, claiming happiness to be the only intrinsic good, and yet he is a nonhedonist in distinguishing between happiness and pleasure. Likewise, Nietzsche's monistic value of power as good is nonhedonistic. He states: "What is good? Everything that heightens the feeling of power in man, the will to power, power itself. What is bad? Everything that is born of weakness" (12, p. 570).[2] Kant's assertion that a "good will" is the only thing that is good without qualification is also an example of monistic nonhedonism.

Basic Categories of Normative Value

The most useful categories of intrinsic value are (a) qualitative hedonism, (b) quantitative hedonism, and (c) nonhedonism, because these three categories are comprehensive, accounting for all types of monism and pluralism, and yet are specific enough to convey definite meaning. Furthermore, they subsume all of the values of which instrumentalists speak, allowing them to use these broad categories with the simple qualification that they are not meant as ultimate intrinsic goods but as instrumental goods only. These categories will therefore be used henceforth in this book to specify various value theories and to assist in the definition of moral theories of obligation.

NORMATIVE OBLIGATION—THE RIGHT

Whereas normative value theory is concerned with the good, theories of normative obligation are concerned with the right. Given that one knows what is good and to be sought in life (whether it is pleasure or freedom or power, etc.), the question still remains, What makes particular actions morally right or obligatory? What is it about an act that makes one say it ought or it ought not to be performed? As opposed to the questions of normative value, these are the questions of normative obligation.

Theories of normative obligation are either teleological or deontological. As will presently be seen, revolving around this division is one of the most fundamental moral issues—the argument about the means versus the end. The teleological and deontological categories can each be dissected into smaller, more precise units, however, and discussion of these is necessary for a full understanding of the larger categories and thus of the entire moral reasoning process. The basic elements of teleological moral thought will be discussed first.

Teleology

The term *teleology* implies direction toward a goal or toward some specific end-state. In ethics the term is very appropriate, for all teleological ethical theories argue that a given act is morally right or obligatory insofar as it tends to produce some desired end. The teleologist first has a definition of the good, whether it be some form of quantitative hedonism, qualitative hedonism, or nonhedonism, and then defines as morally right those acts which lead to that end. Those acts which impede it are morally wrong. Moreover, the rightness of an act depends solely on its consequences.

In the first dialogue about the trapped miners in the Introduction, speaker A apparently holds to this type of theory. From his point of view, disposing of two members is right because such killing would produce the most favorable consequences. Furthermore, by similar reasoning, he decides which two men ought to be allowed to live—the bachelor and the family man. All of his decisions are based on the projected consequences of the act: would it produce happiness or not? This emphasis upon consequences is the essence of teleological theories.

Egoism

One ethical theory that is subsumed under the teleological heading is egoism. The ethical egoist is one who determines the moral rightness of an act specifically in terms of its consequences for himself; his creed is, "do that which promotes the greatest good for oneself." The theory is clearly a form of teleology; it is directed toward promoting some end, and an act is considered morally right or wrong depending on its ability to produce that end. It is called "egoism" because the end which is sought is one's own good.

Max Stirner. Ethical egoism may take several forms. One of the most extreme is exemplified by Max Stirner, a mid-nineteenth-century German philosopher. Although virtually none of the introductory ethics books discusses Stirner, he is of interest because of his passionate insistence on egoism and his consequent diatribe against democracy (as well as communism and socialism). In speaking of human liberty, for instance, Stirner remarks, "I do not want the liberty of men, nor their equality; I want only *my* power over them, I want to make them my property, *material for enjoyment*" (18, p. 11).

Stirner describes the metaphysical identity of what he calls "The Unique One." Briefly, this is an individual who is absolutely solitary and independent of others. Paterson (13) describes this aspect of Stirner's thought:

> The total egoism of The Unique One consists in this: that his subjectivity is affirmed by denying the subjectivity of others, by treating other persons as if they were simply natural phenomena to be studied and manipulated without regard to their existential claims as persons—in short, by reducing others to the status of *objects*. . . . The egoist's conduct is not governed by the interests or wishes of others, except in so far as some consideration of these is found to be technically advantageous; the interests or wishes of others may require to be taken into account as a datum on which his managerial decisions need to be based, and a studied deference to the feelings of others may be found to facilitate the egoist's own purposes. But in themselves, for their own sakes, the needs and interests of others count for nothing in his eyes. [13, p. 257]

And Stirner himself says of egoism: "To the egoist nothing is high enough for him to humble himself before it, nothing so independent that he would live for love of it, nothing so sacred that he would sacrifice himself to it. The egoist's love rises in selfishness, flows in the bed of selfishness, and empties into selfishness again." (13, p. 259).

Stirner's egoism and his consequent views on human relationships lead to extreme positions regarding governments and political philosophy. In one place Stirner says, "I think nothing of Nature, men and their laws, human society and its love, and I sever every general connection with it" (13, p. 255), and in another he says: "Let us therefore not aspire to community, but to *onesidedness*. Let us not seek the most comprehensive commune, 'human society,' but let us seek in others only means and organs which we may use as our property! . . . No one is *my equal*, but I regard him, equally with all other beings, as my property" (18, p. 214).

Clearly Stirner's ethical philosophy is a form of egoism.[3] The Unique One (an epithet which Stirner claimed for himself) admits the existence of others, but he denies others' corresponding subjectivity and uniqueness. In this ethical philosophy, therefore, all energy is directed toward realizing oneself as The Unique One and then fulfilling one's own needs and interests—at the expense of others if necessary.

Enlightened egoism. Not all types of egoism, however, take the form represented by Stirner. An individual may be motivated egoistically—for his own advantage—and yet do nothing in our ordinary way of talking that is selfish or narcissistic, or even indifferent. It may simply be that he considers it to be in his own long-range interests to be kind, considerate, honest, helpful, and so on. Indeed, ethical egoism does not require that one not help others when so helping supports one's own interests. For example, if one helps a neighbor, he will be more likely to help in return; if one gives liberally to charity, others will respond with high praise and social esteem; if one helps a professor correct papers, the professor will likely help one get into graduate school. In all these cases the interests of the involved parties overlap so that one may very effectively pursue one's own interests by the very means of helping others pursue theirs—and this is entirely consistent with ethical egoism. All that ethical egoism denies is that one should do these things when it is not in one's own interests to do so.

Thus, in the name of his own interests the egoist could do many things that are not considered selfish or unkind. For instance, a Christian may be attracted by the ultimate union he envisions with God and thus be motivated to do those things he has been told will help him achieve that union. He attends church, avoids sexual improprieties, is kind and charitable, diligent, and abides by the other requirements of his moral code—not because each of these things is considered morally right in itself or because they are beneficial to others, but because if observed they will enable him to achieve the sublime union he desires. In his normal everyday actions this individual will not be seen as selfish or indifferent but instead is likely to be looked up to and considered a pillar of the community. Similarly, the individual who desires only to be a pillar of the community, or at least to be seen as such, may do all the things others consider exemplary to gain their approval, but his motivation is egoistic.

Perhaps Plato is the best example of this "enlightened egoism." Plato's discussion of the topic occurs in *The Republic*; Glaucon and Adeinonantus challenge Socrates to refute the Sophistic theory of morality, to prove that justice is better or more advantageous than injustice, even apart from the benefits of reputation and the like that accrue to one who performs the usual moral actions. Plato's task is to show that justice does not in fact result in a loss to the individual but rather results in his advantage. In the following excerpt from *The Republic* Socrates likens an individual to a state and takes tyranny to be the epitome of injustice—and then reaches his conclusions.

"Beginning with the State," I replied, "would you say that a city which is governed by a tyrant is free or enslaved?"

"No city," he said, "can be more completely enslaved."

"And yet, as you see, there are freemen as well as masters in such a State?"

"Yes," he said, "I see that there are a few; but the people, speaking generally, and the best of them are miserably degraded and enslaved."

"Then if the man is like the State," I said, "Must not the same rule prevail? his soul is full of meanness and vulgarity—the best elements in him are enslaved; and there is a small ruling part, which is also the worst and maddest."

"Inevitably."

"And would you say that the soul of such a one is the soul of a freeman, or of a slave?"

"He has the soul of a slave, in my opinion."

"And the State which is enslaved under a tyrant is utterly incapable of acting voluntarily?"

"Utterly incapable."

"And also the soul which is under a tyrant (I am speaking of the soul taken as a whole) is least capable of doing what she desires; there is a gadfly which goads her, and she is full of trouble and remorse?"

"Certainly."

"And is the city which is under a tyrant rich or poor?"

"Poor."

"And the tyrannical soul must be always poor and insatiable?"

"True."

"And must not such a State and such a man be always full of fear?"

"Yes, indeed."

"Is there any State in which you will find more of lamentation and sorrow and groaning and pain?"

"Certainly not."

"And is there any man in whom you will find more of this sort of misery than in the tyrannical man, who is in a fury of passions and desires?"

"Impossible."

"Reflecting upon these and similar evils, you held the tyrannical State to be the most miserable of States?"

"And I was right," he said.

"Certainly," I said. "And when you see the same evils in the tyrannical man, what do you say of him?"

"I say that he is by far the most miserable of all men." . . .

"He who is the real tyrant, whatever men may think, is the real slave, and is obliged to practice the greatest adulation and servility, and to be the flatterer of the vilest of mankind. He has desires which he is utterly unable to satisfy, and has more wants than anyone, and is truly poor, if you know how to inspect the whole soul of him: all his life long he is beset with fear and is full of convulsions and distractions, even as the State which he resembles: and surely the resemblance holds?"

"Very true," he said.

"Moreover, as we were saying before, he grows worse from having power: he becomes and is of necessity more jealous, more faithless, more unjust, more friendless, more impious, than he was at first; he is the purveyor and cherisher of every sort of vice, and the consequence is that he is supremely miserable, and that he makes everybody else as miserable as himself."

"No man of any sense will dispute your words."

Then, having proved his point, Socrates triumphantly asks:

"Need we hire a herald, or shall I announce that the son of Ariston (the best) has decided that the best and Justest is also the happiest, and that this is he who is the most royal man and king over himself; and that the worst and most unjust man is also the most miserable, and that this is he who being the greatest tyrant of himself is also the greatest tyrant of his State?" [14, pp. 463–64, 466, 467]

The notable quality of Plato's approach to this problem, which Prichard (15) is exercised to point out, is that he answers the Sophists on their own terms. Plato accepts without qualification the assumption that just acts must be advantageous to the individual and that it is their very advantageousness that makes those acts just.[4] Thus, Plato's thought fits neatly into the category of egoism as an ethical philosophy, for his entire defense of the commonly held moral standards is based on their utility in providing advantages, i. e., happiness, for oneself.

Such reasoning is clearly a form of egoism but, in contrast to those forms typified by philosophers like Stirner (who are generally considered rather crude), this is often called "enlightened" egoism. Much of the motivation we see and experience is, indeed, of this type. Hospers (8) points out the pervasiveness of enlightened egoism.

The most usual answer, and the most popular answer, to the question "Why should we do right acts?" is "Because it *pays* to do so—because it will, later if not immediately, turn out to be *to our interest* to do so." This motive is appealed to so constantly that we are hardly aware of it. We are told to be honest, but not because honesty is a good thing: we are told that "Honesty pays" and "Honesty is the best *policy*"—the best policy, of course, being the one that most benefits us in the long run. "Be helpful to people when they need help, for then they'll help you when you need it." "Drive safely—the life you save may be your own"—the implication being that if the life you save were *not* your own you need not be so anxious to drive safely. Even Biblical commands often include such an appeal: "Cast thy bread upon the waters and it shall return to thee after many days." But suppose it didn't return to you, should you still cast it upon the waters? The president of a large American corporation, who gives two hundred fifty thousand dollars every year to cancer research, was asked why he did so, and he replied, "It costs more than a yacht, but I have more fun out of it." Here at any rate is an unabashedly egoistic motive. Not every such appeal to morality is as crudely egoistic. "Be helpful to others, for if you do they'll help you in turn" is egoistic in a perfectly straightforward way. "Be helpful to others, for it will give you peace of mind" is perhaps less crudely egoistic, but it is egoistic none the less. If you are to be helpful because it will give you peace of mind, the implication still is that if being helpful did *not* give you peace of mind, there would be no obligation to be so. [8, p. 175]

This excellent statement of enlightened egoism helps show that indeed this type of thinking is at the heart of Plato's defense of the usual moral actions.

Two further points about ethical egoism need to be made. First, in setting forth his philosophy, the ethical egoist may be saying one of two things: one, "I, and only I, ought to do what will further my own self-interests," or two, "Each person ought to do what will further his own self-interests." Plato and, less obviously, Stirner both advocate a philosophy of the second type. The same is also true of other egoists such as Epicurus (2) and Hobbes (7).

Stirner and Plato. This "everyone" approach to ethical egoism, however, has an interesting consequence: Stirner's philosophy becomes entirely and conspicuously inconsistent, while Plato's philosophy does not—it remains consistent and viable. That Stirner's egoism so disintegrates is easily seen. For if The Unique One categorically denies the subjectivity of others, is indifferent toward them, and is willing to be vicious, brutal, and deceitful in dealing with them, how can he at the same time wish them likewise to become Unique Ones and thus adopt the same attitudes toward him? But this is precisely what Stirner does. Speaking specifically of Stirner's exhortations to others to overcome their narrow morality, Paterson concludes: "In exhorting others to become, like himself, invincible to moral strictures and appeals, The Unique One is pointlessly relinquishing an instrument of exploitation which was ready to his hand, and is thereby showing himself to be less than the total egoist which he claims to be" (13, pp. 266–67). In holding this "everyone" view of egoism, Stirner is obviously inconsistent.

The same is not true of Plato's philosophy, however. Plato can say that all people ought to do what will further their own self-interest and not be committing them to mutually self-defeating action because each person's self-interest, as defined by Plato, does not entail obstructing or destroying another's. This introduces the final point to be made about egoism: egoists' definitions of the good (or of self-interest) differ. It is this difference that separates Stirner and Plato. For Stirner self-interest or the good is defined in terms of supreme independence—independence typified by the power to deny others their humanity and to treat them insensitively as objects or property. If this is the definition of self-interest, then one cannot avoid obstructing another's pursuit of his interests. But, because Plato defines the good or self-interest as happiness or "the mixed life" and claims that this self-interest is achieved by performing the usual moral acts—payment of debts, honesty, kindness, and so on—Platonic philosophy is free of this inconsistency. The Platonist can pursue his own self-interest without in any way impeding others' similar pursuits. Clearly, then, a crucial difference among ethical egoists is their respective definitions of good, or their theories of moral value.

Egoism and Theories of Value

Here it is useful to return to the three categories of good adopted in the previous section: qualitative hedonism, quantitative hedonism, and nonhedonism. An egoist may define his good in any of these three ways; his choice will profoundly affect the form his egoism ultimately takes. Thus, to understand a given egoist or to develop one's own egoistic philosophy one must have a clear conception of what, in each case, is meant by self-interest, or the good.

For example, the following generalizations can be made about the trapped miners in the Introduction. In making his decision, the quantitative hedonistic egoist would judge matters on the basis of the relative amounts of pleasure available to him. He would certainly insist that he be one of those to live, for dying, presumably, would not be pleasurable. The qualitative hedonistic egoist, on the other hand, would include quality of pleasure in his considerations and would balance the relative moral values, perhaps, of the spiritual pleasure to be gained from knowledge of his noble self-sacrifice against the combined physical and spiritual pleasures to be gained if he prolonged his life. Finally, the nonhedonistic egoist might range from Plato to Stirner in his deliberations. If, like Stirner, he values independence and power over others, he would certainly insist that he be one to live. Suppose, however, that he includes in his definition of the good, honor and a good reputation—both of which he would likely receive for his self-sacrifice. In this case it is possible that he would proudly lay down his life—but again, for his own ultimate good. The important point is that in all three cases the individual is egoistically motivated. His behavior differs according to his definition of good and, perhaps, whether he has his short- or long-term interests at heart, but his moral decisions are entirely self-oriented. This is the essence of egoistic theories.

Summary

To this point teleology has been identified as a category of strictly end-oriented reasoning, the end being either qualitative hedonism, quantitative hedonism, or nonhedonism. As a subset of teleology, egoism is the view that one ought to seek one of those ends exclusively for himself. Figure 1 depicts the relationship of these elements with one another:

FIGURE 1. TELEOLOGY—EGOISTIC ELEMENT

	Egoism	
Qualitative Hedonism	Quantitative Hedonism	Nonhedonism

Egoism may be directed toward any one of three definitions of the good and it is always teleological.

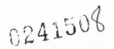

NOTES

1. See 2, pp. 87–91, for statements by Epicurus himself corroborating Mill's interpretation of his philosophy.

2. Nietzsche did not limit his meaning of *power* to "authority," but included all strengths and "excellences" of the human spirit.

3. Paterson (13) denies that Stirner's egoism is a moral philosophy. He contends that Stirner was a complete amoralist and his philosophy "a repudiation of any and every moral imperative" (p. 264). However, in Stirner's philosophy the "egoistic self" itself becomes an absolute ideal of a rather moral nature. Thus, the point that Stirner repudiates the usual moral imperatives and claims to repudiate the very concept of morality itself does not negate the fact that he proclaimed his own theory of the egoistic self, or The Unique One, in morally relevant ways. Thus, even if he did so only unwittingly, Stirner did, it seems, end up propounding a moral philosophy of his own.

4. Prichard (15) substantiates this point.

2 / Normative Ethics II: Utilitarianism

A second ethical theory that is subsumed under the general heading of teleology and is opposed to ethical egoism is ethical universalism, commonly called utilitarianism. Whereas the egoist asks, "What will maximize my own good or further my own self-interests?" the utilitarian asks, simply, "What will maximize the good?" The thesis of the utilitarian is that good should be promoted and it is one's moral obligation to so act that one always promotes the greatest possible amount of good. No emphasis is placed upon oneself as the agent for whom the good is to be realized; simply, the greatest possible good is to be realized. And since the good for ten persons generally results in a greater total amount of good than the good for only one person, the utilitarian is generally obligated to strive for the good for everyone if he expects the good to be maximized. Also, utilitarianism is clearly teleological, for the sole criterion for regarding any act as morally obligatory is its utility in producing the desired result—maximization of intrinsic good. This principle of utility is the foundation upon which all utilitarian theories are based and is the single criterion for judging matters of right and wrong, good and bad.

MAXIMIZATION OF THE GOOD

Before giving a more complete description of utilitarianism, an important question can be asked: Does the utilitarian say, simply, "One ought to maximize the good" or does he say, "One ought to maximize the good *for the greatest number*?" The difference between the two can be substantial. For instance, imagine fifteen units of the good (whatever it is) divided among five people in two different ways. In the first, one person has seven units of good, the second has five, the third enjoys three, and the fourth and fifth persons must do without; in the second, all five persons enjoy equal amounts of the good—three. Both schemas represent the same amount of the total good, fifteen units. The second one, however, represents the greatest good for the greatest number—more individuals are able to enjoy the good, at least to some extent, than in the first one. Thus, while both schemas represent equal amounts of total good, they do not by any means represent the same situation, as the individuals involved would certainly attest.

But which concept is intended by the utilitarian—the single-aspect view, which emphasizes maximization of intrinsic good per se, or the double-aspect view, which emphasizes the per capita maximization of intrinsic good? Both views have been emphasized by different utilitarians and so a definitive answer cannot be given. A possible compromise, however, (and a view that Bentham apparently held) is suggested in the preceding paragraph: if the greater good is to be realized then the greater number *must* be involved. The single-aspect view is restated: one cannot say that the maximum possible amount of good per se has been realized unless the maximum possible number of people are included. Not all utilitarians have taken this view, however—many have held to an unqualified double-aspect view—and thus still no definitive answer can be given to the question posed above. The issue is an important one, and though it admits of no definitive answer, it is an issue in utilitarian theory of which the reader should be aware.

BASIC FEATURES OF UTILITARIANISM

Several clarifications are needed to insure a reasonably complete and accurate understanding of utilitarianism. Following, therefore, are some basic features of ethical theory which all utilitarians share.[1]

First, time is not a relevant consideration in determining the rightness of an act. If one act will result in a certain amount of good today but another act would result in a greater amount tomorrow, or next week or next year, then the second act should be performed, regardless of the remoteness of its results. The only relevant consideration is the actual amount of good produced. In choosing among possible acts to perform, one's moral obligation is always to perform that act which will maximize intrinsic good, regardless of when its results will actually be realized.

Second, in the phrase "maximizing the good," it is the net good that is meant. For instance, if one act will produce five units of intrinsic good and no units of evil while a second act will produce ten units of good but similarly ten units of evil, then the first act is to be preferred because its net result of good is higher than that of the second act, five to zero. This is a significant consideration because it implies that a utilitarian must consider a multitude of factors besides simply the possibilities for good in order to determine the rightness of a given act. For instance, one might envision the good that would result from the assassination of a world leader and conclude from this that the act is morally right. However, if the various types of evil or negative consequences that would also follow from the act are also considered, it might well be concluded that its net results would be negative and that the act would therefore be morally reprehensible.

Third, and in conjunction with this second point, it is not simply enough that an act produce greater good than evil to be morally right; it must do so more than any other act that could have been performed instead. Thus, rather than assassinate the leader one might choose simply to ignore him, but, even supposing that this would lead to greater good than the alternative, it is not morally obligatory unless it leads to greater good than any other alternative, e.g., becoming involved in government and working for desired reforms.

Fourth, utilitarianism is not, like egoism, an ethics of self-interest, but neither is it, like altruism, an ethics of self-sacrifice. For the utilitarian, there is no self in the decision-making process. The utilitarian is concerned solely with maximizing the good; his judgment must be impartial and disinterested. If it happens that the good is maximized by an act which hurts him personally, he is nevertheless bound by the utilitarian principle to aim at or perform that act. Similarly, if the good is maximized by an act that is favorable to him, then he is likewise bound to choose *it*. His only concern is with maximization of the good. The determination of the morality of an act always rests on the net good realized and never on the personal interests of a single individual. Thus, self-interest and self-sacrifice can both be the consequence of utilitarian behavior but neither can consistently be a motive for a utilitarian's moral decisions.

LIMITED VERSUS UNIVERSAL UTILITARIANISM

There are also major points of disagreement among utilitarians. One of these has already been mentioned—whether maximization of good implies maximizing the total good per se or maximizing the average, or per capita, good. Another difference is that between limited and universal utilitarianism.

Limited Utilitarianism

Limited utilitarianism is an unusual, but necessary, ethical category. It is unusual because it fits neatly under neither egoism nor utilitarianism but it is necessary because it describes many people's moral thinking. Briefly, the assumption behind limited utilitarianism is that the good should be maximized for a specified, or limited, class. Rather than including everyone, the limited utilitarian includes only a specified group and argues that the good ought to be maximized for that group only. For example, suppose that during World War II when the Germans were killing the Jews, a Nazi had said: "This extermination is justified because it will rid us of those troublesome Jews, and the Third Reich and all the German people will rise to greater heights of glory as a result." This thinking is utilitarian insofar as it is not egoistic; the individual is apparently not directly concerned with his own personal interests, but with those of all the German people. However, it is limited insofar as it emphasizes the interests of one group of people to the exclusion or deprivation of another. Similarly, suppose a senator researches a bill proposed in Congress and finds that although it would have a favorable effect on the nation as a whole it would have an unfavorable effect on his home state. If, for this reason, he should vote against the bill, his reasoning is a form of limited utilitarianism—he seeks to maximize the good for a particular group, his constituency, rather than for everyone who is involved.

This type of moral thinking is widespread; we will often emphasize the interests of our own country over that of the rest of the world and we often protect the interests of our own university, church, or race with little thought for other groups. Most individuals care and provide for their own families before they help care for others. All of these are examples of a type of utilitarianism—the agent is not particularly concerned with his own interests—but it is limited utilitarianism in that one group for whom the good is to be maximized is singled out over others.

It should be noticed, however, that limited utilitarianism is really no further removed from egoism than it is from the universality implicit in most discussions of utilitarianism. That is, there is little reason, except precedent, for calling this form of moral thinking limited utilitarianism rather than generalized egoism. Why would one single out a certain group for favors unless one felt some allegiance or identification with it himself? Certainly, a person cares for his own family before caring for others because it is *his* family, and this seems as close to egoism as to utilitarianism. Nevertheless, this type of thinking has come to be termed "limited utilitarianism."

Universal Utilitarianism

In contrast to this, a second form of utilitarianism is the pure form. However, to emphasize the distinction between this and limited utilitarianism, some authors refer to this as "universal utilitarianism." Briefly, the central belief of this type of utilitarianism is that maximizing the good should not be limited to a particular group or class but should be extended to include all people. Some would extend this further to include all creatures, and others to include additional parts of nature. The minimum statement of universal utilitarianism, however, is that the good is to be maximized for all people on earth. This has interesting implications for many issues: one would have to sacrifice his country's interests for the interests of the rest of the world if there were a conflict between the two; one would have to sacrifice his own community's interests when they conflicted with the interests of the majority of people of the state; and perhaps most strikingly, in times of crisis one could not favor one's own family over others. In Bentham's terms, "everyone is to count for one and no one for more than one," a dictum that is a great equalizer. The principle insures that all of humanity is taken into consideration every time a moral choice is made. It then insures a strictly universal, as opposed to a limited, form of utilitarianism.

UTILITARIANISM AND INTRINSIC GOOD

To understand still another difference among utilitarians, it is important to remember that utilitarianism is a teleological theory. Thus, like egoism, much rests on the individual utilitarian's definition of the good, for the moral rightness of an act depends entirely on its utility in maximizing that good, whether for a limited class or for all of humanity. But what exactly is the good to be maximized? As is the case with egoism, the various answers to this question reveal wide divergences among utilitarians in response to specific moral questions.

As explained in chapter one, it is convenient to classify definitions of the good under three headings: (*a*) quantitative hedonism, most closely associated with physical pleasures, (*b*) qualitative hedonism, most closely associated with mental and spiritual pleasures, and (*c*) nonhedonism, which encompasses all pluralistic theories of good as well as such monistic concepts as power, freedom, and good will. Utilitarians fall into any one of these categories according to their definitions of the good that is to be maximized.

Quantitative Hedonistic Utilitarianism

The best example of a quantitative hedonistic form of utilitarianism is that held by Jeremy Bentham (1), for he was not only an adamant quantitative hedonist but also one of the premier figures in the development of utilitarian theory. Bentham was an active political theorist and reformer and was concerned with the morality of governmental action. In the following excerpts Bentham's emphasis on both hedonism and the principle of utility are revealed. It should be recalled that Bentham includes several types of pleasure in his discussion of pleasure and pain—not only those of a physical nature. The important distinction between Bentham and qualitative hedonists is that he admits of no independent qualitative differences among the various types of pleasure.

Nature has placed mankind under the governance of two sovereign masters, *pain* and *pleasure*. It is for them alone to point out what we ought to do, as well as to determine what we shall do. On the one hand the standard of right and wrong, on the other the chain of causes and effects, are fastened to their throne. . . . The *principle of utility* recognizes this subjection, and assumes it. . . .

A thing is said to promote the interest, or to be *for* the interest, of an individual, when it tends to add to the sum total of his pleasures: or, what comes to the same thing, to diminish the sum total of his pains . . .

[And] a measure of government . . . may be said to be conformable to or dictated by the principle of utility, when in like manner the tendency which it has to augment the happiness of the community is greater than any which it has to diminish it. . . . [1, pp. 1, 2]

Later in the same work, Bentham argues that "pleasure is in *itself* a good: nay even setting aside immunity from pain, the only good: pain is in itself an evil; and, indeed, without exception, the only evil; or else the words good and evil have no meaning" (1, p. 48). Thus Bentham explains his form of utilitarianism: pleasure and pain define the limits of good and evil, and what is good ought to be sought for the whole community. An act is morally right if it increases the total pleasure of the entire community. This conclusion also implies the two corollaries of Bentham's philosophy: (*a*) one must strive for the greatest happiness for the greatest number, and (*b*) everyone must count for one and no one for more than one. These points combined, then, lead Bentham to a form of ethical philosophy that may be called quantitative hedonistic utilitarianism.

Qualitative Hedonistic Utilitarianism

John Stuart Mill is another of the premier figures in the historical development of utilitarian theory and was also the primary exponent of qualitative hedonism. It will be recalled that although, as a disciple of Bentham, Mill accepts the proposition of hedonism, as a disciple of Epicurus he also believes that pleasures are of different qualities. To maximize the good, the criteria of quality as well as of quantity must be met. The core of both Mill's qualitative hedonism and his utilitarianism can be seen in these excerpts from his work *Utilitarianism* (5).

The creed which accepts as the foundation of morals Utility or the Greatest Happiness Principle holds that actions are right in proportion as they tend to promote happiness, wrong as they tend to produce the reverse of happiness. By happiness is intended pleasure, and the absence of pain; by unhappiness, pain, and the privation of pleasure. . . .

According to the Greatest Happiness Principle, as above explained, the ultimate end, with reference to and for the sake of which all other things are desirable—whether we are considering our own good or that of other people—is an existence exempt as far as possible from pain, and as rich as possible in enjoyments, both in point of quantity and quality; the test of quality and the rule for measuring it against quantity being the preference felt by those who, in their opportunities of experience, to which must be added their habits of self-consciousness and self-observation, are best furnished with the means of comparison. This, being, according to the utilitarian opinion, the end of human action, is necessarily also the standard of morality, which may accordingly, be defined "the rules and precepts for human conduct," by the observance of which an existence such as has been described might be, to the greatest extent possible, secured to all mankind, and not to them only, but, so far as the nature of things admits, to the whole sentient creation. [5, pp. 8, 14]

From these excerpts it can be seen that, although Bentham and Mill are both utilitarians, their discrepant definitions of the good that is to be sought and maximized would likely cause them to disagree on many issues.

Nonhedonistic Utilitarianism

A third form of utilitarianism is nonhedonistic utilitarianism, the broadest form of utilitarianism since nonhedonism is the broadest category of definitions of the good. This category can include anything from endorsement of the monistic concept of freedom to be maximized for everyone to a pluralistic concept of many different goods, e.g., beauty, knowledge, wisdom, temperance, to be maximized for everyone. The most notable form that nonhedonistic utilitarianism has taken, however, is the latter, a pluralistic notion of the good. Hastings Rashdall (6) calls this "Ideal" utilitarianism:

The right action is always that which (so far as the agent has the means of knowing) will produce the greatest amount of good as a whole. This position implies that all goods or elements of the good are in some sense and for some purposes commensurable. . . . This view of Ethics, which combines the utilitarian principle that Ethics must be teleological with a non-hedonistic view of the ethical end, I propose to call Ideal Utilitarianism. According to this view actions are right or wrong according as they tend to produce for mankind an ideal end or good, which includes, but is not limited to, pleasure. [6, p. 184]

Rashdall proposes a pluralistic view of the good which includes pleasure. This pluralism of goods becomes the definition of good and evil and is that which ought to be sought for all of mankind and against which all acts are to be judged as to their moral rightness or wrongness. It is primarily in terms of this pluralism that Rashdall differs from both Bentham and Mill. All three of these philosophers are utilitarians, but all three use a different definition of the good, and this is sufficient to insure that there will be many instances of disagreement among them.

If anything is more important than theories of the good in distinguishing among utilitarians, it is the difference between act-utilitarianism and rule-utilitarianism. Briefly, the distinction may be put this way. Although the ultimate test for the moral rightness or wrongness of any action is the principle of utility, there is a question whether this principle should be applied to particular acts themselves or to general rules instead. That is, should each particular act be judged individually on the basis of its own consequences, or should there instead be general rules of morality against which, then, particular acts are to be judged? Should the principle of utility be applied to particular acts or to general rules? Those who hold to the former view are called act-utilitarians and those to the latter view, rule-utilitarians.

Act-Utilitarianism

The act-utilitarian phrases his moral inquiry in such a way that he is concerned specifically with how a particular act in a particular situation will affect maximization of the good in the world. He maintains that general rules such as "killing is wrong" are valuable only as guides; the most pertinent question in any specific situation is whether or not killing *in this instance* will produce evil—might it not, in this instance, result in the greatest good? For example, to borrow from Hospers (4), an act-utilitarian will generally agree that killing is wrong, not because there is anything inherently wrong in killing, for then he would not be a teleologist, but because killing results in a decrease of the good: the individual whose life is taken almost certainly loses whatever chances he may have had of enjoying the good; his family and other loved ones surely suffer; people who hear of the killing become fearful at the prospect of a murderer on the streets; if the individual is caught and convicted he gains little apparent good from either a lifelong imprisonment or his own death; and certainly the whole foundation of law upon which a society is built is weakened by every violation of it—particularly by a crime as serious as murder. Clearly, in most cases of killing, the negative consequences outweigh any good consequences there might be, and thus the act-utilitarian will agree that killing is generally wrong and that the rule "Do not kill" generally should be followed.

There are, however, exceptions which prevent this and any general prescription from becoming an absolute rule. Suppose, for instance, that an individual had had the opportunity to kill Hitler in 1941 but did not do so. The act-utilitarian, assuming certain things about his definition of the good, could contend that *not* killing Hitler was immoral, for by not doing so many thousand Jews would continue to be tortured and killed and, similarly, many thousands of soldiers (on both sides) would continue to die, not to mention all the misery and grief accompanying these deaths. It would seem that the good would have been maximized had Hitler been killed, and doing so, therefore, would have been the moral alternative. Indeed, this is likely what an act-utilitarian would recommend. And while this goes against the rule "Do not kill," the act-utilitarian would simply observe that that rule is not absolute. He would claim the rule is considered a rule at all only for the sake of convenience; it is a statement of what is generally the case—that killing usually produces evil consequences. However, when the situation arises where the maximum possible good is produced by killing, then the rule is irrelevant because it does not fit the case at hand.

Rule-Utilitarianism

The rule-utilitarian, on the other hand, applies the principle of utility to general rules rather than to particular acts. "The question is not which *action* has the greatest utility, but which *rule* has" (2, p. 39). That is, rather than asking which possible action will most maximize the good in a given situation, one must consult a prior set of rules about what most maximizes the good. The act chosen in any situation, then, must be the one which is in conformity with that set of rules. The rule-utilitarian asks, "What rules, if followed by everyone all of the time, will maximize the good in the world?" The rules settled on are those having the greatest utility; they are those, therefore, to which all particular acts ought to conform. Thus, a rule-utilitarian is very likely to reason that the good would be maximized if everyone, all of the time, obeyed the rule "Do not kill." On this basis, he would condemn all killing and would contend, against the act-utilitarian, that killing Hitler would be immoral, even though he might admit that favorable consequences would result from such a deed. The rule-utilitarian would ask, "What if everyone went around killing people every time they thought it was useful or needful? Certainly that would not be a world in which good could be realized or enjoyed. No, the best possibility for maximizing the good is for everyone to refrain from killing all of the time—and that includes me in this particular situation." In this way, the rule-utilitarian applies the principle of utility to various rules. Alternative acts in particular situations, then, are not themselves measured against the principle of utility (i.e., against the consequences they will elicit), but solely against those rules whose utility is already established.

The difference between act- and rule-utilitarians is seen in the following example suggested by Taylor (8). Suppose two rules are proposed, one of which says, "Never lie to a person who asks you a direct question," and another of which says "Always lie to a person who asks you a direct question." Clearly, the first rule has greater utility than the second, for many of the advantages of society are due precisely to the benefits of truth-telling. Thus, a rule-utilitarian may reason that everyone telling the truth all of the time will most maximize the good and therefore adopt the first proposed rule, asserting that all particular acts must conform to it. It is not difficult, however, to imagine circumstances in which an act-utilitarian would gladly violate this rule. Suppose, for instance, that during the height of the Jewish genocide in Nazi Germany someone was hiding a family of Jews in his home. Suppose further that one night the Gestapo stopped at that home and asked him if he knew the whereabouts of any Jews. As an act-utilitarian he would weigh the consequences of his specific act: if he did not tell the truth, there would be few direct consequences except that the family of Jews would continue living and hiding in his home; if he told the truth, however, they would be sent to a concentration camp and probably be executed, and he and his own family would be punished for their role in assisting them. Clearly, the good would appear to be maximized by lying in this case, and the act-utilitarian would probably consider any act of truth-telling here not only wrong, but morally reprehensible.

The rule-utilitarian, conversely, would not weigh the consequences of this specific act but would simply measure it against the rule "Never lie to a person who asks you a direct question." The utility of that rule has already been determined and so all that remains is to assess the degree to which the alternative actions conform to it. In this case, obviously, truth-telling is enjoined by its conformity to that rule and thus revealing the hiding place of the Jewish family is the required moral action. Clearly, people who adhere to an act-oriented utilitarianism and to rule-oriented utilitarianism can be committed to making drastically different moral decisions.[2]

Consider another case, also suggested by Taylor (8). Suppose a person finds a wallet containing two hundred dollars. Suppose further that the owner's name and address are clearly written on a card inside the wallet and that he is recognized by the finder as being a very wealthy man. Finally, suppose that the finder himself is very poor and that it would be very easy for him to remove the money from the wallet and walk away without anyone's ever finding out. In this case the consequences seem to favor his taking the money, and it is possible that this is what the act-utilitarian would recommend as the moral course of action. A rule-utilitarian, however, would probably reach the opposite conclusion. He would likely assume the rule "Thou shalt not steal" to be of great utility and thus conclude that, regardless of any favorable consequence that may arise, taking the money would be wrong because of its nonconformity to that rule.

The distinction between rule and act orientations can cause profound differences of moral opinion among utilitarians. Accordingly, this is one of the most important theoretical and practical distinctions to which attention can be drawn and should be kept in mind in all discussions of utilitarian ethical theory.[3]

THE FEATURES OF UTILITARIANISM: SUMMARY

All utilitarians hold basic features of moral thought in common. First, all utilitarians are teleologists—the sole criterion of the moral rightness of an act is its consequences. Second, they share the principle of utility, asserting that maximization of intrinsic good is the result an act or rule must have in order to be morally right. Third, they assert that time is irrelevant to moral considerations, that the net good is what is sought, that to be morally right an act must produce more good than any other act that could have been performed instead, and finally, that in making moral judgments one must be totally impartial and disinterested regarding his own personal interests.

Utilitarians also disagree on important points, however. For instance, some believe that it is the maximum good per se that is to be sought, while others contend that it is the maximum average or per capita good. Some insist that nothing less than the entire universe (or at least all of humankind) is that for which the good must be sought, while others specify smaller, more distinct groups to which they direct their concern. Utilitarians also differ in their conceptions of what constitutes intrinsic good. Some, like Bentham, are quantitative hedonists; others, like Mill, are qualitative hedonists; and still others, like Rashdall, are nonhedonists. Finally, utilitarians differ on their attitudes toward moral rules. Act-utilitarians admit the usefulness of rules in moral choices, but only as summaries of what past situations have shown to be moral. The principle of utility is applied to particular alternative acts and not to rules. Rule-utilitarians apply the principle of utility to rules; those rules then become the definition of morality and therefore cannot be superseded in any specific situation. Thus, while the act-utilitarian is concerned with the utility of particular acts, the rule-utilitarian is concerned with the utility of general rules.

To understand utilitarianism fully one must be familiar with all these distinctions. However, one can focus only on the broader distinguishing features of the theory, and pay less attention to the finer ones. Accordingly, the difference between act- and rule-utilitarianism and the differences among conceptions of the good require specific focus. Figure 2 represents these features.

FIGURE 2. UTILITARIANISM

Act-Utilitarianism		Rule-Utilitarianism	
Qualitative Hedonism	Nonhedonism	Qualitative Hedonism	Nonhedonism
Quantitative Hedonism		Quantitative Hedonism	

In future discussions of utilitarian theory these are the features that will receive specific attention.

SUMMARY OF TELEOLOGICAL THEORY

A teleological theory of obligation asserts that the moral rightness of an act is solely a function of its consequences. The teleologist first has a definition of the good and then defines as morally right those acts leading to it. Within this general framework of teleology, egoism and utilitarianism constitute broad ethical categories. Each of these, however, can be further subdivided by introducing concepts of normative value, or definitions of the good. Utilitarianism can be subdivided even further, by identifying either an act or a rule orientation, as depicted in the following diagram.

It can be seen that there are two broad types of teleological moral reasoning, egoism and utilitarianism, and that utilitarianism may be further defined as either act or rule oriented. These dimensions—egoism, act-utilitarianism, and rule-utilitarianism—are further defined as directed toward either qualitative hedonistic ends, quantitative hedonistic ends, or nonhedonistic ends. Thus, by identifying where an individual stands with respect to these few features of ethical theory, much may be understood concerning his entire network of moral thought. These few variables, then, have great heuristic value in identifying and classifying elements of moral reasoning.

FIGURE 3. TELEOLOGY—EGOISM AND UTILITARIANISM

Egoism

Qualitative Hedonism	Quantitative Hedonism	Nonhedonism

Utilitarianism

Act-Utilitarianism	Rule-Utilitarianism
Qualitative Hedonism Nonhedonism	Qualitative Hedonism Nonhedonism
Quantitative Hedonism	Quantitative Hedonism

NOTES

1. The following points are suggested by Hospers (4).

2. Moral philosophers, of course, in order to avoid obvious objections to rule-utilitarianism, quickly become more subtle in their discussions of it than this treatment implies. For psychological purposes, however—studying the moral reasoning of the man on the street—this level of discussion is probably sufficient.

3. One way to make this difference between act and rule orientation explicit is to employ Rawls's (7) concept of two different types of rules, summary rules and practice rules. Summary rules are simply rules that summarize conclusions drawn from past specific situations. For instance, to the act utilitarian, "Do not kill" is a summary rule because it summarizes the conclusions, drawn on many past occasions, that killing is

not productive of the maximum good. There is no allegiance to this rule as a rule, however, and it can be superseded at any time as a new specific situation requires. Practice rules, on the other hand, are not just generalizations about what has been found to be moral in the past; instead they serve to define what is moral. To use Garner and Rosen's example (3), the rules of chess do not serve simply to report how people have played chess in the past, they serve to define what it is to be playing chess; simply, if one is not playing according to the rules then one is not playing chess. Similarly for morality. For the rule-utilitarian, "Do not kill," if a rule, is a rule that defines the very practice of morality and if one is not obeying the rule then by definition one is not being moral.

3 / Normative Ethics III: Deontology

Ethical deontology, the other major category of normative obligation, is quite simply a denial of the basic proposition of teleology. Teleologists, whether egoists or utilitarians, assert that moral obligation is solely a function of consequences—that an act or a rule is morally right or wrong depending solely on its results. This, however, is precisely the point that the deontologist denies. He asserts instead that a given act is judged not only by the consequences it will elicit, but by the nature of the act itself.

NATURE OF THE ACT

The words *nature of the act* may mean a number of things. For instance, suppose one believes that moral principles are eternal and immutable and that these principles at least partially define moral action. Then, to determine the rightness of a given act one must determine its degree of conformity to moral principle(s). For instance, it may be that one such principle is that it is wrong to lie. In that case, an important feature of morality for any truth-relevant act is its conformity to truth. This conformity is at least partially involved in determining whether the act is in fact moral or immoral. Thus, the rightness of the act is not dependent solely upon its consequences—whether they are favorable or unfavorable—but also upon its truth-conforming nature *as an act*. This is the "nature of the act." Not all deontologists argue for conformity to moral principles as the feature which pertains to the nature of the act and which figures into the calculation of its rightness, but some do, and this is sufficient at present to provide an immediate idea of what is meant by the "nature of the act." Other possible meanings will become clear in this chapter.

45

PURE AND MIXED DEONTOLOGY

It should be noted that, as a denial of teleological theory, the basic statement of deontology is simply: Moral obligation is not solely a function of consequences. But this essentially negative definition embraces a rather wide range of possible ethical positions. By saying, "moral obligation is not solely a function of consequences," one may mean either that consequences should play no role in the determination of moral rightness, in which case the morality of an act depends entirely upon its nature alone, or one may mean that consequences are not the only relevant consideration, in which case the morality of an act depends both upon its consequences and upon certain features of the act itself. The complexity entailed by this second possible view combines all of the considerations involved in teleological theories with features of the act itself as well: one must weigh the consequences of one's acts (which for an egoist would include a choice from among the many possible definitions of the good, and, for a utilitarian, would include not only defining the good but also choosing between a limited or a universal view of utilitarianism and deciding whether particular acts or general rules are the objects to which the principle of utility is to be applied) and against all this one must also balance various aspects of the act itself to finally determine its rightness.

Obviously, then, deontology covers a wide range of ethical views. It includes what will be called here a *pure* deontology—theories in which morality is a function solely of the nature of the act itself and to which consequences are irrelevant—and what may be called a *mixed* deontology—theories which combine a consideration of consequences with considerations of the act itself. A pure deontologist, for instance, might contend that since lying is wrong, simply because it is wrong, it would be wrong for him to lie under any circumstances. A mixed deontologist, conversely, might well admit that while there is something wrong about lying itself, in a given circumstance the wrongfulness of lying might be outweighed by the favorable consequences that would result from such a lie. In that case the lie would in fact be morally obligatory rather than wrong. The pure deontologist refers only to the nature of the act itself, while the mixed deontologist considers both the act and the consequences it will elicit.

ACT- AND RULE-DEONTOLOGY

A second distinction between deontologists is, as for utilitarians, that between act and rule orientations. A rule-deontologist adopts one or more rules which, at least partially by their very nature, are considered to be right and against which particular acts are to be judged. An act-deontologist, on the other hand, judges particular acts at least partially by their very nature and uses rules only as does the act-utilitarian—as mere summary rules or guidelines. The rule and act distinctions thus serve essentially the same function for deontologists as for utilitarians.

These two basic distinctions, pure versus mixed and act versus rule, provide four basic complexions of deontological theory: pure rule-deontology, mixed rule-deontology, pure act-deontology, and mixed act-deontology.

PURE RULE-DEONTOLOGY

The following elements are included in all forms of pure rule-deontology: (*a*) one or more rules make up the foundation of morality and particular acts are determined to be right or wrong by the degree to which they conform to those rules, and (*b*) consequences are irrelevant in determining the morality of those rules, and hence in determining the morality of particular acts.

Kant

The most notable example of this form of deontology is the philosophy of Immanuel Kant (4, 5). Kant's system of ethics defies any simple description but for present purposes it is sufficient to state that Kant acted from one central moral rule, which he called the "categorical imperative." The categorical imperative is a principle of universalizability, stating: "Act as if the maxim of thy action were to become by thy will a universal law of nature" (4, p. 229). Simply, this means that to determine the morality of any action one must determine what the nature of the act would be if it were to become a universal law—if everyone were required to act the same way. Would the act be self-consistent or self-contradictory? Kant gives the following explanation of this reasoning:

[One] finds himself forced by necessity to borrow money. He knows that he will not be able to repay it, but sees also that nothing will be lent to him, unless he promises stoutly to repay it in a definite time. He desires to make this promise, but he has still so much conscience as to ask himself: Is it not unlawful and inconsistent with duty to get out of a difficulty in this way? Suppose, however, that he resolves to do so, then the maxim of his action would be expressed thus: When I think myself in want of money, I will borrow money and promise to repay it, although I know that I never can do so. Now this principle of self-love or of one's own advantage may perhaps be consistent with my whole future welfare; but the question now is, Is it right? I change then the suggestion of self-love into a universal law, and state the question thus: How would it be if my maxim were a universal law? Then I see at once that it could never hold as a universal law of nature, but would necessarily contradict itself. For supposing it to be a universal law that everyone when he thinks himself in a difficulty should be able to promise whatever he pleases, with the purpose of not keeping his promise, the promise itself would become impossible, as well as the end that one might have in view in it, since no one would consider that anything was promised to him, but would ridicule all such statements as vain pretences.[4, p. 230]

It should be noted that Kant's basis for morality is found in reason, or logical consistency with a universalized maxim. His concern is not with the consequences of such a maxim, i.e., "What would happen if everyone broke promises merely when it was self-advantageous to do so? No one could trust anyone and total chaos would result." That is how a rule-utilitarian would argue, but Kant's concern is not with these consequences but with inconsistency or a contradiction of will. For example, he says: "That action is immoral whose intent cancels and destroys itself when it is made a universal rule. It is moral, if the intent of the action is in harmony with itself when it is made a universal rule" (5, p. 44). Given this distinction it can be seen that it is contradictory to believe both that promises should be made and that they should be broken at will, for if promises may be broken at will what sense does it make to speak of promise making at all? Since the maxim "Everyone ought to break promises when it will serve his advantage to do so" is self-contradictory—its intent "cancels and destroys itself"—it does not meet the requirement of the categorical imperative. Promise breaking is morally wrong—no individual at any time may break a promise, because that act, when made a universal maxim, is self-contradictory.

Of all philosophers it is perhaps Kant to whom it is most difficult to do justice in a short discussion. However, at least the basis of his form of ethical deontology should be clear. He adopted a moral rule, the categorical imperative, as the basic criterion of moral rightness against which all particular acts must be judged. All universalized maxims must meet the test of reason or self-consistency. It should be especially noted that for Kant, consequences (as the teleologist speaks of them) are irrelevant to moral considerations; the sole criterion of morality is whether an act can be made a universal maxim without contradiction—if it cannot it is immoral. This places reason rather than results at the heart of moral matters and, because reasonableness is a feature of the act itself, defines the theory as deontological. Furthermore, because of Kant's formulation of a single ultimate rule, the categorical imperative, as the criterion of morality, and the total absence of the role of consequences in his ethical system, his philosophy is an excellent example of pure rule-deontology.

Cudworth

Not all examples of pure rule-deontology take the form of Kant's philosophy, however. For instance, the English philosopher Richard Cudworth (2) seems to have held this general type of ethical theory, but rather than emphasize the role of reason and a single rule, Cudworth spoke instead of intuition and several rules or laws as the basis of morality. Briefly, Cudworth held that moral laws are eternal and immutable and that logically, or by nature, they are prior even to God. No one, not even God, makes a principle right or wrong, because a principle is, by its own nature, right or wrong, much the way a square simply is a square. Speaking on this point, Cudworth says:

Neither can Omnipotence itself . . . by mere will make a thing white or black without whiteness or blackness; that is, without such certain natures. . . . Omnipotence itself cannot by mere will make a body triangular, without having the nature and properties of a triangle in it. Omnipotent will cannot make things like or equal one to another, without the natures of likeness and equality. [2, pp. 14, 15][1]

Thus, moral laws simply exist and they are eternal and unchangeable. These eternal laws are understood and known by intuition; they constitute the basis for moral action—performance in accordance with the perceived moral laws. For these reasons Cudworth's philosophy is also an example of pure rule-deontology.

To qualify as pure rule-deontology, a philosophy must have two characteristics: (a) rules rather than particular acts are the test of morality, and (b) consequences must count for nothing in that test. The specific test of morality varies. Kant asserted the test must be reason, or self-consistency of the universalized maxim or rule. Cudworth said it must be the rule's existence as an eternal and immutable moral principle. In both cases, however, morality is set on a foundation of one or more rules and the consequences of following the rule are irrelevant to its moral status. For these reasons each is an example of pure rule-deontology.

MIXED RULE-DEONTOLOGY

Like pure rule-deontology, mixed rule-deontology emphasizes rules over particular acts, but unlike it, consequences are allowed a role in moral determinations. In all forms of mixed deontology it is most accurate to say that although consequences are a relevant consideration in determining the rightness of a rule (or an act, as the case may be), they are not the only relevant consideration. As in teleology, consequences are considered in determining moral rightness, but certain features of the act itself are also considered and it is the balance between the two that finally determines whether the rule or act in question is moral.

Ross

Perhaps the best example of this mixed rule-deontology is the ethical philosophy of W. D. Ross (6, 7). Ross outlines seven prima facie rules, rules which ought to be followed other things being equal. This means that there are seven duties, each of which, if no intervening circumstances arise, ought to be performed. But when such circumstances do arise, then one duty may take precedence over another. These obligations or duties are as follows: (a) The obligation of fidelity—of keeping promises and of telling the truth; (b) the obligation of reparation, of making amends for any previous wrongs one may have done others; (c) the obligation of gratitude, of repaying the services rendered to one by others; (d) the obligation of justice, of insuring the distribution of happiness according to merit; (e) the obligation of beneficence, of doing whatever can be done for others to improve them "in respect of virtue, or of intelligence, or of pleasure"; (*f*) the obligation of self-improvement, of improving oneself as well as others "in respect of virtue or of intelligence"; and finally, (*g*) the obligation of not injuring others, of refraining from harming them as well as of actively promoting their good (7, p. 21).

The important thing to see in Ross's list of duties is the mixture of both teleological and deontological obligations. Indeed, one of Ross's greatest concerns in his writings is to show the inadequacy of a purely teleological, particularly utilitarian, ethical theory. This is precisely his reason for introducing the concept of prima facie, or conditional, duties into ethical theory. For instance, Ross says, suppose that fulfillment of a promise to A would produce 1,000 units of good for him, but that by performing some other act, which would entail breaking the promise, a person could produce 1,001 units of good for B. Is it right to break the promise to A in order to achieve the greater good for B? The utilitarian would say yes, assuming the other consequences of both acts are the same, but Ross says no. It is one's prima facie duty to promote the greatest good, but in this case there is an intervening circumstance of promise keeping, which is also a prima facie duty and which in this case outweighs the difference to be obtained if the promise were broken. Moreover, Ross maintains that even if breaking the promise to A would result in 1,001 units of good to A himself, instead of the 1,000 obtained if the promise is kept, it still would be wrong to break the promise in order to achieve the greater good. In other words, one has a prima facie moral obligation to keep promises. There is something about the very nature of promise keeping or fidelity that is right and this cannot be easily outweighed by consideration of consequences. This is clearly a deontological feature in Ross's philosophy.

Although these points serve to illustrate the differences between Ross and the utilitarians, there is also, of course, a significant difference between Ross and the pure deontologists, as can be seen in the following passage, in which Ross makes explicit the distinction between prima facie (parti-resultant) duties and actual (toti-resultant) duties:

It is necessary to say something by way of clearing up the relation between *prima facie* duties and the actual or absolute duty to do one particular act in particular circumstances. If, as almost all moralists except Kant are agreed, and as most plain men think, it is sometimes right to tell a lie or to break a promise, it must be maintained that there is a difference between *prima facie* duty and actual or absolute duty. When we think ourselves justified in breaking, and indeed morally obliged to break, a promise in order to relieve some one's distress, we do not for a moment cease to recognize a *prima facie* duty to keep our promise, and this leads us to feel, not indeed shame or repentance, but certainly compunction, for behaving as we do; we recognize, further, that it is our duty to make up somehow to the promisee for the breaking of the promise. We have to distinguish from the characteristic of being our duty that of tending to be our duty. Any act that we do contains various elements in virtue of which it falls under various categories. In virtue of being the breaking of a promise, for instance, it tends to be wrong; in virtue of being an instance of relieving distress it tends to be right. Tendency to be one's duty may be called a parti-resultant attribute, i.e. one which belongs to an act in virtue of some one component in its nature. *Being* one's duty is a toti-resultant attribute, one which belongs to an act in virtue of its whole nature and of nothing less than this. [7, p. 28]

Ross makes two important points in this passage. First, the obligation of fidelity is not so firm as never to be outweighed by consequences. Thus, promise keeping is a prima facie obligation, but in Ross's example it is outweighed by the good to be achieved by relieving someone's distress. As a pure rule-deontologist, Kant would argue that breaking a promise cannot be willed to be a universal maxim and is therefore immoral, but Ross, as a mixed rule-deontologist, would argue that consequences can be considered in moral situations, and that when they are, they can sometimes outweigh such purely deontological considerations as the inherent rightness of promise keeping. The crucial problem in making moral choices is to balance maximization of the good against several other prima facie duties.

Second, and related to the above point, a prima facie duty is one that ought to be performed all other things being equal, and an actual duty is one that actually ought to be performed in a particular circumstance—it emerges in a given situation after all the necessary balancing has been performed and the proper course of action becomes clear. For instance, in Ross's first example of the 1,000 units of good, it is one's prima facie duty to maximize the good, but after all the balancing is finished, it is one's actual duty to keep his promise— at the expense of maximizing the good. And in Ross's second example, quoted above, promise keeping is still a prima facie duty, but it must be sacrificed in order to fulfill one's actual duty which, in this case, is to maximize the good. Thus, exactly which prima facie duty emerges as one's actual duty is highly variable and depends upon the situation at hand; again, the problem is to weigh the various duties against one another until the obligation to be performed in a particular circumstance becomes apparent.

Ross's ethical philosophy, then, is an example of a mixed rule-deontology. Rules rather than particular acts are the primary subject matter of moral inquiry—acts are judged solely by their relationships to the various moral rules—and the consequences of the rules, as well as certain aspects of their very natures as rules, are relevant in determination of their moral rightness or wrongness. Ross satisfies these conditions by positing seven prima facie rules, which combine elements both of teleology and deontology. In this way, the primacy of moral rules is combined with a view both to consequences and to inherent rightness in determining the moral course of action, and this results in a form of mixed rule-deontology.[2]

RULE-DEONTOLOGY: SUMMARY

Rule-deontologists, then, such as Kant, Cudworth, and Ross, all share the attitude that morality is a function of rules and that particular acts, to be moral, must conform to a particular moral rule or set of rules. In this sense, Rawls's category of the practice conception of rules applies here as well as in rule-utilitarianism. In both cases it is a rule or set of rules that defines what it is to be moral; morality is made up of those particular prescriptions. These philosophers differ, however, in the extent to which consequences are allowed a place in moral determinations. All would agree on the basic deontological thesis that consequences are not the only relevant consideration in assessing (and determining) moral rightness, but a mixed deontologist, such as Ross, would be content to leave it at that, allowing consequences some relevance, while a pure deontologist, such as Kant, would take the thesis further and insist that consequences have no relevance in moral determinations. Hence, these philosophers are similar in their emphasis upon moral rules but somewhat dissimilar in their attitudes toward consideration of consequences. It is not adequate to say simply that they are deontologists, or even that they are rule-deontologists; it is quite as important to make explicit their differences as well. For this reason, the distinction between a pure and a mixed deontology is necessary theoretically as well as practically in understanding the various types of moral reasoning.

PURE ACT-DEONTOLOGY

In contrast to the rule-deontologist the act-deontologist holds that particular acts are the proper subject matter of moral inquiry and that rules, rather than defining the very practice of morality, serve only as guidelines derived from past experience. For the act-deontologist (as for the act-utilitarian) moral rules are merely summary statements of the particular kinds of acts that have been found to be moral in the past. Thus, in a specific moral situation, the act-deontologist may well refer to moral generalizations derived from past specific situations; they may serve as helpful guidelines as to what has been generally found to be moral in the past. But the question is still, "What is moral in this particular situation?" and the answer to that is never defined by generalizations and indeed can easily contradict them. Thus, while for the rule-deontologist the very rightness of a particular action depends on its conformity to a certain rule or set of rules, for the act-deontologist, the rightness of a given action is independent of such rules.

The pure act-deontologist, therefore, is concerned with particular acts in particular situations and not with any transcendant and definitive moral rules. But because he is also a *pure* act-deontologist, consequences are irrelevant to him in the determination of a given act's moral rightness. But if the morality of an action is determined neither by its conformity to a moral rule nor by the consequences it will elicit, how is its morality to be determined? What criterion remains?

Sartre

The pure act-deontologist adopts the attitude that the rightness of each act must be judged without recourse to its projected consequences or to its conformity to any moral rules. The net result of this is the ethical "invention" or "choice" of which many existentialists, particularly Sartre, speak. The necessity of such a choice follows from one of Sartre's basic theses that since God does not exist, neither can there exist any absolute moral code: man must create his own values. He cannot simply discover those that "exist," for they do not exist; they must be invented. Thus, Sartre is led to say: "What art and ethics have in common is that we have creation and invention in both cases" (8, p. 51).

To illustrate his ethical position Sartre relates the story of a student who approached him for advice on an important decision during the war. The student was faced with the choice of leaving his mother (who found in him her only consolation in life) and fighting in the war, or staying with his mother and essentially abandoning the cause. Moreover, he knew that if he stayed with his mother his assistance would be specific and concrete, while if he chose to fight, his assistance would be vague and perhaps even wasted since he might be stuck with a useless desk job. To this student Sartre had only one answer to give: "You're free, choose, that is, invent" (8, p. 33). This element of invention is crucial and its meaning is to be taken literally. It is not even precisely correct to say that one should follow his instincts or intuitions, as this student eventually did, in deciding the proper course of action to follow. Sartre says one cannot be certain that intuition prescribes a certain action unless one in fact performs that action, but similarly, one will say that one cannot perform an action unless intuition tells him to do so—so the whole argument from instinct is circular. That is why the element of invention is so crucial: there is no God, no eternal and immutable moral code, and instinct introduces problems of its own; so nothing is left but a creation or invention of ethical values and obligations: "I can neither seek within myself the true condition [intuition or instinct] which will impel me to act, nor apply to a system of ethics for concepts which will permit me to act" (8, p. 32). One must create one's own ethical system and this necessitates active invention. Sartre says that

[Kant] believes that the formal and the universal are enough to constitute an ethic. We, on the other hand, think that principles which are too abstract run aground in trying to decide action. Once again, take the case of the student. In the name of what, in the name of what great maxim do you think he could have decided, in perfect peace of mind, to abandon his mother or to stay with her? There is no way of judging. The content is always concrete and thereby unforeseeable; there is always the element of invention. [8, pp. 55–56]

Sartre's essential ethical position seems to be that of a pure act-deontology. Consequences seem to be considered irrelevant, presumably because the principle of utility itself is so abstract that it would "run aground in trying to decide action," and Sartre clearly rejects the use of any definitive moral rules, apparently including even the principle of utility. The moral act is invented (though not arbitrarily) in each particular situation and not simply deduced from a set of moral laws. For this reason, Sartre's philosophy seems to be the best example of pure act-deontology; few others abandon the use of moral rules, as well as consideration of consequences, as totally as Sartre appears to do.

MIXED ACT-DEONTOLOGY

As with the pure act-deontologist, the mixed act-deontologist is concerned primarily with particular acts in particular situations. For him moral rules are simply summary statements of past experience and, strictly speaking, not rules at all. Mixed act-deontological theory, however, differs from the pure form in that here the consequences of a given act are considered a relevant feature of its moral status. That is, both the consequences as well as certain features of an act are relevant to that act's moral rightness and therefore both must be considered when that act's morality is being questioned.

Carritt

One example of this type of ethical theory is the philosophy of E. F. Carritt (1). In discussing the nature of moral rules Carritt argues that they are only generalized from specific cases and are not in a strict sense rules at all.

> I cannot persuade myself that I first morally apprehend the obligation of several rules, then intellectually apprehend one of alternative actions to be an instance of one and the other of another, and finally, by a second moral intuition, see which rule ought now to be followed. I rather think that I morally apprehend that I ought now to do this act and then intellectually generalize rules. [1, p. 116]

And in discussing the role of consequences and other factors involved in a given act's moral rightness, Carritt says:

If an action cannot be right unless it afford somebody some satisfaction, a fortiori it follows that utilitarians are also correct in maintaining that we must consider the "consequences of action." . . .

[However] we must also consider the antecedents. Whether I ought to initiate a certain change in a given situation depends upon what that situation is. Whether I ought to pay a sum of money to A or B depends not only upon whether A's or B's possession of it will result in more pleasure, but on whether A or B is my creditor, my government, my parent, my benefactor, or a stranger, and upon how they and I have behaved in the past. [1, pp. 42, 43]

By this reasoning, Carritt sets out a form of mixed act-deontology as the proper ethical position. First, one does not act upon rules that are definitive of morality; instead, one acts in particular moral situations and derives moral generalizations from them. Second, consideration of consequences is an important feature of moral determinations but it is not the only relevant feature. Thus, suppose again, for example, that an individual is hiding Jews in his home in Nazi-ruled Austria and that one night the Gestapo stops at his home and asks him if he knows the whereabouts of any Jews. If Carritt were that individual he could be supposed to assume three things: (*a*) the common rule "lying is wrong" is not really a moral rule and is not necessarily applicable to this situation; (*b*) the consequences of the alternative course of action are relevant to its moral rightness; and (*c*) other features of the act (for example, one's relationship to the one asking for information, i.e., does the relationship require or deserve truthfulness?) are also relevant. Given these considerations, regarding (*b*), Carritt would likely argue that the consequences of telling the truth would only be disastrous, and regarding (*c*), he would likely claim that the relationship between the Gestapo and individual Austrian citizens during Nazi control was such that no obligation of trust and faithfulness existed between them. Regarding (*a*), Carritt would probably conclude that the generalization "lying is wrong" has no application at all and that the moral course of action in this case is to lie. Here Carritt (presumably) has appealed to consequences as well as to features of the act itself to determine the moral rightness of alternative courses of action, and he has appealed to moral generalizations only as helpful guidelines. This is the essence of mixed act-deontological theory.

Garner and Rosen

A more recent example of mixed act-deontology comes from Garner and Rosen (3). That which sets their theory off from even the mixed act-deontology of Carritt is the assertion that not only are consequences to be taken into account, but sometimes *only* consequences are to be taken into account. Whereas Carritt apparently holds that both consequences and certain act features are to be considered in every case, Garner and Rosen assert this is not so and that one may consider only one of these in a given case. The only essential point is that one be *willing* to consult either or both criteria, not that he actually do so in each case that arises. Thus, whereas the teleologist claims that one should consider only the consequences of an act, and the pure deontologist claims that one should consider only certain features of the act itself, and most mixed deontologists claim that one must consider both criteria in every case, Garner and Rosen claim only that one should be willing to consider both criteria, but that they each need not be employed in every case. The wide latitude that this dimension introduces into ethical choice is clear. For instance, it is not as easy to infer the solutions such a theorist would offer for various moral dilemmas, for he may do any of a number of things in making that choice. However, the basic foundation for this type of mixed act-deontologist should be clear; he is concerned with particular acts in particular situations, and he considers consequences as well as certain act features in determining moral courses of action.

SUMMARY OF DEONTOLOGICAL THEORY

The basic thesis of deontological ethical theory is that consequences are not the only relevant consideration in determination of moral questions. As has been seen, however, this thesis may lead in either of two directions: the pure deontologist asserts that consequences play no role in determining the rightness of a given act, and the mixed deontologist asserts that while consequences play some role, they are not the sole criterion of moral rightness. Furthermore, a deontologist may have either a rule or an act orientation. For the rule-deontologist there exists a rule or set of rules that defines the practice of morality and to which particular acts must conform in order to be moral, while for the act-deontologist, moral rules are simply generalizations and the primary concern is with the morality of particular acts. These features of deontology combine to form four basic variants of the theory: pure rule-deontology, mixed rule-deontology, pure act-deontology, and mixed act-deontology.

It should also be noted here that mixed deontologists, because they also consider consequences, can be categorized in the same way as are teleologists. That is, if the deontologist considers consequences at all, he must have some definition of the good to which he can refer in determining the desirability of the consequences under consideration. Thus, the categories of qualitative hedonism, quantitative hedonism, and nonhedonism are applicable to mixed deontologists as well as to egoists and utilitarians. The difference, again, is that for teleologists the consequences are the sole consideration, while for the mixed deontologist they constitute only one of the relevant considerations.

Another important point is that it is not sufficient for the mixed deontologist to simply have a definition of the good; an essential feature of consideration of consequences is a concern for the person(s) for whom the good is sought. Insofar as the mixed deontologist is concerned with consequences, part of his concern must be with the consequences *for* someone, and insofar as he must take this position he falls into either a quasi-egoist or a quasi-utilitarian camp. Although it is not necessary to examine this point in detail here, it is important to see its clear implication: mixed deontology is a very broad ethical position and involves almost every consideration made in every other ethical theory.

Figure 4 depicts the most relevant features of deontological theory.

FIGURE 4. DEONTOLOGY

Mixed

Act-Deontology	Rule-Deontology
Qualitative Quantitative Nonhedonism	Qualitative Quantitative Nonhedonism
Hedonism Hedonism	Hedonism Hedonism

Pure

Act-Deontology	Rule-Deontology

SUMMARY OF NORMATIVE ETHICS

As was seen in chapter one, normative value theory is theory of the good, or that which has value and ought to be sought. Three basic theories of intrinsic good can be identified: quantitative hedonism, qualitative hedonism, and nonhedonism. Quantitative hedonists define pleasure as the sole intrinsic good and assert that all types of pleasure are of the same kind; thus, quantity is the sole criterion for choosing between types of pleasure. Qualitative hedonists also define pleasure as the sole good but claim that types of pleasure differ in quality and, thus, that quality as well as quantity must be considered in choosing between pleasures. They maintain that less of a high quality (e.g., mental) pleasure is preferable to more of a low quality (e.g., purely physical) pleasure. Finally, nonhedonists simply deny that pleasure is the sole good and assert instead either that some one other thing is the sole intrinsic good, or that several things combined constitute the good. Thus, whereas both types of hedonists are monists (i.e., pleasure is the sole good), nonhedonists may be either monist (i.e., something other than pleasure is the sole good) or pluralist (i.e., several things combined constitute the good). Also, it should be noted that because of its emphasis upon quantity, quantitative hedonism has become most closely associated with pursuit of physical pleasures, presumably because quantity is most easily increased among these types of pleasure. Conversely, qualitative hedonism has become most closely associated with pursuit of mental or spiritual pleasures, presumably because of their inherently higher quality.

These theories of normative value become extremely important in the discussion of teleology, the first major theory of normative obligation. The teleologist, it will be recalled, is concerned solely with consequences—an act is judged to be right or wrong depending solely on the consequences it produces. Theories of the good are important here because they define the consequences to be sought. If one is a quantitative hedonist, then one will define as morally right those acts which increase the quantity of pleasure, and one will define as morally wrong those acts which decrease it. Within this paradigm, the ethical egoist measures the balance of good in relation to himself and the utilitarian simply seeks to maximize the good, with no reference to himself or to anyone else in particular. (Universal utilitarianism is implied in all unqualified discussions of this theory; that there is most certainly a limited form of utilitarianism, however, should also be noted.) Both egoism and utilitarianism are further clarified by reference to the specific good that is sought, either qualitative hedonism, quantitative hedonism, or nonhedonism. Finally, utilitarianism is also further defined by delineation of either an act or a rule orientation.

The second major theory of normative obligation is deontology. Whereas the teleologist judges the rightness of acts by the consequences they elicit, the deontologist asserts that consequences are only one relevant feature of the rightness of an act (mixed deontology), while to some deontologists, consequences are not relevant at all (pure deontology). Also, as with utilitarianism, deontology can be classified according to rule and act orientations.

Figure 5 depicts the major theories of normative ethics and how they are related to the fundamental elements of ethical theory, providing a quick summary of the information presented in these chapters.

NORMATIVE ETHICS

TELEOLOGY

Egoism

| Qualitative Hedonism | Quantitative Hedonism | Nonhedonism |

Utilitarianism

Act-Utilitarianism — Rule-Utilitarianism

| Qualitative Hedonism | Quantitative Hedonism | Nonhedonism | Qualitative Hedonism | Quantitative Hedonism | Nonhedonism |

DEONTOLOGY

Mixed

Act-Deontology — Rule-Deontology

| Qualitative Hedonism | Quantitative Hedonism | Nonhedonism | Qualitative Hedonism | Quantitative Hedonism | Nonhedonism |

Pure

Act-Deontology — Rule-Deontology

NOTES

1. Spelling and punctuation have been updated in this quotation.

2. There is one sense in which Ross's philosophy may seem to be a form of act rather than rule deontology. In a given circumstance, one cannot simply appeal to a fast rule or set of rules to guide one's choice of actions; one must first determine which

of the seven rules best achieves moral rightness in that particular situation. This has the effect of making morality situation-specific, and this seems, at first glance, to violate the principle of any rule theory that morality is a function of rules and not of particular actions. However, it should be noted that the question is not "which *action* best achieves moral rightness in this situation" but "which *rule* best achieves moral rightness in this situation." Once this is determined, particular alternative actions must then be measured against this rule to determine their moral rightness; thus the rule is still the foundation of morality and so the philosophy is properly called a form of rule-deontology.

4 / Metaethics

In the previous chapters, our concern has been with normative ethics—the ethics of obligation and value. Metaethical issues,
however, have often been involved. It will be remembered that
metaethics is divided into two basic issues: how ethical statements are
justified and how ethical terms are defined. The reader will recall the
sometimes circular nature of the discussion of normative value and
obligation in the previous chapters. For instance, a utilitarian theorist
would conclude that an action is right and thus ought to be performed if it maximizes the good more than any other act that could be
performed instead. The definition of *right*, in this case, obviously
depends on the definition of *good*; *right* is defined in terms of *good*.
This is a definitional matter and as such it is metaethical.

A similar case can also be made for the reverse of this. A. C. Ewing
(3), for instance, takes the position that something is intrinsically
good if it *ought* to be desired. In this case, *good* is defined in terms of
ought. This, likewise, is a definitional matter and is thus metaethical
in nature.

However, as stated previously, our treatment of metaethics involves two questions: first, exactly what is meant by moral judgments—by the terms *good*, *bad*, *right*, and *wrong*? How are these terms
defined? Second, and perhaps more important, how does one justify
one's basic moral assumptions of right or good? How does a person
know his assumptions are correct? In dealing with these issues,
Sellars offers an appropriate guideline:

The philosopher is *particularly* concerned with criteriological questions [ques-
tions of justification]. Thus, he wishes to know whether it makes sense to say
of a set of moral first principles that they are not only accepted, but correct or

true, and how one would go about defending by rational means the assertion that they are true. In short, he wants to know whether moral principles can be rationally justified, and if so, how. [20, p. 6]

In other words, our main concern in this chapter is with epistemology, the theory of knowledge or "how one knows" and justification, rather than with the meanings of terms.

The field of metaethics is traditionally divided into three major categories: naturalism, nonnaturalism, and noncognitivism. Before discussing these directly, however, it is important to introduce two further dimensions of moral reasoning: objectivism-subjectivism and relativism-absolutism. These dimensions will then be helpful in describing the metaethical theories themselves.

OBJECTIVISM-SUBJECTIVISM

Because moral philosophers have used the terms *objectivism* and *subjectivism* in different ways in the past, it is impossible to give the one common definition of these terms that will apply to all philosophical literature. However, a rule can be proposed that may come the closest to doing this and will thus be useful in interpreting the various metaethical positions.

By this rule, the term *subjectivism* is used to signify that a given ethical theory basically rests on attitudes. That is, subjectivism makes a given attitude the sole criterion of morality or moral truth. For example, if something is said to be wrong "because God disapproves," then that judgment is a subjective one, because the disapproval of God is obviously an attitude. A subjectivist theory is one in which all ethical assertions are merely statements of attitudes which one holds, or which someone else (e.g., God) holds; moral truth is defined in terms of those attitudes.

Simply stated, an objectivist theory is one in which this is not the case: ethical assertions are not believed to be mere statements of attitude, but rather are held to reflect an "objective," transcendent moral truth that is independent of anyone's feelings. Attitudes are thus irrelevant to the truth or falsity of ethical statements.

It is important to note the role that definition, or criterion, plays in the distinction between these two concepts. For instance, to say that something is wrong "because God disapproves" is subjectivist precisely due to the *because*—the clear meaning is that God's disapproval is what makes it wrong, it is the criterion of wrongness. But suppose someone says that if something is wrong, then you or someone will have a certain feeling or attitude toward it. Then the theory is not subjectivist because, although attitudes are involved in the analysis, they constitute no criterion for the wrongness itself but merely provide a means for apprehending that wrongness. Thus the theory is objectivist; the actual wrongness of the act transcends and is independent of any of the feelings toward it. This is an important distinction in this chapter and should therefore be kept in mind.

ABSOLUTISM-RELATIVISM

In discussing the distinction between absolutism and relativism, we must first make clear what ethical relativism is not; briefly put, ethical relativism is not synonymous with situational ethics, as is so often supposed. To speak of relativism is to speak of a difference in basic moral assumptions, whereas to speak of situational ethics is generally only to speak of a difference in circumstances, which leads one to prescribe contradictory courses of action although one is using the same basic moral assumptions. For instance, one is not necessarily a relativist merely because he believes it is wrong for a group of Eskimos to strip a man of his clothing twenty miles from home on January 1, but that it is not wrong for a tribe at the equator to do the same thing (2, p. 271). In this case, only the facts of each situation are different, and there is no evidence that there is a change in any of the underlying moral assumptions. Likewise, that I will lie to Grandmother about her new hat, but that I will not lie to cover up crashing into my neighbor's car is not necessarily an example of relativism, because my underlying normative assumption, concern for others, is unchanged. The facts of the situation are changed, not the moral beliefs, and so this cannot be spoken of as ethical relativism,[1] although it may perhaps be called an instance of situational ethics. Such a distinction is obviously important, for if it were not clearly made, nearly everyone would be a relativist and the category would be meaningless.

What then, is relativism in ethics? Actually, there are two types of relativism that concern us. The first may be termed "normative relativism."[2] Normative relativism is the view that: (a) there are conflicting ethical opinions—not merely situational differences—about precisely the same moral subject among individuals; (b) there is a rational, reliable method for objectively answering ethical questions; but (c) in spite of this rational method, it is still sometimes impossible to declare one ethical opinion more valid than another. Thus, it is possible to have conflicting but equally valid moral judgments about precisely the same subject. Furthermore, the claim is not merely that according to present knowledge the two opinions must be considered equally valid, but that given a *complete* set of facts including future evidence and a totally rational method of determination, it is still possible that two conflicting moral judgments will be equally valid. This leads to interesting consequences, as described by Frankena. "What is right or good for one individual or society is not right or good for another, even if the situations involved are similar, meaning not merely that what is thought right or good by one is not thought right or good by another . . . but that what is really right or good in the one case is not so in another" (5, p. 109).

The second type of ethical relativism with which we are concerned is termed "metaethical relativism."[3] This view agrees with the above assertion that conflicting ethical opinions may be equally valid, but for a different reason—there is no rational method for distinguishing between them. Obviously, if there is no way of establishing one moral judgment over another conflicting one, if there is no unique conclusive method of determination, then it follows that they must be considered equally valid. As Brandt (2) states, this relativist gives up the task of finding the right answers to ethical questions and is content merely to find agreement.[4]

The simple claim of absolutism, contrary to all forms of relativism, is that it is impossible for conflicting ethical opinions to be equally valid. If two ethical opinions differ in their basic moral assumptions, it is impossible for both of them to be right.

The two dimensions of moral reasoning discussed thus far provide us with four terms that are important to an understanding of metaethical theories:

subjectivism: moral assertions are statements of attitude.
objectivism: moral assertions are independent of attitude.
relativism: two conflicting ethical opinions may be equally valid.
absolutism: two conflicting ethical opinions cannot be equally valid.

NATURALISM

A clear and succinct statement of the central thesis of naturalism is given by R. B. Brandt. He comments:

Ethical statements can, after all, be confirmed, ethical questions answered, by observation and inductive reasoning of the very sort that we use to confirm statements in the empirical sciences—and for a reason that the other theories overlook or do not take seriously: because of what ethical statements *mean*. In other words, it is held that on reflection, we can see that the *meaning* of ethical statements is such that we can verify them just like the statements of psychology or chemistry. [2, p. 152]

To the uninitiated, the naturalist's claim appears ludicrous, but consider the following: If ethical terms are defined in such a way that *good*, for instance, means "being an object of favorable interest (desire)" (14), then all that must be done to determine if something is good is to discover if it is an "object of favorable interest." That is an achievable empirical task and means, therefore, that ethics itself is subject to scientific observation and calculation in determining moral truth. The naturalist claims that all ethical terms and statements can be defined in *non*ethical terms (as above) and that these can then be put to empirical test. Because of this view, ethics is thus considered a department of empirical science, or part of what "is." For this reason, naturalism has often been characterized by the phrase "Ought can be defined in terms of Is, and Value in terms of Fact."

It should also be added that the naturalist claims that there is moral truth—ethical statements are either true or false. This is an important point because one of the metaethical theories to be considered later discards the notion of truth in ethics.

Briefly, then, the theory of naturalism asserts that: (*a*) there *is* moral truth; (*b*) all ethical terms can ultimately be defined in nonethical terms; and (*c*) ethical questions can therefore be answered empirically. To illustrate the theory of naturalism it may be helpful to discuss briefly several moral philosophers who hold a naturalist position.

Edward Westermarck

One example of naturalism is the ethical theory of Edward Westermarck (25,26). Westermarck's theory is totally subjectivist; all ethical judgments are seen as statements of attitude. For instance, to say that x is wrong is merely to say "I have a tendency to feel disapproval of x." Similarly, to say that something is right (or good) is merely to

express an attitude—"I have a tendency to feel approval of x."
Speaking directly on subjectivism and objectivism, Westermarck
observes:

I have thus arrived at the conclusion that neither the attempts of moral
philosophers or theologians to prove the objective validity of moral judgments, nor the common sense assumption to the same effect, give us any
right at all to accept such validity as a fact. So far, however, I have only tried
to show that it has not been proved; now I am prepared to take a step further
and assert that *it cannot exist*. The reason for this is that in my opinion the
predicates of all moral judgments, all moral concepts, are ultimately *based on
emotions*, and that, as is very commonly admitted, *no objectivity can come from
an emotion*. [25, p. 60] (Emphasis ours.)

Thus, Westermarck clearly asserts subjectivism in moral theory and
this leads him to a normative relativism. Normative relativism does
not always follow from subjectivism, e.g., in the case of appeal to
God's attitudes, but it is clear that in this instance it does. Obviously,
if moral or ethical truth is defined solely in terms of one's attitudes on
certain issues (and Westermarck does specify that these attitudes
must be impartial and disinterested), and if people have different
attitudes on those issues (regardless of their impartiality and disin-
terestedness), then patently the truth varies—two conflicting ethical
opinions are equally valid. Brandt's following comment illustrates
this point. According to Westermarck,

my ethical statement is true if I have a corresponding tendency to feel
emotion. . . . [Westermarck] was concerned to emphasize that there is no
such thing as absolute truth in morals in the sense of there being moral
statements that everyone must accept *independently of how he feels*. We cannot
establish the statement, say, "Homosexuality is a bad thing". We can show
that it is correct for you to say this, or for me, depending on our feelings; but
if someone comes along who does not get excited about homosexuality, then
he would be mistaken if he said it is wrong. [2, p. 167]

Westermarck's reasoning on this issue would thus likely be: If I feel
disapproval of homosexuality, then my ethical judgment that homosexuality is wrong is true, simply because my impartial disapproval is
the definition of moral truth. If true moral judgments are simply a
function of attitudes, and if I truly disapprove of homosexuality, then
it is truly wrong. But, by the same token, if I feel approval of
homosexuality, then it is right. Hence, my judgment of homosexuality is either right or wrong, depending on how I feel. This example
reveals the normative relativism inherent in Westermarck's theory.

To relate this directly to naturalism and the assertion that there is moral truth, however, requires more discussion. For how can a naturalist, one who believes moral statements are either true or false, be a relativist and thus say that the truth varies? If one believes there is truth, how can he simultaneously believe that it can vary—is it consistent to speak of "varying truth?" In answer to this, these points have already been established: (*a*) Westermarck's theory is a sub-jectivist one—ethical statements are statements of attitude; (*b*) if one actually does have the attitudes he expresses, then his statement is true; and (*c*) attitudes differ from person to person; thus, the truth differs from person to person and is relative. The subtlety which classifies the theory as a form naturalism is found in the second point. On each *individual* basis, we can speak of empirically knowable moral truth, for the definition of truth for Westermarck is merely *the congruence between one's statement and his actual attitude*, and this is scientifically testable. If a person makes a normative statement that does not correspond with his real attitude, then the ethical statement is false. If he makes a normative statement which does correspond with his real attitude, then the ethical statement is true. There is, then, individual moral truth, and it is on this basis that Westermarck is properly classified as a naturalist.

Roderick Firth

Another example of a naturalist theory is Roderick Firth's ideal observer theory (4).[5] The basic proposition of this theory is that if an ideal observer existed, his "ethically significant reactions," or moral emotions, would be the determining property of moral truth and falsity. By appealing to what an ideal observer would feel in a moral situation one may know the proper course of action.

But what characteristics constitute an ideal observer? Firth lists six such characteristics. First, the ideal observer is omniscient with respect to the nonethical facts of any situation. That is, he is in possession of all the factual information, both past and future, that can influence his moral emotions and the determinations of right and wrong. He has all the facts of the case. Second, the ideal observer is omnipercipient, or he possesses an unlimited imagination, allowing him to visualize "all actual facts, and the consequences of all possible acts in any given situation" (4, p. 214). Third, the ideal observer is disinterested. This means that he does not have interests in the outcome of the case and he is entirely impartial. Fourth, the ideal

observer is dispassionate; he has no particular attachments or emotions such as jealousy or hatred which are directed toward any
individuals. A fifth characteristic is that the ideal observer is consistent. This means that his moral emotions in response to any particular
act will always be exactly the same; his attitude concerning that act,
which includes its time and place and the alternatives associated with
it, would never change. The sixth and final characteristic of the ideal
observer, in order to cover all the other necessary characteristics
which defy precise definition, is that he is in all other respects entirely
normal.

That Firth's ideal observer theory, like Westermarck's, is naturalist
can be seen from the fact that it satisfies the three primary conditions
of naturalism. First, all ethical terms can be defined in nonethical
terms, i.e., in the attitudes of the ideal observer. Firth says that
"ethical statements are statements about an ideal observer and his
ethically-significant reactions [moral attitudes]" (4, p. 221). Second,
ethical issues can be answered empirically by appeal to what are (or
would be) the ideal observer's attitudes. Finally, there is moral truth,
and it is defined by the ideal observer's attitudes.

It should also be noted that, by our definitions, this theory, like
Westermarck's, is subjectivist. For instance, Firth objects to speaking
of what he calls the ideal observer as being an ideal *judge* because that
term implies that the function of this ideal being is to pass judgment
on ethical issues and that there is objective moral truth which is
independent of the being and which he merely taps in order to pass
judgment on specific ethical issues. What Firth proposes, however, is
that the being's attitude *is* the truth. The ideal observer, Firth says,
must be capable of "reacting in a manner which will determine *by
definition* whether an ethical judgment is true or false" (4, p. 203,
emphasis added). Clearly, the ideal observer's attitude is the definition of moral truth and thus by our definitions the theory is
subjectivist.[6]

While, like Westermarck's theory, Firth's may be considered subjectivist, unlike Westermarck's it is clearly absolutist rather than
relativist. Although in Westermarck's theory attitudes must be impartial and disinterested, it is nevertheless allowed, even assumed,
that such attitudes, and thus the truth, will vary from person to
person. In Firth's ideal observer theory, however, if the individual is
"ideal," that is, if he is omniscient, fully imaginative, impartial,
dispassionate, consistent, and otherwise normal, he will necessarily

have exactly the same attitude as any other individual who fits that description. There is no variance from ideal observer to ideal observer, and thus there is no variance in truth. Firth states that "if ethical statements are ever true, they are true only because we have defined an ideal observer in such a way that . . . *any* ideal observer would react in the same way to a particular act" (4, p. 219). Firth states that his theory is "unquestionably absolutist" and that it implies that ethical statements are true or false "without special reference to the people who happen to be asserting them" (4, p. 202). Truth is determined by the moral emotions of an ideal observer irrespective of the attitudes of any others; because ideal observers will always agree, the theory is clearly absolutist.

It is this distinction that makes one of these subjectivist theories relativist and the other absolutist. The ideal observer theory assumes that any person under any circumstances who is endowed with the characteristics of an ideal observer will respond exactly the same and experience exactly the same moral emotions as any other ideal observer in the same circumstance. It is impossible, then, to have conflicting ethical statements which are equally valid, and thus the theory is absolutist. In Westermarck's theory, however, although moral truth is similarly defined by attitudes, no requirement is placed upon agreement among those with the qualifying (i.e., impartial and disinterested) attitudes. Thus, since attitudes vary from person to person, so does the truth, and thus it is that two conflicting ethical opinions can be equally valid.

That both theories are naturalist, however, can be seen from the fact that each fulfills the three requirements of naturalist theories. First, each defines all ethical terms in nonethical terms, someone's attitudes; second, ethical issues are thought to be empirically answerable, by appeal to the specified attitudes; and third, each claims that there is moral truth, that ethical statements lend themselves to issues of truth and falsity. We have seen, though, that beyond satisfying these three conditions, theories of naturalism may vary considerably. Like Westermarck's theory, they may be relativist, in a normative sense, but never in a metaethical one, or, like this version of the ideal observer, they may be absolutist. Also, although both of these theories are subjectivist, naturalist theories may also be objectivist (2). Thus, various theories of naturalism differ considerably in one or more dimensions of moral thought, but their basic manner of justification is always the same: First, define all ethical terms in nonethical ones, and then by inductive reasoning and/or empirical observation, determine their truth or falsity.

Nonnaturalism, as the name implies, essentially denies the postulates of naturalism. All nonnaturalists agree on the following points:

    (a) There is moral truth; ethical statements are either true or false.

    (b) Ethical terms *cannot* be defined in nonethical terms and are ultimately indefinable.

    (c) Ethical issues can be answered, but not by empirical observation.

Except for the first point, nonnaturalism is a fundamental denial of the postulates of naturalism.

It follows from the first point that ethical terms refer to actual properties. In some naturalists' theories, e.g., Westermarck's, the term *right* refers to the property of "my tendency to approve." In this sense ethical terms refer to properties, and on this basis, ethical statements are either true or false; they correctly identify the property or they do not. The same is true for the nonnaturalist. However, there is one very important difference. The nonnaturalist claims that some of the properties to which ethical terms refer are simple and irreducible and cannot be defined into something like an attitude. The most common example of this point is G. E. Moore's use of "yellow"; he states: "My point is that 'good' is a simple notion, just as 'yellow' is a simple notion; that, just as you cannot, by any manner of means, explain to anyone who does not already know it, what yellow is, so you cannot explain what good is" (12, p. 7). Thus, it will not do to say simply that *good* means "is desired by someone," for it does not mean that at all. *Good* refers to some other property which cannot be explicated or explained; it is indefinable because there is no more basic or more simple phrase that means the same thing. It is simple and irreducible. Nonnaturalists disagree about which ethical term is indefinable, and they also disagree about whether there is more than one term that fits into this category. However, they do agree that there is at least one such term.

Nonnaturalists believe that although ethical terms refer to properties, these properties are not directly observable, as the naturalist claims. Thus, although "good" may be like "yellow" in the sense that it is a simple unanalyzable notion and that it may in fact be known, it is unlike "yellow" in the sense that it cannot actually be observed or perceived. This is why the nonnaturalist denies the efficacy of empiricism in ethics; terms like *good* and *ought* do not refer to empirical qualities such as "yellow" and "attitude"; instead, they refer to nonnatural, nonempirical qualities that cannot be observed. The nonnaturalist claims that ethical terms refer to actual properties but that these properties cannot be known by observation.

Intuition

The nonnaturalist asserts, however, that these simple properties are intelligible and can be known. How is this possible without scientific observation? Nonnaturalists generally postulate two methods of obtaining moral knowledge. The first of these is intuition or direct knowledge. The nonnaturalists who are intuitionists argue that because moral properties, at least ultimately, are simple and irreducible and because they cannot be perceived or sensed, they can only be known by direct awareness. If a person knows something due to sensory presentation, through visual appearance, touch, smell, and the like, he knows it indirectly or by inference from that sense experience. But between moral principles and the person's knowledge of them, there is no such intervening sensory process; he knows moral principles directly. He intuits or feels moral principles and thus has direct awareness of particular ethical facts, e.g., the Spanish Inquisition was wrong, without the intervention of any sensory experience.

In a sense, the intuitionist is released from answering the "whys" in moral argument. He knows something is right or wrong because of intuition; however, that intuition need not include a reason for its rightness or wrongness. For instance, one might argue that complete chastity before marriage is right, not because it leads to something in particular or prevents something in particular, but simply because intuition tells one that it is right. A person does not feel obligated to offer reasons but merely to share his intuitions. This, apparently, is Thomas Jefferson's intent as he begins the Declaration of Independence with the statement "We hold these truths to be self-evident." There is no need to offer legal or logical arguments for these truths because they are self-evident, or directly apprehended, and all men can test their verity in the same way—by appeal to their natural intuition.

Rational Insight

The second mode of knowledge claimed by many nonnaturalists is that of rational insight. It is claimed by these theorists that pure reason alone is capable of establishing moral truth and, further, that it is impossible for empirical observation to do so. The rational nonnaturalist claims: (*a*) that moral truths are "synthetic"; they are "about the world" and not merely about the meanings of words (as our final metaethical theory will claim); and (*b*) these truths are necessary; they don't just happen to be true—they *must* be true. Brandt explains the nature of these necessary truths:

[Ethical principles] are, it is said, like the principles of logic or mathematics. Or, more exactly, they are like the proposition that space has three dimensions, that a cube has twelve edges, that anything that is red is colored . . . and so on. All these propositions, it is said, are not only true . . . they *could not* be false. . . . Once one sees what "red" means and what colored means, one sees that any red thing *must* be colored. [2, p. 187]

In other words, a necessary truth states what must be the case, e.g., all red things must be colored because it is impossible for them to be otherwise. Not all truths are of this nature, however. For instance, if one measures a pencil and finds it is six inches long, then the statement "This pencil is six inches long" is true. But it only happens to be true; it does not follow that because this instrument is a pencil that it must be six inches long, for it could be many different lengths and still be a pencil. This is true of most things in our experience: this table has four legs, this room is hot, London is the capital city of England, etc. They only happen to be true, there is no logical necessity that requires them to be true.

The rational nonnaturalist, however, asserts that all moral truths are, like logical and mathematical principles, necessarily true; they do not merely happen to be true, they could not be otherwise. Ordinarily the naturalist agrees that moral statements are synthetic, meaningful statements about the world, but he denies that they are necessary. He claims, instead, that moral truths merely happen to be true and that there is no logical necessity entailed in them.

This, obviously, is an important difference between naturalists and nonnaturalists and suggests how each would seek to justify ethical statements. This is because it is impossible for empirical, sensory experience to yield, or justify, necessary truths. David Hume (8) was the first to point this out; his argument is concisely stated by A. J. Ayer:

No general proposition whose validity is subject to the test of actual experience can ever be logically certain. No matter how often it is verified in practice, there still remains the possibility that it will be confuted on some future occasion. The fact that a law has been substantiated in n-1 cases affords no logical guarantee that it will be substantiated in the nth case also, no matter how large we take n to be. [1, p. 72][7]

Thus, if one considers moral truths to be necessary, one must give up verifying them through empirical observation, for if they are necessary, empirical methods simply do not apply. That which applies to necessary truths is pure reason or rational insight. Thus, naturalists believe that moral truths only happen to be true. These are called "contingent" truths and naturalists attempt to discover them empirically. Conversely, rational nonnaturalists believe moral truths are necessary—they must be true—and that they can be apprehended only rationally or logically, as are mathematical principles. Thus, in their ideas about the nature of moral truths the naturalist and the rational nonnaturalist are in direct opposition. This partially explains the different ways in which each seeks to justify moral statements.

In summary, then, there are two basic nonnaturalistic modes of moral knowledge: intuition and rational insight. Although one appeals to the direct awareness of simple indefinable moral properties and the other to the logical necessity of moral principles as necessary truths, they are both in absolute opposition to naturalistic empiricism as justification of ethical statements. For this reason, they are both generally included under the heading of nonnaturalism.

To understand nonnaturalism, we do not need to refer to statements of its specific theorists as much as we did in the case of naturalism. This is because nonnaturalists deny the necessity, even the possibility, of ultimately defining ethical terms, and it is the difference caused among naturalists by such "definism" that requires discussion of specific theorists in order to understand naturalism itself. However, there are nonnaturalist theorists such as Kant (9, 10),

Prichard (17), Ross (18,19), Ewing (3), Moore (11,12), and Sidgwick (22) with whom the interested reader may want to become more familiar.

Nevertheless, it is important to see how the moral dimensions described a⁺ the first of this chapter relate to nonnaturalism. For instance, it should be clear that all forms of nonnaturalism must be objectivist. Since ethical terms are ultimately simple and indefinable properties of some kind, they obviously transcend or at least reside outside of emotion and cannot therefore be thought of as mere expressions of attitude. Thus, there is something objective about moral truth that is independent of feelings. For this reason, nonnaturalist theories are objectivist. Also, it should be equally clear that nonnaturalist theories are absolutist. If two individuals disagree about the nature of an absolute and indefinable property (or even if they disagree about whether a given act or quality possesses that property), it is impossible for both of them to be right. This point is especially obvious in the case of the rational nonnaturalist who claims that all moral truths are necessary; it would be impossible for those truths to be other than they are. How could two opposing statements about such logically necessary truths both be considered valid? It would be impossible, and so the theory must be absolutist.

To summarize: nonnaturalism consists of three major propositions: (a) there is moral truth—ethical statements are either true or false; (b) ethical terms are ultimately indefinable; and (c) ethical issues can be answered, but not empirically. Within this general framework, some nonnaturalists, intuitionists, propose that ethical properties are directly apprehended, while others, rationalists, assert that moral truths are necessary and are objects of the understanding. Further, all nonnaturalist theories are objectivist and absolutist; there is no relativist form of nonnaturalism, either normative or metaethical. Historically, perhaps the most important feature of nonnaturalism is its fundamental denial of most of the major postulates of naturalism.

NONCOGNITIVISM

As we have seen, both naturalists and nonnaturalists accept the notion that ethical judgments are, in one way or another, statements of fact. For instance, naturalists or nonnaturalists could say "Stealing is wrong," and they would be stating what they believe to be a justifiable and verifiable fact—that stealing is wrong. Likewise, they believe that all normative statements—"pain is bad," "killing is wrong," "gossip is evil"—are assertions or declarations that simply state facts. The manner of justifying such statements of fact will vary depending on their naturalistic or nonnaturalistic inclinations, but they will never deny that they *are* either true or false. This is the first proposition of both of these theories.

Noncognitivists, however, such as Ayer (1) and Stevenson (23,24) who emphasize logical positivism, or Hare (6,7) and Nowell-Smith (13), who focus on linguistic analysis, escape both naturalism and nonnaturalism by flatly denying this first proposition. The noncognitivist holds that we miss the very point of ethical statements if we think of them as either true or false, or as declarations stating facts. They are, rather, non-fact-stating, and merely express emotions, issue commands, or prescribe certain attitudes. Moral statements cannot be true or false in any fundamental sense. The main proposition of noncognitivism is: There is no moral truth as such; ethical statements are not either true or false. It follows from this proposition that there is no need for a method of ultimate justification, whether it is empirical observation, intuition, or rational insight. All these efforts are misdirected and meaningless exercises since there is no truth to be discovered. For the noncognitivists the primary task in metaethics is analyzing and understanding exactly what we mean by our normative statements, not in justifying them.

A greater understanding of noncognitivism may be gained by briefly discussing three specific theorists. The noncognitive theory known as "emotivism" has been extensively argued by A. J. Ayer (1). Ayer's historically important theory asserts, as do all noncognitivists', that ethical statements are neither true nor false, but he adds that *all* they do is express the speaker's emotion. The following oft-quoted passage from *Language, Truth and Logic* expresses Ayer's ideas:

to say to someone, "You acted wrongly in stealing that money," I am not stating anything more than if I had simply said, "You stole that money". In adding that this action is wrong, I am not making any further statement about it. I am simply evincing my moral disapproval of it. It is as if I had said, "You stole that money", in a particular tone of horror or written it with the addition of some special exclamation marks. The tone, or the exclamation marks, adds nothing to the literal meaning of the sentence. It merely serves to show that the expression of it is attended by certain feelings in the speaker. [1, p. 107]

Again: "In saying that a certain type of action is right or wrong, I am not making any factual statement, not even a statement about my own state of mind. I am merely expressing certain moral sentiments" (1, p. 107). Thus, to say "Stealing is wrong" is like saying "Stealing!!!" Or to say "Mercy is good" is like saying "Hurrah for mercy!" In neither case is there a statement of truth, nor is there even a prescription that others ought to disapprove of stealing and approve of mercy; there is merely the statement of the speaker's emotion. In Ayer's conception of ethics there can be no meaningful moral argument, as all parties are merely expressing their emotions and one cannot be said to be preferable to another.

C. L. Stevenson, another noncognitivist, accepts much of Ayer's position but adds the significant point that not only do moral judgments express the speaker's attitudes,[8] but they also seek to evoke similar attitudes in the audience. His definitions of ethical terms, then, are these.

1. "This is wrong" means I disapprove of this; *do so as well*.
2. "He ought to do this" means I disapprove of his leaving this undone; *do so as well*.
3. "This is good" means I approve of this; *do so as well*. [23, p. 21]

Thus, Stevenson preserves the concept of ethical statements as expressions of attitude but further defines them as attempts to get others to share those attitudes.

Another important point made by Stevenson is that although moral judgments are expressions of attitudes, these attitudes are largely based upon our beliefs. This means that it is possible, at least to some extent, to have meaningful moral debates. Frankena offers this example:

I may favor a certain course of action because I believe it has or will have certain results. I will then advance the fact that it has these results as an argument in its favor. But you may argue that it does not have these results, and if you can show this, my attitude may change and I may withdraw my judgment that the course of action in question is right or good. In a sense, you have refuted me. [5, p. 106]

This, of course, is not the type of moral argument a naturalist or nonnaturalist would consider very fundamental or significant, but it is a significant revision of Ayer's position in that moral argument is considered meaningful and worthwhile.

A third example of noncognitivism is that of R. M. Hare (6,7). He has referred to his theory as "universal prescriptivism"; the job of ethical statements is not merely to express emotions (Ayer's view) or merely to influence others' attitudes (Stevenson's view), but to prescribe certain moral principles and thus guide human conduct. This view, in contrast to the other noncognitivists' views, implies that there must be some rational bases for morals. Obviously, if the task of ethical statements is to be a guide to human conduct, then there must be a degree of rationality in ethics that the other noncognitivists who speak merely of expression and influence deny.

The question to ask Hare is: "Given that moral judgments can be rational and thereby in some sense justified, how does one determine the rationality of moral judgments?" That is, if one cannot claim that his basic moral assumptions are true (either through empirical observation, intuition, or rational insight), how can he defend them as rational?

Hare answers this question by postulating that moral judgments are universalizable and that a speaker's ethical statement is thus rational if he is willing to universalize it to all logically possible cases. For example, if a burglar breaks into a house in order to rob it, the owner cannot rationally say that the burglar ought to be shot and then shoot him, unless he is willing to say that everyone ought to be shot in similar circumstances, including himself. If he is unwilling to admit that he ought to be shot under the same circumstances, then his moral judgment that the burglar ought to be shot is irrational and unjustifiable. By this definition it is possible to speak of rational moral statements that justifiably prescribe and guide human conduct. In this sense, ethical statements are subject to proof. Obviously, this type of proof is broader than that used by naturalists and nonnaturalists, because there is no assertion that universalized ethical statements are true; there is only the statement that they are rational and justified. Only in this sense are they subject to any proof, but in terms of the meaningfulness of moral debate, this is a significant revision of other noncognitivist theories. Here, rationality and sincerity are made strict requirements of moral judgments, and they can thus at least be evaluated on that basis.

Hare's position is not that ethical statements can be ultimately justified in the sense of being demonstrably true, but only that they can be justified more broadly in the sense of being rational and sincere. Clearly, this maintains the noncognitivist's proposition that ethical statements are neither true nor false, but it does, in lieu of truthfulness, offer some rationale for making and justifying moral judgments.[9]

It can be seen from the discussion of these three theorists that all noncognitivists maintain that there is no truth value in ethics. It may be that in some cases, and by some definitions, one ethical statement may be more rational than another, but it is never the case that one may be true and the other false. It is in this fundamental sense that all noncognitivists disagree with both the naturalists and nonnaturalists.

SUMMARY

The three major metaethical theories have been discussed in this chapter, and it may be well to summarize the basic propositions of each.

Naturalism: (a) There is moral truth; ethical statements are either true or false.
                       (b) Ethical terms can be defined in nonethical terms.
                       (c) Ethical questions can be answered by empirical observation.

Nonnaturalism: (a) There is moral truth; ethical statements are either true or false.
                       (b) Ethical terms cannot be defined in nonethical terms and ultimately are indefinable.
                       (c) Ethical questions can be answered, but not by empirical observation.

Noncognitivism: (a) There is no moral truth; ethical statements are neither true nor false.
                       (b) The function of ethical statements is to express emotions, or influence others' attitudes, or rationally guide human conduct.

It is within one of these three philosophical contexts that philosophers explain and justify their moral assumptions or normative reasoning. Thus, if one says "pain is bad," he is responsible both for explaining what he means and for explaining why he said it, even if this involves only Ayer's emotivism. It is the combination of these two things that establishes an individual's metaethical foundation. This foundation combined with one's normative principles constitutes the essential nature of his total moral thought. It is with an interest in the individual's total moral thought as described and explained.by philosophy, then, that we now turn to a discussion of psychology and its role in the study of moral reasoning.

NOTES

1. See Brandt's comments, for instance (2, pp. 99–103, 271–72).

2. This is Frankena's term (5, p. 109), but it is equivalent to Brandt's "nonmethodological relativism (2, pp. 278–84).

3. This is Frankena's term (5, pp. 109–10), but it is equivalent to Brandt's "methodological relativism" (2, pp. 275–78).

4. A third type of relativism is called "descriptive relativism" (5, p. 92). This is the assertion that people and societies differ in their basic normative assumptions and not merely in their factual ones. Brandt (2, pp. 99–103, 273, 275) discusses this point and accepts it, while Frankena (5, pp. 109–10) discusses it and seriously doubts it.

5. F. C. Sharp (21) has also proposed an ideal observer theory, but it is different in some significant respects from Firth's theory, presented here.

6. It is important to note here that, using different definitions than those we have used above, Firth described his theory as objectivist. He defines as subjectivist any theory which implies that for moral truth to exist there must be experiencing subjects, and as objectivist any theory which does not imply this. By these definitions Firth's theory is objectivist because it does not imply that an ideal observer must exist in order to define moral truth, but only that if he *did* exist then moral truth would be defined in such and such a way. Firth's discussion is based entirely on an ideal observer as a possible, hypothetical being to whom, nevertheless, we can appeal in a conditional way (e.g., "if he existed, then . . . "). By this definition the ideal observer theory is rightly considered objectivist. Firth's definitions, however, do not seem to have been widely accepted, and so we have used definitions that seem of greater heuristic value to beginning readers.

7. Many authors, including Popper (15, 16), make extended use of this principle.

8. Stevenson distinguishes between his term *attitude* and Ayer's term *emotion*, but this distinction is not essential to our discussion.

9. It may be asked in what substantial way the naturalist theory of Edward Westermarck and other relativists differs from the noncognitivist theory of R. M. Hare. The answer is this: Westermarck's ethical statements are assertions about one's state of mind. Thus, if one's ethical assertions are congruent with one's state of mind, then those ethical assertions are true, and this truth is empirically demonstrable. The ethical statements of the noncognitivist, however, assert nothing about one's state of mind; they merely express, influence, or prescribe. There is nothing the noncognitivist says with which these acts must be congruent; thus, it is meaningless to speak of them as being "true"; they are simply "there." This is a subtle distinction and perhaps makes Westermarck somewhat difficult to classify, but there is a basic difference over truth in ethics, and this is sufficient reason to make the distinction.

11

THE PSYCHOLOGIST
AND MORAL REASONING

5 / Psychological Theories of Moral Reasoning

We have briefly explored the philosopher's struggle with morality. One aspect of this struggle is his endorsement of some normative theory. The serious moral philosopher generally embraces a normative stance that, at least for him, directs the issue of morality—what is right or wrong, good or bad—allowing him to approach specific situations with an established moral sense and a philosophical rationale for making moral choices. Thus, Stirner, an egoist, approaches moral choices with a strict, "What's in it for me?" rationale (24, 33); Jeremy Bentham, a utilitarian, approaches the same issues inquiring, "What will produce the greatest amount of pleasure?" (6); and Kant, a deontologist, begins with the query, "What is my duty?" (10). In each case, with the exception of some deontologists, the issue of what constitutes right and good has already been decided and needs only to be applied to the situation at hand. This adoption of a normative stand with which one can settle moral issues and within which one can propose *the* moral attitude and *the* definition of *right* and *good* is the first part of the philosopher's struggle with morality.

The second major portion of this struggle is to justify the normative stand that one adopts. The moral philosopher must eventually defend his advocacy of the basic moral attitude: for instance, on what basis does one come to believe that morality is defined as the greatest good for the greatest number rather than as pleasure for oneself? Justifying such a choice, the most important concern of metaethics, is a difficult, complex task that philosophers have wrestled with for centuries. Sidgwick (29), for instance, appeals to the nonnaturalistic

85

method of intuition to justify his acceptance of utilitarianism; Westermarck (35, 36) includes actual empirical observations, a naturalistic method, to justify normative theory; and, Stevenson (31, 32) and others use an appeal to linguistic analysis, or principles such as "universalizability," essentially noncognitive methods, to provide justification for given normative theories.

The psychologist's discussion of morality and moral reasoning is quite different from the philosopher's. Whereas the moral philosopher asks, "Why should people believe or do something?" the psychologist more commonly asks, "What do people believe or how do they act?" This makes the psychologist's task different from the philosopher's. The essential difference is that the moral philosopher's work is prescriptive, while the psychologist's is largely descriptive. The main work of the psychologist concerned with moral reasoning consists of observation and explanation. The psychologist wants to observe the natural phenomenon of moral development either through naturalistic observation or through more direct experimental manipulation of significant variables. He then wants to explain, in the most meaningful but parsimonious terms, the facts that he has observed. Finally, once the explanation seems satisfactory, the applied psychologist may wish even to influence the actual development of moral reasoning.

At this time, the most important concern among psychologists interested in moral reasoning is explanation. There are two major theoretical approaches, both claiming to be the best explanation of available data. The first, associated with various social learning theories of moral development, is behaviorism. Bandura (3,4) and others (2,7,9,22) are divergent examples (see 17). Behaviorists assert their ability to explain all behavior, including moral thinking, by using a single, broad paradigm.

In their explanation of behavior, behaviorists identify two basic causes. The first is the collection of all individual differences, such as sex, health, and especially inherited genetic traits, the individual brings to any situation. The second is the pattern of learning contingencies generally called "experience." Therefore, subject to any biological and/or physiological limitations, an individual's behavior is contingent upon his reinforcement and learning history. The development of moral reasoning is explainable in the same way any behavior is explained: one comes to adopt a given normative theory because its adoption has resulted in more reinforcing events; it is a quantitative accumulation of data which is organized into a pattern of reasoning according to the reinforcements one has experienced.[1]

The second major theory, which departs from the behavioristic analysis and is presently the most popular theory for explaining moral development, is the cognitive-developmental approach. The primary architects are Piaget (25, 26, 27) and Kohlberg (11, 12, 13, 14, 15, 16, 17, 18, 19). This theory, while accepting and including some of behaviorism, focuses primarily on the interaction of the individual with his environment, an interaction that produces another unique and separate factor to be considered in the explanation of any behavior, including moral reasoning. Kohlberg explains: ". . . cognitive-developmental theories are 'interactional', i.e., they assume that basic mental structure is the product of the patterning of the interaction between the organism and the environment rather than directly reflecting either innate patterns in the organism or patterns of events (stimulus contingencies) in the environment" (18, p. 350). Further, "the cognitive-developmental assumption is that basic mental structure is the result of an interaction between certain organismic structuring tendencies and the structure of the outside world, rather than reflecting either one directly" (18, p. 352).

The cognitive-developmental theory postulates the existence of innate structuring tendencies in the individual which, when coupled with the environmental contingencies, result in a new entity and explains the individual's basic mental structure. This, in turn, forms the governing unit of an individual's moral development. Cognitive-developmentalists further theorize that the individual actually proceeds through a series of stages in reaching mature morality. Discussion of these stages and further details of cognitive-developmental theory can best be presented in a discussion of the work of Piaget and Kohlberg. Piaget's work will be discussed first, as his laid the foundation for Kohlberg's.

JEAN PIAGET

Piaget wrote more and in greater detail about children's thinking than anyone else. Using both observation and experiments, often with his own children, he developed a comprehensive theory of children's moral thought. Piaget began by studying the rules of children's games, which led him to a more explicit study of moral development itself. He first examined the rules for playing marbles, because marbles is a very simple yet definitely social game in which the rules are devised by the children themselves and are not imposed upon them by others. Understanding Piaget's findings concerning children's use of such rules lays a foundation for understanding his insights into moral development.

Children's Use of Rules

Using Rules, Stage One

Early in his investigations, Piaget noted three characteristics in the behavior of the three-and-a-half-year-old child who is given a handful of marbles to play with. First, the child exhibits a lack of organization or direction, performing a number of different, unconnected actions with the marbles. Second, the child soon begins to repeat certain acts more frequently than others, producing a regularity of behaviors. Third, the marbles eventually become symbols or are used as representatives of other events in the child's environment, such as candy, eggs, or automobiles. All three of these typical acts, particularly the symbolism, occur without any instruction or help from adults. These elements constitute the first stage and are identifiable by both consciousness and regularity, even if they are only simple motor responses. This basic stage is considered to be amoral in nature.

Using Rules, Stage Two

The second stage of development Piaget calls "egocentricism." In this stage, a later one occurring between three and five years of age according to Piaget, children become aware that there are rules for the game. Piaget found that older children know that in order to play the game, one must first make a square, place some marbles inside the square, and then expel some of the marbles by hitting them with another marble. Each child then proceeds to practice the game in almost any way that fits his needs, believing he is playing the game fully and completely, not recognizing that other people do not play the game as he plays it. Piaget's inquiries reveal that the child is unable to comprehend that other persons do not play the game as he plays; he is unable to comprehend the social nature of the interactions. For example, there is no awareness of the idea of winning; to win means simply playing on one's own. Basically, also, there is no interaction with other people, but only attempts to imitate adults or older children from a distance. Finally, their conversations are not attempts at communication, but mere repetitions of expressions the child has himself overheard.

Using Rules, Stage Three

Piaget found that the third stage begins about age seven or eight and continues until age ten. During the third stage, the child tries to obey the common rules shared with other players. In this stage communication develops between the players, and each child tries to adhere to the same rules, expecting other children to do the same. A child no longer simply tries to get marbles out of the square in a ritualistic manner but tries to do it according to a set of laws or rules adhered to by all participants.

Using Rules, Stage Four

In this stage all participants agree upon and comply with common rules. The new element is an ability to generalize or to apply the rules to more than one game or situation. This stage begins about age eleven or twelve. Codes of rules are developed, and the codes are applied to all games.

In order to understand Piaget's concepts, one should know that he believes that one of the first concepts children learn is the concept of order or regularity in the universe. Almost everything becomes a law of regularity to the child, and as he grows, he continues to be aware of regularity as additional rules continue to be imposed upon him. Piaget believes that when a child first encounters any new object or a game, he tends to believe that there is a set of rules which must apply to these new objects. Thus, without being able to understand the rules in marbles, for example, and even in the absence of any modeling, the child engages in the practice of ritualization during play. The child thereby produces a regularity or lawfulness, even in the simplest play, which corresponds to his awareness of rules in all aspects of life. Moreover, this awareness or consciousness could occur without any verbalization on the child's part.

The practice of rules at stage two implies a desire to imitate or copy the actions of others engaging in the game. Here the consciousness of rules usually seems to be verbalized. At this stage, Piaget investigated consciousness of rules by asking three questions.

Can rules be changed?

Have rules always been the same as they are today?

How did rules begin?

Although the child sometimes ignores and breaks rules freely, Piaget found that the child's conceptions or consciousness is more rigid than is his practice or actions. The child has an almost mystical respect for rules, attributing their origin to elders, to God, or to the government. The child will not consider changing or altering any rules, stating that they have always been as they are today. One girl believed that the rules were put in her head by God: "Before I was born he put it there." The children Piaget questioned were four, five and six years old.

After the age of ten, however, an almost complete transformation concerning rules develops. Rules no longer appear to be sacred; external laws may be laid down by authority, but they are viewed as conventions made by free decision in cooperative activity. From his discussions, Piaget found that children believe that rules can be changed if everybody votes for it. Thus, since laws can be changed by consensus, they are no longer considered eternal. Many rules are therefore conceived as resulting from free discussion and agreement; they can be modified, changed, or discarded. Piaget also found, contrary to the expectation that such an attitude would weaken obedience to rules, that with this attitude the rules are seen as moral laws and actually serve as even more effective guides to behavior. He says:

> But is it the consciousness of autonomy that leads to the practical respect for the law, or does this respect for the law lead to the feeling of autonomy? These are simply two aspects of the same reality: when a rule ceases to be external to children and depends only on their free collective will, it becomes incorporated in the mind of each, and individual obedience is hence forth purely spontaneous. [25, p. 71]

This stage is said to appear and develop toward the end of age ten and eleven, and this is also the age when cooperative activities—the third stage of cooperative practice of rules—occurs. Piaget notes that children of twelve and thirteen prefer a democratic process of deciding rules. Opinions are held in respect and are clearly considered; people have the right to challenge existing rules. Piaget relates that when a child is making a democratic decision about the acceptance or rejection of values, he has in mind an ideal or spirit of the game against which rules are evaluated. For example, rules favoring skill are preferred to those favoring luck.

Piaget maintains that the democratic basis and the cooperative nature of rules in the game of marbles is a result of peer interaction. While this same basic approach is not always apparent in other aspects of an eleven- or thirteen-year-old's life, it is apparent in the game of marbles because he is allowed to participate and to discuss fully the rules with peers who are equals. In other aspects of life, he is not given this opportunity.

Two Moralities

Piaget's observations of these patterns in children's use of rules allow us to appreciate more fully his conception of moral development. He identifies two separate moralities: one, a more primitive morality of constraint, or heteronomy; the other, a morality of cooperation, or autonomy. Although these two moral processes can overlap considerably in a child's life (and thus they do not constitute precisely distinct stages) Piaget asserts that the second eventually replaces the first and that this pattern is invariant: autonomy always follows heteronomy and never precedes it. These two stages also include substages of development. An egocentric stage precedes the first morality.

Egocentrism

Before the child is aware of his existence as a distinct self and other people as selves, he is in an undifferentiated alogical and amoral state. He is egocentric and, if it were not for social interaction and cognitive growth in later years, the individual would remain in this state. In this stage, he is not able to distinguish between his own perspective and those of other people and is not aware that there are distinct others who have other perspectives; thus he cannot be conscious of his own thought and has nothing with which to compare it. He makes no evaluation of his thoughts; ideas and perspectives for him do not require verification. Consequently, tenderness can coexist with a naive selfishness, and the child cannot consider one of them to be superior to the other. He simply does not submit his feelings to any evaluation. He is nonmoral and simply reacts to his environment.

Heteronomy

It is only through adult constraint and unilateral respect for the adult that the child first establishes and begins to form logical and moral control. This early moral control is a "morality of constraint," which Piaget calls intellectual "realism." The child ceases to affirm every thought that he might want to believe and begins, for example, to distinguish between truth and falsehood, recognizing that some ideas are valid and that others are not. The simple criterion for validity, however, is confirmation by an adult; the things that are true are those spoken by an adult authority. This represents some advance in reasoning over the egocentric stage, but actually it is not as different from the alogical mentality as it seems at first. Formerly, the child would accept *any* idea without questioning; now he accepts statements he is told *by an adult* without question. The self's pleasure has been replaced by the authority's pleasure; there is still no objective evaluation or thinking.

Piaget calls this morality "heteronomy," or "subject to another's law." The child gives the adult's will the rank of supreme importance, the position that was formerly held by his own desires and feelings. At this point, there is no real concept of good; right is defined as obedience to the will of authority. As a result of this characteristic, the child views issues in absolute terms; shades of gray do not exist. He cannot perceive the intentions behind an act to determine rightness; he judges solely on the basis of consequences. Thus, a child who breaks fifteen cups with good intentions is judged naughtier than a child who breaks only one cup while having bad intentions. Viewing the world in such absolute terms, the child at this stage of morality sees rules as eternal and unalterable. Rules must be obeyed; they cannot be changed, broken, or even established through the mutual agreement of the parties involved. Rules are external to him; they are revealed and imposed on him by the adult and they should be treated sacredly. At this stage of morality, the child views values of right and wrong as absolute rules. This moral realism does not, however, entirely replace the child's original egocentrism; the child's absolutism still prevents him from assuming the role of another person and seeing things from another perspective.

Transition

The child next enters an intermediate stage in which he no longer gives his allegiance to the adult authority but gives it instead to the rules themselves. He begins to comprehend rules, differentiate between them, and apply them in original ways. This moves the child halfway toward a moral autonomy. He no longer appeals to adult authority, but he nevertheless appeals to rules that are still imposed from outside and that are not a product of his own mind. Piaget says very little about this stage, and its only importance for him is as a steppingstone to autonomous moral reasoning.

Autonomy

Piaget concluded that an authoritarian approach to morality could never eliminate the egocentrism of the first three stages and produce the sense of justice that is considered necessary for mature moral reasoning. This mature morality develops only from the give-and-take of peer interaction with concomitant discussion, criticism, equality, and mutual respect. Through these influences, a new and more mature "morality of cooperation" develops. Piaget called this stage "moral autonomy" or being "subject to one's own law." As the child develops new logical skills and experiences cooperation in peer interaction, he realizes that his perspective is not the only possible one, that even adult authorities and the ideas they enunciate are not the only alternatives and need not be accepted unquestionably as *the* right. Ideas, whether by-products of one's spontaneous egocentric convictions or faith in adult authority, need to be verified. Fortunately, cooperation and peer interaction produce the criticism and discussion which lead the child to compare his motives and rules with those of others. He begins to evaluate his own and others' moral rules, including those of adults. Rather than relying upon adult restraint, he begins to see morality in terms of social necessity and mutual respect among equals. He no longer sees rules as being absolute and sacred and instead begins to see them in terms of peer agreement and mutual benefit. The child becomes more autonomous in moral reasoning, depending less on the imposition of rules from the external world. This leads to a suppression of both egocentrism and moral realism. At this point, the child can objectively judge the acts and commands of others; moral judgments at this stage come from within rather than from without.

Autonomy versus Heteronomy

Piaget described at least seven dimensions of moral judgment that distinguish the morality of constraint (heteronomy) from autonomous morality.

1. Younger children tend to make absolute moral judgments, not realizing that there may be several relative points of view.
2. The heteronomous child tends to judge an act to be bad if the actor is punished, not recognizing the possibility of an unjust punishment.
3. Younger children tend to have an immature conception of reciprocity, using it as an exact return of good or evil instead of considerate treatment of others as a basis.
4. The heteronomous child tends to view punishment as having only a punitive function and tends to favor severe punishments, whereas the autonomous child believes that punishment is justified only if it has a reformative or restitutive function.
5. Using moral realism, the child tends to base his judgment about the badness of an act solely on the consequences of the act instead of considering the intention of the person performing the act.
6. Younger children tend to believe in immanent justice, which is the belief in automatic punishment which emanates from things themselves or which flows from God's will.
7. Younger children do not consider the importance of the intentions or purpose in evaluating an action. [13, pp. 396–98]

In explaining these differences, Piaget postulated a correlation of general cognitive development with the moral stages that have just been discussed. Understanding this correlation is important in understanding Piaget's theory. He believes that there can be no significant moral movement without significant cognitive movement; cognitive development is a necessary (though not sufficient) condition for moral development. This relationship is detailed in table 2. The other condition necessary for mature moral development is social experience—the movement from adult constraint and authoritarianism to the mutual equality and reciprocity typified by peer interaction. Piaget explains the growth from heteronomous to autonomous modes of moral thought as being the result of both cognitive development and social experience.

AUTONOMOUS MORAL THOUGHT: CLARIFICATIONS

Piaget sees autonomy as the goal of development and as partly the product of an active environment, particularly the social interaction in which the child individuates himself and experiences mutual respect and cooperation. In the cognitive realm, this social interaction produces a more accurate perception of the world and gives the child the necessary intellectual tools with which to interpret the world. It increases the child's ability to analyze the situations he encounters. Morally, it leads to a sense of justice, an internalization of morality, and an increased maturity in a variety of specific moral judgments.

In this higher, autonomous stage of moral reasoning which follows realism, the child no longer obeys the rules or commands given him by adults; he obeys himself. One of Piaget's first clear statements about the development of autonomy is this:

> We see the first signs of it when [the child] discovers that truthfulness is necessary to the relations of sympathy and mutual respect . . . autonomy. For moral autonomy appears when the mind regards as necessary an ideal that is independent of all external pressure. Now, apart from our relations to other people, there can be no moral necessity. The individual as such knows only anomy and not autonomy. Conversely, any relation with other persons, in which unilateral respect takes place, leads to heteronomy. Autonomy therefore appears only with reciprocity, when mutual respect is strong enough to make the individual feel from within the desire to treat others as he himself would wish to be treated. [25, p. 196]

According to Piaget justice is the essential element in the investigation of autonomous morality. He believes that children learn justice not from adults or their rewards and punishments, or even from example, but automatically, through the interaction and respect children develop with each other. In fact, he finds that it is often in spite of the adult that children acquire a sense of justice.

> It is often at the expense of the adult and not because of him that the notions of just and unjust find their way into the youthful mind. In contrast to a given rule, which from the first has been imposed upon the child from outside and which for many years he has failed to understand, such as the rule of not telling lies, the rule of justice is a sort of immanent condition of social relationships or a law governing their equilibrium. [25, p. 198]

Piaget proposes three steps in the development of this sense of justice.

First Step of Justice: Obedience to Authority

In the first period, justice cannot be distinguished from duty or conforming to adult authority. Punishment is accepted, even when

TABLE 2. PIAGET'S STAGES OF MENTAL-MORAL DEVELOPMENT

Stage of Development and Approximate Age	Cognitive Development	Moral Development with Focus on Rules
1. SENSORI-MOTOR Age: 0–2 years Amoral	Child can differentiate himself from objects, gradually becoming aware of the relationship between actions and their effects on the environment. He learns that objects continue to exist even though no longer visible (object permanence).	Child handles materials, e. g., marbles, in an individual way to see what he can do with them. Motor activity is best characterization.
2. PREOPERATIONAL Age: 2–7 years Egocentric	Child sees language can represent objects by images and words, but is still *egocentric*. He has difficulty taking the viewpoint of others and will classify objects by single salient features. Toward the end of this stage he begins to use numbers and develop conservation concepts.	Child has only a general idea of what rules are, but he plays by his own idiosyncratic systems and changes rules when it suits his purpose.
3. CONCRETE OPERATIONAL Age: 7–12 years Heteronomous	Beginning of logical thought; child can use concepts of number (age 6), mass (age 7), weight (age 9). He can classify objects in series along a dimension and understand relational terms (A is longer than B), but must have *concrete* examples to work with.	Child is constrained by respect for adults and older children; whatever these authorities say must be so. He refuses to accept any change in rules. His ideas are still vague; three children playing together will give three different explanations of the rules.

the punishment produces inequality. Expiation rather than reciprocity is the type of punishment that is preferred, and the child still believes in immanent justice. If obedience and equality conflict, the child will favor obedience. Authority, in this case, is preferred to justice. This period is characterized by unilateral respect, a result of laws imposed by an adult.

TABLE 2. CONTINUED.

Stage of Development and Approximate Age	Cognitive Development	Moral Development with Focus on Rules
4. FORMAL OPERATIONAL Age: 12–adult Autonomous	Child can think in abstract terms, using logical propositions. Reasons by hypothesis. Becomes concerned with the hypothetical, the future, and ideological problems.	Child sees rules as laws due to mutual consent. Has set aside belief in the infallibility of parents, and other authority figures. Sees himself as equal of others and believes that since people made the rules, people can change them. And sees himself as equally able to change them. No longer accepts adult authority without question. All children in a group know and play by the same rules.

Second Step of Justice: Equality

The second step is a period of development toward autonomy; equality gradually supercedes authority. The child no longer accepts expiatory punishment and proposes reciprocal punishments instead. Belief in immanent justice decreases and morality is defined independently of punishment. The child now sees justice in terms of equality.

Third Step of Justice: Equity

Now equity replaces equality, equity being a judgment of equality that takes into account other human circumstances. Justice is tempered so that punishment is not given until all factors are considered. Now that the child takes into account personal circumstances in his conception of justice, simple equality may disappear from his thinking.

Piaget notes the importance of action by teachers and parents to the development of higher forms of justice:

Authority as such cannot be the source of justice, because the development of justice presupposes autonomy. This does not mean, of course, that the adult plays no part in the development of justice, even of the distributive kind. In so far as he practices reciprocity with the child and preaches by example rather than by precept, he exercises here, as always, an enormous influence. [25, p. 319]

To summarize: Piaget has proposed two causes of moral development: (*a*) cognitive development, and (*b*) social interaction, characterized first by adult authority and later by mutual peer respect and reciprocity. The combination of these factors leads to the development of moral autonomy and to a mature sense of justice. Piaget has skillfully systematized these two origins of moral thinking into a coherent theory which is not only internally consistent but also compatible with his independent theory of cognitive development and logical thinking. The following statement by Piaget is perhaps the best summary of his theory:

Thus adult authority, although, perhaps it constitutes a necessary moment in the moral evolution of the child, is not in itself sufficient to create a sense of justice. This can develop only through the progress made by cooperation and mutual respect—cooperation between children to begin with, and then between the child and adult as the child approaches adolescence and comes, secretly at least, to consider himself as the adult's equal. [25, p. 320]

LAWRENCE KOHLBERG

Early Development

Building within this basic cognitive-developmental framework of Piaget, Lawrence Kohlberg has elaborated and specified various aspects of moral development (11, 12, 13, 14, 15, 16, 17, 18, 19). There have been two major periods in the development of Kohlberg's theory. In his early theoretical formulations Kohlberg was guided by an "aspect" approach to moral development. He identified twenty-five aspects of moral reasoning which were subsumed under the following major categories: rules, conscience, welfare of others, self's welfare, sense of duty, role taking, punitive justice, positive justice, and motives. He also identified six stages of development which were defined in terms of these aspects, each stage representing a more highly developed, integrated, and autonomous conception of these aspects than the preceding stage. For example, the issue "motive given for rule obedience or moral action," was seen in the following manner for the six stages:

Stage 1: Obey rules to avoid punishment.
Stage 2: Conform to obtain rewards, have favors returned, and so forth.
Stage 3: Conform to avoid disapproval or dislike of others.
Stage 4: Conform to avoid censure by legitimate authorities and resultant guilt.
Stage 5: Conform to maintain the respect of the impartial spectator judging in terms of community welfare.
Stage 6: Conform to avoid self-condemnation. [11, p. 111]

In another of these moral issues, "the value of human life," the six stages were defined thus:

Stage 1: The value of a human life is confused with the value of physical objects and is based on the social status or physical attributes of its possessor.
Stage 2: The value of a human life is seen as instrumental to the satisfaction of the needs of its possessor and of other persons.
Stage 3: The value of a human life is based on the empathy and affection of family members and others toward its possessor.
Stage 4: Life is conceived as sacred in terms of its place in a categorical moral or religious order of rights and duties.
Stage 5: Life is valued both in terms of its relation to community welfare and in terms of life being a universal human right.
Stage 6: Belief in the sacredness of human life as representing a universal human value of respect for the individual. [11, p. 111]

These moral issues were seen to share certain basic elements. Kohlberg stated that the most important moral elements, particularly with reference to early development of children, are comparable to Piaget's dimensions of moral judgments, for example, intentionality, reciprocity, independence of sanctions, and so forth. Also, Kohlberg claimed that the child's reasoning about these moral elements has a stagewise progression. Thus, when the child is evaluating a situation in moral terms, he will make references to and use certain moral issues. His conclusion will depend upon which issues he considers appropriate and on what level he is reasoning.

Table 3 depicts Kohlberg's basic six-stage model as it was postulated in that earlier period.

TABLE 3. DEFINITION OF MORAL STAGES

I.

PRECONVENTIONAL LEVEL

The child is responsive to cultural rules and labels of good and bad, right or wrong, but interprets these in terms of either the physical or hedonistic consequences of action (punishment, reward, exchange of favors), or in terms of the physical power of those who enunciate the rules. The level is divided into two stages:

Stage 1: Punishment and obedience orientation. The physical consequences of action determine its goodness or badness regardless of the meaning or value of these consequences. Avoidance of punishment and unquestioning deference to power are valued in their own right, not in terms of respect for an underlying moral order (the latter being stage 4).

Stage 2: Instrumental relativist orientation. Right action is that which instrumentally satisfies one's own needs and occasionally the needs of others. Human relations are viewed in terms of the marketplace. Fairness, reciprocity, and equal sharing are present, but are always interpreted in a physical, pragmatic way. Reciprocity is a matter of "you scratch my back and I'll scratch yours," not of loyalty, gratitude, or justice.

II.

CONVENTIONAL LEVEL

Maintaining the expectations of the individual's family, group, or nation is perceived as valuable in its own right, regardless of consequences. The attitude is not only one of *conformity* to personal expectations and social order, but of loyalty to it, of actively *maintaining,* supporting, and justifying it, of identifying with the persons or group involved in it. This level has two stages:

Stage 3: Interpersonal concordance or "good boy—nice girl" orientation. Good behavior is that which pleases or helps others and is approved by them. There is much conformity to stereotypical images of what is majority or "natural" behavior. Behavior is frequently judged by intention—"he means well" becomes important for the first time. One earns approval by being "nice."

Stage 4: "Law and order" orientation. Orientation is toward authority, fixed rules, and the maintenance of the social order. Right behavior consists of doing one's duty, showing respect for authority, maintaining the social order for its own sake.

III.

POSTCONVENTIONAL, AUTONOMOUS, OR PRINCIPLED LEVEL

The person makes a clear effort to define moral values and principles which have validity and application apart from the authority of the groups or persons holding these principles, and apart from the individual's own identification with these groups. This level has two stages:

Stage 5: Social-contract, legalistic orientation, generally with utilitarian overtones. Right action is defined in terms of general individual rights and

TABLE 3. CONTINUED.

standards which have been critically examined and agreed upon by society. The person is clearly aware of the relativism of his values and opinions and so he emphasizes procedural rules for reaching consensus. Aside from what is constitutionally and democratically agreed upon, right is a matter of personal "values" and "opinion"; emphasis is thus on the "legal point of view," but with the possibility of changing law in terms of rational considerations of social utility rather than freezing it in terms of stage 4. Outside the legal realm, free agreement and contract is the binding element. This is the "official" morality of the American government and constitution.

Stage 6: Universal ethical principle orientation. Right is defined by the decision of conscience in accord with self-chosen *ethical principles* appealing to logical comprehensiveness, universality, and consistency. These principles are abstract and ethical (the Golden Rule, the categorical imperative); they are not concrete moral rules like the Ten Commandments. At heart, these are universal principles of *justice* of the *reciprocity* and *equality* of human *rights*, and of respect for the dignity of human beings as *individual persons.*

Source: Adapted from: 15, pp. 164–65.

Kohlberg concluded at that time, and still maintains, that moral development is sequential and directed. The pattern of individual development is an invarying sequence starting with stage one and progressing without skipping a stage until the point at which one culminates one's moral thinking is reached. He also believes that the sequence is culturally universal. However, young people in various cultures develop at different rates and may not reach the same final stage as that reached by youth in other cultures.

Kohlberg made the following specific points about his stages and their sequence (adapted from 12, p. 192): (*a*) They are qualitatively different modes of thought rather than increased knowledge of, or internalization of, adult moral beliefs and standards. (*b*) They form an invariant order or sequence of development. Movement through these stages is always forward and always step-by-step. (*c*) The stages form an integrated whole. There is a general factor of a moral stage cross-cutting all dilemmas, verbal or behavioral, with which an individual is confronted. (*d*) The stages are hierarchical integrations. Subjects comprehend all stages below their own and not more than one above their own. Each new stage represents a synthesis between the prior stage and new elements; in this way a given stage serves as a prerequisite for a higher stage, or a later mode of thought. Also, (*e*) Stages are viewed neither as the direct reflection of maturation nor as the direct reflection of learning in the sense of specific environmental stimulus exposures, reinforcements, and the like. "Stages represent, rather, the equilibrated pattern of interaction between the organism and the environment."

In one article (19) Kohlberg also described an even higher stage. This seventh stage, it was said, involves "the sense of being a part of the whole of life and the adoption of a cosmic as opposed to a universal humanistic (Stage 6) perspective" (19, p. 501). His example is Spinoza (30), who saw all finite things, even man, as parts of an infinite cosmic whole. In more recent times the writings of Bateson (5) and Taylor (34) seem to reflect a similar view. Such a perspective, Kohlberg adds, does not quite fit the form of the other stages because of its ambiguity; it is a religious orientation, in the broadest sense of the term, but it implies no single religion or ethical philosophy. Because of this difference, Kohlberg never actually incorporated it into his stage model, although it is discussed as a possible further stage.

Recent Developments

More recently, Kohlberg has made an important change in his characterization of moral development (17). His postulation of six stages and their invariant developmental nature has remained intact, but he has abandoned the aspect approach to the scoring of moral development. Instead, Kohlberg focuses on "social perspective," or the view one has of his relationship to society, as the basic structural element in the development of moral maturity. From this view, a level one, preconventional person is one who views rules and various adult-social expectations as external to himself. Rules are imposed from without, or "above," and are not objectively considered or evaluated. A level two conventional person is one who has internalized the expectations of society and authorities. He no longer considers rules as external to the self, but views himself as a member of society who has simply internalized the appropriate guidelines for conduct. A level three postconventional person is one who has differentiated himself from others' expectations and rules and who adopts self-chosen principles instead. His principles may coincide with the expectations of his society, but they are not chosen because they do so. Here the individual is seen as logically prior to society.

Morality is a matter of individual choice and commitment, not simply the internalization of others' expectations and rules.

It is important to note how Kohlberg's recent emphasis on social perspective as the basic structural element of moral development approximates Piaget's emphasis much more closely than his previous works. Piaget stresses the development of an individual from immature heteronomy, or dependence on external sanctions, to a mature autonomy characterized by independence and the willingness to evaluate objectively others' expectations or rules. Kohlberg's more recent stage characterization seems also to do this. The individual is seen as developing from a position of blind reliance on adult and social influences to a position of self-reliance and individual commitment to self-chosen principles. This development is implicit in the earlier model but becomes entirely explicit only in the later one.

Kohlberg made the change because of his recognition that the previous model had confused content and structural elements of moral thought. In his attempt to examine only structural elements, content had become involved, confusing the issue of underlying structural changes—the primary concern of cognitive developmental theory. In focusing too much attention on what the person believes (content), Kohlberg had obscured the underlying thought structures behind the beliefs. His more recent model explicitly attempts to deal primarily with structural concerns. Apparently, this explains its closer similarity to Piaget's formulations, for concepts such as heteronomy and autonomy are clearly ones of structure. The importance of this distinction between content and structure will be made more explicit in chapter ten.

Kohlberg's recent stage characterization is presented in table 4. It should be noted that he lists the topics "what is right" and "reasons for doing right" under content. Social perspective is seen as the structural dimension which underlies these content elements and provides their common element. He says: "What underlies these characteristics of reasoning and holds them together? What fundamentally defines and unifies the characteristics [of a given stage] is its *social perspective* . . ." (17, p. 36). Thus the egocentric perspective of stage one is that which explains the child's conception of the right as the avoidance of rule breaking, and his reason for doing right as the fear of punishment. Similarly, the "moral" perspective of stage six explains the individual's adherence to self-chosen ethical principles

TABLE 4. THE SIX MORAL STAGES

	Content of Stage		
Level and Stage	What Is Right	Reasons for Doing Right	Social Perspective of Stage
LEVEL I— PRECONVENTIONAL Stage 1— Heteronomous Morality	To avoid breaking rules backed by punishment, obedience for its own sake, and avoiding physical damage to persons and property.	Avoidance of punishment, and the superior power of authorities.	*Egocentric point of view.* Doesn't consider the interests of others or recognize that they differ from the actor's; doesn't relate two points of view. Actions are considered physically rather than in terms of psychological interests of others. Confusion of authority's perspective with one's own.
Stage 2— Individualism, Instrumental Purpose, and Exchange	Following rules only when it is to someone's immediate interest; acting to meet one's own interests and needs and letting others do the same. Right is also what's fair, what's an equal exchange, a deal, an agreement.	To serve one's own needs or interests in a world where you have to recognize that other people have their interests, too.	*Concrete individualistic perspective.* Aware that everybody has his own interest to pursue and these conflict, so that right is relative (in the concrete individualistic sense).

and his emphasis upon universal justice as motivations for and conceptions of the right. The same, of course, follows for the other stages as well. It should be noted, given the importance of the distinction between content and structure, that what are considered content elements here are the same dimensions, essentially, that are used as the sole criteria of stages in Kohlberg's earlier stage model. This is an important difference between the two models and will be seen in chapter ten to take on added importance.

Kohlberg also describes four "moral orientations" or decisional strategies that are involved in any social situation. These are:

1. *Normative order*: Orientation to prescribed rules and roles of the social or moral order. The basic considerations in decision making center on the elements of *rules*.
2. *Utility consequences*: Orientation to the good or bad *welfare consequences* of action in the situation for others and/or the self.

TABLE 4. CONTINUED.

	Content of Stage		
Level and Stage	*What Is Right*	Reasons for Doing Right	*Social Perspective of Stage*
LEVEL II— CONVENTIONAL Stage 3—Mutual Interpersonal Expectations, Relationships, and Interpersonal Conformity	Living up to what is expected by people close to you or what people generally expect of people in your role as son, brother, friend, etc. "Being good" is important and means having good motives, showing concern about others. It also means keeping mutual relationships, such as trust, loyalty, respect and gratitude.	The need to be a good person in your own eyes and those of others. Your caring for others. Belief in the Golden Rule. Desire to maintain rules and authority which support stereotypical good behavior.	*Perspective of the individual in relationships with other individuals.* Aware of shared feelings, agreements, and expectations which take primacy over individual interests. Relates points of view through the concrete Golden Rule, putting yourself in the other guy's shoes. Does not yet consider generalized system perspective.
Stage 4—Social System and Conscience	Fulfilling the actual duties to which you have agreed. Laws are to be upheld except in extreme cases where they conflict with other fixed social duties. Right is also contributing to society, the group, or institution.	To keep the institution going as a whole, to avoid the breakdown in the system "if everyone did it," or the imperative of conscience to meet one's defined obligations (Easily confused with Stage 3 belief in rules and authority . . .)	*Differentiates societal point of view from interpersonal agreement or motives.* Takes the point of view of the system that defines roles and rules. Considers individual relations in terms of place in the system.

3. *Justice or fairness*: Orientation to *relations* of liberty, equality, reciprocity, and contrast between persons.
4. *Ideal-self*: Orientation to an image of actor as a *good self*, or as someone with conscience, and to his motives or virtue (relatively independent of approval consequences from others). [17, p. 40]

For research purposes, Kohlberg combines the normative order and utilitarian orientations into a single Type A. The just and ideal-self orientations are combined into a Type B. Type A judgments are more descriptive and predictive, usually directed toward the situation "out there." Type B judgments are more prescriptive or ought-oriented and are stated in terms of what is internally acceptable to the self. Kohlberg asserts that each moral stage can be divided

TABLE 4. CONTINUED.

	Content of Stage		
Level and Stage	*What Is Right*	Reasons for Doing Right	*Social Perspective of Stage*
LEVEL III— POSTCONVENTIONAL, OR PRINCIPLED Stage 5—Social Contract or Utility and Individual Rights	Being aware that people hold a variety of values and opinions, that most values and rules are relative to your group. These relative rules should usually be upheld, however, in the interest of impartiality and because they are the social contract. Some nonrelative values and rights like *life* and *liberty*, however, must be upheld in any society and regardless of majority opinion.	A sense of obligation to law because of one's social contract to make and abide by laws for the welfare of all and for the protection of all people's rights. A feeling of contractual commitment, freely entered upon, to family, friendship, trust, and work obligations. Concern that laws and duties be based on rational calculation of overall utility. "the greatest good for the greatest number."	*Prior-to-society perspective.* Perspective of a rational individual aware of values and rights prior to social attachments and contracts. Integrates perspectives by formal mechanisms of agreement, contract, objective impartiality, and due process. Considers moral and legal points of view; recognizes that they sometimes conflict and finds it difficult to integrate them.
Stage 6— Universal Ethical Principles	Following self-chosen ethical principles. Particular laws or social agreements are usually valid because they rest on such principles. When laws violate these principles, one acts in accordance with the principle. Principles are universal principles of justice: the equality of human rights and respect for the dignity of human beings as individual persons.	The belief as a rational person in the validity of universal moral principles, and a sense of personal commitment to them.	*Perspective of a moral point of view* from which social arrangements derive. Perspective is that of any rational individual recognizing the nature of morality or the fact that persons are ends in themselves and must be treated as such.

SOURCE: 17, pp. 34–35.

into these A and B substages. For instance, in the Heinz dilemma (see pp. 161–62), where the task is to decide whether or not Heinz should steal in order to save his wife's life, a stage 3A subject reasons in terms of "What does a good husband do? What does a wife expect?" Conversely, a stage 3B subject thinks in terms of "What does a husband who is a partner in a good mutual relationship do? What does each spouse expect of the other?" (17, p. 41). Thus, although each is a stage three response (sharing, meeting expectations), the B response shows a greater concern for a balance, or fairness. Kohlberg says:

Because of this balance, B's are more prescriptive or internal, centering more on their judgments of what ought to be. They are also more universalistic, that is, more willing to carry the boundaries of value categories, like the value of life, to their logical conclusion. As an example, a Stage 3 subject responded to Heinz's drug-stealing dilemma by giving a standard A response, "A good husband would love his wife enough to do it." Asked whether a friend would steal a drug for a friend, he said, "No, a friend isn't that close that he has to risk stealing." He then added, "But when I think about it, that doesn't seem fair, his friend has just as much right to live as his wife." [17, p. 41]

Kohlberg finds that, within any moral stage, there is a progression from A to B type judgments. The B substage is more mature than the A substage; a 3A subject, for instance, can move to 3B, but a 3B subject cannot move to 3A. However, individuals can skip the B substage altogether, for example, move from 3A to 4A; but within any given stage, the movement is always from A to B. Kohlberg suggests this is evidence for the notion that justice is the primary criterion of morality: the highest stage of moral development (stage six) culminates in a concern for principles of justice, and within each stage there is also movement toward a concern for justice. This is evidence, he says, that justice is the ultimate standard of morality, a claim which has been more fully described, and criticized, elsewhere (1, 2, 15, 21, 23).

Kohlberg's Stages: General Considerations

While Kohlberg gives no specific age guidelines for each of his stages, he does state that attainment of a stage level is dependent upon underlying cognitive development (17). A person whose logical stage is only concrete operations would be limited to reasoning within stages one and two. A person who is able to reason only within the low strata of formal operations would be limited to moral stages three and four. A full understanding of formal operations is necessary for stages five and six. This would indicate that stage five and six reasoning could not occur until after approximately age twelve, and usually not even until much later. As will be pointed out in later chapters, however, attainment of the logical stage of cognitive development does not insure that one will reason at the higher moral levels. Basic cognitive development is a necessary, but not a sufficient, condition for mature moral development.

Kohlberg similarly maintains that attainment of a higher level of reasoning will not necessarily insure that behavior will match the moral reasoning processes. He states:

> To act in a morally high way requires a high stage of moral reasoning. One cannot follow moral principles (stages 5 and 6) if one does not understand or believe in them. One can, however, reason in terms of such principles and not live up to them. A variety of factors determines whether a particular person will live up to his stage of moral reasoning in a particular situation, though moral stage is a good predictor of action in various experimental and naturalistic settings. [17, p. 32]

It is important to note that Kohlberg makes the same claims for his recent stage sequence as for his earlier one: that is, the stages are qualitatively different modes of thought; they form an invariant sequence of development; each stage forms an integrated cluster or whole; the stages are hierarchical, each one laying a necessary foundation for the ones following; and finally, the stages are a reflection of interaction between the individual and his environment.

Incorporating these features, Kohlberg lists the following as basic assumptions in the cognitive-developmental approach to moral development:

1. Moral development has a basic cognitive-structural or moral judgmental component.
2. The basic motivation for morality is a generalized motivation for acceptance, competence, self-esteem, or self-realization, rather than for meeting biological needs and reducing anxiety or fear.
3. Major aspects of moral development are culturally universal, because all cultures have common sources of social interaction, role taking, and social conflict, which require moral integration.
4. Basic moral norms and principles are structures arising through experiences of social interaction, rather than through internalization of rules that exist as external structures; moral stages are not defined by internalized rules, but by structures of interaction between the self and others.
5. Environmental influences in moral development are defined by the general quality and extent of cognitive and social stimulation through-

out the child's development, rather than by specific experiences with parents or experiences of discipline, punishment, and reward. [17, p. 48]

Perhaps Kohlberg's most important contribution has been, and will continue to be, his stimulation of an enormous amount of research on human morality. His earlier stage characterization and moral reasoning test gave researchers a common basis for discussion and opened the way for measurement in an extremely elusive, but important, area of human behavior. Although that test has been criticized (20), it nevertheless offered a common ground for researchers and served as a springboard for the development of further measurement instruments, notably that developed by Rest (28). However, with this latest and most important change in approach to the study of moral development, Kohlberg's work will likely take on even more significance than it held in the past.

NOTES

1. For a general discussion of behaviorism see Hilgard and Atkinson (8).

6 / Selected Issues in Moral Reasoning

So far in our examination of the psychology of moral reasoning our primary concern has been with theoretical issues rather than with empirical findings. Experimental literature dealing with moral reasoning will now be presented and interpreted in this chapter. The topics are broad, and discussion is sometimes detailed. For this reason one need not read the chapter straight through but can use it as an information resource to turn to as interest or necessity dictates. Although this review of research literature is not comprehensive, the discussion under each issue provides a fair representation of present knowledge. To expedite rapid skimming of these research results, each section begins with a statement summarizing the results of the experimental research presented in that section.

IS MORAL REASONING RELATED TO BEHAVIOR?

The research indicates that behavior generally is related to moral thought.

"Sow a thought reap an act." "As a man thinketh so is he." These two proverbs reflect the assumption that most people behave as they think. Does research support this conclusion? The answer is controversial and has been debated among social scientists for decades (1, 69). There are many studies failing to show a relationship between moral knowledge, reasoning, values, and related behavior (e.g., 36, 40, 78, 86, 87), and there are also research reviews critical of this conclusion (81, 114). This skeptical attitude is usually associated with an acceptance of behaviorism in psychology. In the early formulation of behavioral theory, inner variables such as beliefs, cognitions, and the like were discredited as causal factors because evidence for such a relationship was lacking and because such a heavy reliance was placed on them that direct external causes were ignored. Today, however, many behaviorists feel that the past rejection of inner causal agents from their theory was too extreme. Albert Bandura (3, 6), for example, in his continual efforts to refine social learning theory, has provided data and theory arguing that there are cognitive determinants of associative learning, behavioral inhibitions, emotional behavior, and psychotic and other behaviors. He also presents many examples illustrating this contention, suggesting that cognitive factors may well be associated with many behavioral manifestations.

Some reviews, accordingly, have reported modest correlations between moral thought, or attitudes, and behavior (1, 43, 62), and many research results also support this. For example, in one study (41), junior and senior high school students were asked if they agreed with the statements: "Suckers deserve to be taken advantage of" and "To get ahead, you have to do some things that are not right." Those having records of delinquency were more likely to agree with these statements than those who had not committed delinquent acts. These same authors found a similar difference between delinquent and nondelinquent youth when asking questions regarding respect for police authority.

Other researchers (110) have found that they could distinguish delinquent adolescent boys and girls from other public school children by asking them certain questions. The public school children who were more likely to support the following values were typical of happy, successful persons.

(*a*) "To treat other people with kindness and sympathy" (nurturance)

(*b*) "To accept the leadership of people he admires" (deference)

(*c*) "To make as many friends as one can" (affiliation)

However, delinquent boys and girls were more likely to choose the following precepts:

(*a*) "To supervise or direct the actions of other people whenever he can" (dominance)

(*b*) "To tell someone off when he thinks that person has wronged him" (aggression)

(*c*) "To be the center of attention in a group" (exhibition)

It was also found (28) that delinquents score lower than other children on Kohlberg's Moral Reasoning Scale[1] (see also [16]) and that those delinquents who scored lowest were more willing to yield when someone attempted to change their minds about a moral decision they had previously made. The same researcher also found greater yielding to social influence among nondelinquents who scored low on Kohlberg's Moral Reasoning Scale (29).

In another type of experiment, Rubin and Schneider (99) found that seven-year-old children who scored high on a Piaget test of moral judgment involving less egocentricism were more likely to engage in two types of altruistic behaviors, to donate candy to poor children and to help a younger child complete a task.

Among preadolescents, Keasey (59) found that higher stages of moral reasoning were associated with social participation and mature leadership. (Teachers and peers provided data about leadership and social participation.) And others have found indications (not always substantiated—85,86) that children who tend to be more mature in moral judgments are also less likely to cheat (35, 106).

The relationship between reasoning and behavior seems to grow stronger with age. For example, it was found (45) among Canadian girls in the fourth to seventh grades that those with lower levels of moral valuing and knowledge also engaged in more cheating, and the strength of this relationship increased with age.

In at least one study it was found that beliefs can inhibit moral behavior (109). Fourth-grade children were taken into an empty room to do some drawing. They were aware that another child occupied an adjoining room. They then heard a tape recording of a sequence of sounds which seemed to come from the next room; something crashed, followed by sobbing and calls for help, such as "Help, please help! I fell off my ladder, my foot is caught, please help!" This lasted for seventy seconds. The experimenter wanted to know if the children would go into the adjoining room to help the child in distress. It was found that help was offered only when a child understood that he could leave the room. When leaving the room had been prohibited or when no information was given about leaving the room, the results were the same: in neither case would the child leave the room to help. Nevertheless, even in the group where permission to leave the room was understood, only half of the children attempted to help. Staub has repeated this same type of experiment and has reported similar findings (107, 108).[2]

A most provocative group of studies report the investigation of the levels of moral reasoning and contemporary social behavior using the Kohlberg scale. A study which fostered much subsequent research, as well as controversy, was conducted shortly after the Berkeley sit-ins (38). These researchers found they could divide their sample into two groups: (*a*) The protestors who engaged in sit-ins, peace marches, or picketing and various forms of social disruption, and who took direct action in issues regarding freedom of speech, war in Viet Nam, racism, and so forth. (*b*) All nonprotesting students, especially those who were politically inactive, fraternity and sorority members, etc., but including those who engaged in special service activities. Having divided their sample into these two categories, they administered Kohlberg's Moral Reasoning Scale and found that 56 percent of the activists were at the higher levels of moral reasoning, whereas only 12 percent of the nonprotestors were. In fact, 85 percent of the nonprotestors were at level four, which is characterized by adherence to law and order or social conformity. Only 36 percent of the protestors were at this level. However, 60 percent of those at level two participated in the sit-in.

Continuing the same approach, other researchers at Yale University, Fishkin, Keniston, and MacKinnon (27), found that an individual's political ideology was related to his stage of moral reasoning. For example, stage four reasoning, law and order, was associated with the least radical ideology, and other correlations were found as well. In this case the research describes a relationship between one cognition and another. This of course does not technically demonstrate a cause-and-effect relationship between reasoning and behavior, but if moral reasoning is related to another cognition which has a known and predictable relationship to behavior, such as liberalism has to voting behavior, then it is highly suggestive that there is a tie between moral reasoning and some actions as well.

Using another short test called the Survey of Ethical Attitudes (which measures whether a person prefers to use a utilitarian view of the law as opposed to personal intuitive principles) Hogan (44) found that he could discriminate vocational choices. The utilitarian persons were located in vocations that reflected a belief in law and established social procedures, such as police work, ROTC programs, and so forth. Persons who believed in intuition preferred activities geared to promoting social change and held more radical ideological beliefs. They were also more independent, innovative, and creative, but tended toward impulsiveness and irresponsibility. On the other hand, the utilitarians appeared to be more reasonable and dependable but more conventional and resistant to change. Hogan concluded that the more mature individuals tended to cluster toward the center, but that how an individual thinks is related to very critical choices and behavior (45).

In a related manner, it was found that subjects at Kohlberg's stages five and six were more likely to make liberal as opposed to conservative choices on an authoritarian-libertarian dimension. For example, persons at the higher level of reasoning were less willing to advocate excessive powers to authorities and endorsed more statements supporting civil rights and the importance of individual welfare. Although it should be noted that this single finding was related to the specific choices in this research (it is, of course, the researcher's choice of words that defines the category of *liberal*) nevertheless, there appears to be a difference associated with the level of reasoning and judgments concerning authoritarianism (90, 91).

When people say they would or would not do something, there is, of course, no assurance that they would actually behave this way. Kohlberg reports, however, that actual behavior is related to moral reasoning, stating that 75 percent of the stage six reasoning subjects disobeyed orders to continue shocking a victim in Milgram's laboratory experiment involving obedience to authority, while only 13 percent of lower-stage reasoning subjects disobeyed (64; see also 89).[3]

In another study (73), reasoning of high school students who participated in a sit-in against a principal's warning and threat of suspension was different than that of students not engaged in the sit-in. While these findings are similar to those of other studies, such as that concerning Berkeley students, it was also found that a larger percentage of stage three subjects also participated. Using a technique similar to a Gallup opinion poll, Rest (92), found that stances on current public policy issues were related to whether a person was principled (levels five and six), or conventional (levels one, two, three, and four) in moral reasoning.

Another finding showing a relationship between the level of moral reasoning and cheating has been reported (106). Schwartz also reports some association between helping behaviors and the belief that one is responsible and/or obligated in a situation (102, 104, 105). Schwartz (103) concludes that an individual will be socially responsible and be more inclined to help those in distress when he: (a) recognizes that others are confronted by a situation that has serious consequences for them, (b) is aware of the moral norms that are pertinent to the given situation, and (c) believes he has a personal responsibility to take action. Schwartz (105) focused on the third condition as one of primary interest. He suggests that individuals who ascribe responsibility to themselves, that is, take responsibility for their own actions as they affect the welfare of others, are more likely to help those in distress. Individuals are less willing to hurt someone in compliance with the orders given them if they have to take personal responsibility for their actions (103, p. 130).

These studies suggest that moral reasoning is related to actual behavior. However, some important qualifications must be made.

In an extremely complex study (27) it was observed that in the university, the norms and work role interacted with the moral reasoning of the student, faculty member, or administrator. In this study leftists used more stage two reasoning, while rightists used more stage four reasoning and less of the higher levels. The results were so complex that they suggest that the relationship of Kohlberg's levels to behavior may sometimes be an artifact of other factors such as social roles, acquaintance with social norms, and/or other social learning factors. For example, these factors are probably necessary to explain the finding that natural scientists employ more level four reasoning and less level five than social science and humanities professors. In other words, this finding is probably a reflection of the content-structure confusion in Kohlberg's early model.

Also, when comparing conformity and moral reasoning of seventh-grade boys and girls, Saltzstein et al. (100) found that stage three subjects were more conforming,[4] but there were no differences between stages four, five, and six. It may be, then, that the findings in the Kohlberg experiments are due not to the subtle distinctions between the six levels but to the differences between the bottom half of the scale (one, two, three) and the top half of the scale (four, five, and six). The emphasis upon using a top half and bottom half of the scale is similar to Rest's approach of simply dichotomizing subjects into conventional and principled moralities (90).

Although we are confronted with some basic methodological and theoretical problems that still need answering, the research findings strongly suggest that how a person reasons about moral issues will in fact affect his actions, choices, and preferences in day-to-day living.

CAN RATIONAL PERSUASION INFLUENCE MORAL BEHAVIOR?

There is some evidence indicating that rational persuasion can influence moral behavior.

We have seen that research indicates that there is some relationship between behavior and moral thought. The next question can possibly also be answered in the affirmative: Will verbal rational persuasion induce or cause moral acts? The assumption is that the verbal persuasion would change something in the mind, such as a belief or a thought, and the change in these cognitive mediators would then produce a change in behavior. Consider, for instance, the research of Joseph Lavoie (70, 71). Lavoie first states that reasoning must be sufficient in focus (central theme) and orientation (the direction of concern, i.e., object- or person-oriented). In one experiment Lavoie allowed a subject to choose his preference between two toys. After the preferred toy was identified, the experimenter said that he remembered he had to make a telephone call and that he would have to leave for a short time. He then asked if the child would be okay by himself. When the child answered, "Okay," he said, "When I return I will knock on the door three times so you will know it's me." This instruction was given so that the child would know that he was alone in the room. The experimenter then left and the child was observed through a television monitor for fifteen minutes. Each child also received one of the following four instructions:

A. *Consequence focus—object orientation*: "That toy is not to be played with because it might get broken or worn out from you playing with it. That toy is a very special toy, and I don't have another toy exactly like that toy to replace it."

B. *Intentions focus—object orientation*: "It is wrong for you to want to play with that toy or to think about playing with that toy. That toy is a very special toy and should not be played with."

C. *Consequence focus—person orientation*: "That toy might get broken or worn out from your playing with it. Since that toy belongs to another boy/girl, how do you think he/she would feel if you played with this toy when he/she is not here?"

D. *Intentions focus—person orientation*: "It is wrong for you to want to play with that toy or to think about playing with that toy because it belongs to another boy/girl. How do you think he/she would feel about you playing with his/her toy?" [70, p. 6]

It was found that subjects who received a person-oriented rationale deviated more briefly than subjects given an object-oriented rationale. Also, girls deviated less than boys. The person-oriented rationale tended to be more effective with older boys and equally effective at all ages with the girls. This effect is similar to that found in another study by Staub (108). He found that verbal persuasion enhanced positive attitudes in delaying gratification for girls, but it had little or no effect for boys. Nevertheless, Staub did find persuasion could be used to effect a type of moral action, i.e., delaying gratification. While complex, the following quote from Lavoie suggests that there is a relationship between persuasion, moral judgment and moral behavior:

Content of the reasoning seemed to be a major determinant in the relationship between the child's level of moral judgment and moral behavior. Reasoning which focused on intentions or was person oriented (i.e., a rationale which implies sufficiency in information and legitimation of inhibition) seemed to be most effective with high moral judgment children clearly indicating a relationship between the cognitive and behavioral aspects of morality. This relationship probably occurred because of the social learning situation in which reasoning commensurate with rules and norms previously acquired by the child was used to legitimate resistance to deviation. In retrospect, it seems quite likely that when physical and cognitive similarity between the present situation and past experiences exists, moral judgment will influence moral behavior. [70, p. 18]

Lavoie points out that most research has focused on the material or object consequences of a deviant act. Research shows that there is less deviation when children are told not to play with the toy because it might get broken or worn out (object orientation and consequence focus with direct punitive outcome in some cases) (18, 19). An example of an intentional argument was given when eight- and nine-year-old children were told they were being punished for *wanting* to pick up a prohibited toy or that their toy choice was inappropriate. This type of rationale produced significant resistance to deviation (2). At least one researcher, Aronfreed (2), has developed an explanation using anxiety, combined with cognition, to explain moral acts of this nature.

Person-oriented rationales appeal to respect of property and rights of others and were found to be more effective in inhibiting deviation than a loud, aversive punishing stimulus. Lavoie also reports that the rationale is more effective with girls, a finding in agreement with other researchers who have shown that mild punishment or persuasion are particularly influential with girls (80).

By adding more information in the persuasion, Cheyne (18, 19) was able to obtain still less deviation in children's behavior. The first group was told simply, "That's bad." The second group was told, "You should not want to play with that toy." The third, "That toy belongs to someone else" (person oriented). There was less deviation among third-grade children in the second and third groups than in the first.

An interesting and practical question arises about influencing others' moral judgments: should the persuader attempt to reason at a level equal to or higher than the person being influenced? In one experiment seventh- and eighth-grade boys decided whether or not to continue taking prize money away from a confederate for making errors on a learning task. The subjects received one moral argument for stopping the punishment and one for continuing it. The researchers found (113) that subjects at Kohlberg's stage two and three chose to continue the punishment regardless of the level of the persuading justifications. Stage four subjects, however, could be persuaded in either direction if the moral argument presented were at stage five. Stage four subjects stopped taking the prize money if they received a stage five argument that they should stop; however, those stage four subjects presented with a stage five argument that they should continue the punishment, continued it. Therefore, the important factor was the higher level of reasoning with which those arguments were presented. It appears, therefore, that rational persuasion should exhibit higher levels of reasoning in order to be most effective. In a similar experiment (72) which yielded generally similar results, a team of college students was led to believe that it was playing games to obtain points. These researchers found that the type of moral reasoning used as justification in a persuasive statement significantly affected the number of points that one partner in the game would voluntarily give to another partner. An interesting addition, however, was that attempts to persuade that were below the level of reasoning of the higher subjects resulted in a negative effect!

Combining these studies, we can suggest three general conclusions. First, there is a relationship between moral judgments, beliefs, values, and behavior. Second, changes through persuasion or verbal instruction can influence behavior. Third, the stage level of the message is important in determining the amount of the behavioral change that occurs.

IS RELIGIOUS BEHAVIOR RELATED TO MORAL REASONING?

Evidence is rather persuasive that religion (if devout) is related to moral reasoning. However, it is unknown whether reasoning influences religious behavior or if religion influences reasoning.

In the last section it was asked if rational persuasion can influence moral behavior. Now it could be asked, "Does religion affect moral thinking or acting?" Although there is little research to encourage the belief that religion affects behavior (42),[5] there are some studies that show a correlation between religious belief and moral evaluations. Strongly religious people, those who attend church regularly, have more stringent and definite moral beliefs than nonbelievers. Also, strongly religious people consider a wider range of actions wrong and are less ready to consider extenuating circumstances (17, 22, 32, 60, 79).

After presenting subjects with a list of thirty-three antisocial items such as cheating on exams or premarital intercourse and petting, London, Schulman, and Black (76) found that Catholics, Jews, and Protestants responded to the questions differently; in addition, they found that Jews and Protestants responded to the questions more liberally in the portrayal of their faiths than Catholics. However, the interaction on an item-to-item basis was very complex; the researchers recorded no general pattern in moral thinking except to note that differences do occur—for example, they concluded that long-term religious practice is a factor in influencing a person's evaluation of moral deeds.

A limitation in the distinction between religious and nonreligious people in their moral judgments is made by Middleton and Putney (79). They separated ascetic morality from social morality. In ascetic

morality the consequences of actions are felt mainly by the wrongdoer; in social morality the consequences are felt by other people. It is
Middleton's and Putney's contention that social morality is an out-
growth of group life and would be equally present among people
with and without religious beliefs. Ascetic morality is said to occur as
a result of religious traditions or teachings and may not be supported
by nonbelievers. Such a distinction between types of morality is often
difficult to maintain since most moral acts usually have elements of
both kinds of consequences. However, Middleton and Putney included sexual activity, gambling, smoking, and drinking in ascetic
morality; their social morality included stealing, cheating, aggression,
and similar acts. As they predicted, a person's religion seemed to be
related to his condemnation of violations of an ascetic or private
morality, but no such relationship between religious belief and
opposition to antisocial acts could be established. Wright and Cox
(115) repeated this study with some changes. They found the same
distinction except that the religious subjects tended to be more
severe, even for social morality. The most interesting aspect of the
Wright and Cox study was their analysis of subjects' comments:

Analysis of the comments made by subjects on all items reveals a clear
difference between the devout and the non-religious. The non-religious tend
to argue that, if a form of behavior has no undesirable consequences for other
people, it is not a legitimate matter for the moral evaluation of others; the
devout claim that the individual's life is not his own, that all his behavior
concerns God, and that hence there is no part of it which may not be the
subject of moral evaluation on occasion. However, from the specific reasons
given by the devout for their moral beliefs, it would seem that these beliefs
may be serving more than one function. Some devout subjects express
considerable disgust for antiascetic behavior, and offer as their reasons for
condemning it the fact that they involve loss of self-control or self-respect,
and the giving way to "animal" instincts of fear and lust. When such
reasons, together with appeals to absolute authority, are given in support of
an unqualified condemnation, we may suspect that the beliefs are serving a
defensive function. On the other hand, some devout subjects are most
concerned with future personal development, and see the ascetic moral rules
as the necessary condition of growth into self-respect and responsibility.
Such subjects, though they condemn antiascetic behavior, are likely to
qualify their judgments with the recognition that under certain circumstances such behavior is not detrimental to personal integrity. These subjects
do draw attention to the fact that religious belief, in addition to all its other
functions, can serve to support a program of personal development. [115,
pp. 142–43]

In further support of the conclusion that religious practice affects the quality of individuals' moral reasoning, a field study conducted by one of the authors (54) revealed a significant difference in moral reasoning between United States Catholic children and children living in a small Hutterite commune in Canada. The greater use of level four reasoning among the Hutterites was particularly obvious. They tended not to use the other types of reasoning, with the solitary exception of level three. The authors concluded that this is primarily because they receive systematic religious training each day. Hutterites hold daily religious services in which one of their group reads and interprets the Bible; all members of the commune are required to attend. The systematic exposure to discussions of right and wrong likely helps them achieve a common point of view about moral problems that would elicit diverse answers among Americans, even among members of a single religious group. It should be noted that the difference that was found could also be attributed to differences in such areas as socioeconomic conditions, housing, family size, or the like. However, it appears that the fact that the religion of the Hutterite youth permeates their entire life is largely responsible for the differences between their moral thinking and that of the American Catholic youth.

These studies suggest that devoutly-held religion has a significant effect on the moral thinking of individuals; it is among members of a faith who are not devout that discrepant results are generally found.

IS MORAL GROWTH DEVELOPMENTAL?

Research indicates that advanced cognitive ability and age are both associated with moral maturity. In particular, cognitive ability is a necessary though not sufficient condition; age (i.e., experience) seems to be the other crucial factor.

At the very heart of the disagreement between cognitive-developmental and behavioristic theories of moral reasoning is the concept of sequential development. If it is true, for instance, that a person follows a general pattern in developing cognitive (qualitative) abilities and that moral reasoning is itself a cognitive ability, then it is reasonable to suppose that moral thinking will develop along a similar, identifiable pattern and, in fact, be dependent upon existing cognitive abilities. It would therefore be impossible for advanced, mature moral thinking to occur in a mind that is otherwise immature and we should discover a specific sequential pattern in the development of moral thought. On the other hand, if cognitive development is not developmental at all, in a qualitative sense, but merely a quantitative addition of newly learned concepts that requires no qualitative reorganization of cognitive functions, then we should expect no such formal sequence. In this case, it should be readily demonstrable that children can learn advanced mature moral concepts without any advancement in their overall cognitive ability, that they need only receive the requisite experience.

This last possibility, that of learning mature moral concepts without evidence of any accompanying cognitive advancement, was tested by one of us (Jensen) in a series of studies (50, 51, 52, 53, 55) with young children ages four through seven. These studies dealt with the effects of direct training techniques. The results revealed that children could apparently learn and retain mature moral concepts without any known alteration in their underlying cognitive abilities. No effort was made to influence general mental development and the short period of experimentation makes belief in a general cognitive change unreasonable. However, although these studies and others like them (e.g., 5, 21) show such changes, they are all open to serious doubt; this will be discussed in some detail in chapter seven so it need not be reviewed now. Other studies, however, are applicable here.

Tomlinson-Keasey and Keasey (111), for instance, performed an important study examining the relationship of cognitive development and moral development in two age groups, twelve- and nineteen-year-old girls. They found high correlations (+.60 for the twelve-year-olds and +.58 for the nineteen-year-olds) between maturity of moral reasoning, as measured on Kohlberg's scale, and cognitive ability on various Piagetian measures. More important, it was found that all subjects who were classified as "principled moral thinkers" also exhibited a substantial amount of formal operational thought, a feature of general cognitive development. The fact that there were no principled thinkers who did not also evidence advanced cognitive ability suggests that such cognitive ability is a requisite, or a necessary condition, for advanced moral thinking. Such evidence is not conclusive, but it does suggest the importance of cognitive factors in moral development. One point that was conclusively established by these researchers, however, is that cognitive development is not a sufficient condition for mature moral thought: many of the subjects who evidenced formal operational thought had not attained principled moral reasoning. This finding indicates that whatever effect cognitive ability may have on moral maturity, it is not, by itself, sufficient for the production of such maturity.

These results suggest that cognitive ability is a necessary, but not a sufficient, condition for mature moral development. A number of additional studies are considered and reported by Keasey (57) in support of this conclusion and it is also supported by at least one study using Piagetian measures of moral maturity (39). In the study discussed above (111), it was found that among the twelve-year-old girls, not one had attained principled moral reasoning despite the fact that several showed substantial amounts of formal operational thought. In the nineteen-year-old group, it was found that a number of those evidencing formal operational thought had attained prin-cipled moral reasoning. Age—as separate from cognitive ability— therefore seems to be a major factor. Furthermore, in a comparison of all twelve-year-olds at the formal operations level with all such nineteen-year-olds, it was learned that the older girls still scored significantly higher on the moral maturity scale. Thus, in spite of similar cognitive scores, the older girls were judged significantly more morally mature. Several other studies (e.g., 25, 36, 66) cor-roborate this conclusion: age is significantly related to various aspects of moral reasoning and maturity. Such age differences, of course, are a function of increased social-emotional experience (9, 88; see also 82).

These studies seem to corroborate the work of Piaget (88) and Kohlberg (65), who maintain that moral development follows a sequence, not because such growth is genetically programmed, but because it follows the progress of the child's adaptation to his environment.[6] The child's assimilation of reality is cognitive growth, which takes time. It is logical to suppose that moral development would also take place over time and be a function of one's environ-mental adaptation, one's cognitive growth interacting with one's experience.

The studies that support the concept of sequential development appear to be reasonably accurate. However, a concept that does not view development as being a sequence of stages is also available. Bandura, the leading social learning theorist, states:

> According to the social learning view, people vary in what they teach, model, and reinforce with children of differing ages. At first, control is necessarily external. In attempting to discourage hazardous conduct in

children who have not yet learned to talk, parents must resort to physical intervention. As children mature, social sanctions increasingly replace their children's behavior. Successful socialization requires gradual substitution of symbolic and external controls for external sanctions and demands. After moral standards of conduct are established by tuition and modeling, self-evaluative consequences serve as deterrents to transgressive acts. As the nature and seriousness of possible transgressions by children change with age, parents alter their moral reasoning. For example, they do not appeal to legal arguments in handling misconduct of preschoolers, but they explain legal codes and penalties to preadolescents in efforts to influence future behavior that can have serious consequences. . . .

Evidence that there are some age trends in moral judgment, that children fail to adopt opinions they do not fully comprehend, and that they are reluctant to express views considered immature for their age can be adequately explained without requiring elaborate stage propositions. [3, pp. 43, 45]

Results are fairly clear, then, in showing moral development to follow general age and cognitive trends. Whether that growth is specifically developmental (sequential and invariant), however, is a different and more complex, question which is still unanswered (e.g., 3, 47, 68, 112). Since the types of reasoning vary in the number of concepts employed, e.g., in abstractness and possibly many other elements related to cognitive complexity, it is expected that younger children with less developed cognitive abilities would have difficulty in comprehending, much less articulating, some of the categories. Some research supports this prediction, at least indirectly. We would also expect to find age differences due to experiential factors, and research also supports this prediction. If children hear no moral discourse at higher levels they will likely respond with what they do hear, ordinarily the more conventional types of thought. Thus, while it is clear that there are both age and cognitive trends in moral development, both behavioristic and cognitive-developmental theories can be shown to account for these observations.

HOW ARE SOCIALIZATION/CULTURAL DIFFERENCES RELATED TO MORAL REASONING?

Although there is some support for the idea that patterns of moral development are universal, there are many differences among cultures in more specific dimensions of moral reasoning.

Kohlberg and the cognitive developmentalists emphasize cultural similarities in moral reasoning. Kohlberg, believing that the developmental pattern of moral reasoning is similar for all humans, argues that one would find the same trends in all cultures. He has studied children in America, Taiwan, Mexico, Turkey, and Yucatan, concluding that the pattern of development is the same in all of these cultures. Some authors (e.g., 68) have pointed to problems with this conclusion, however. For instance, Kohlberg's results showed that 7 percent of the sixteen-year-olds in the United States and Mexico reasoned at stage six, while only 1 percent or less of the sixteen-year-olds in Taiwan reasoned at this stage. Furthermore, "none of the children in either Turkey or Yucatan were able to reach even Stage 5. Thus, Stage 5 reasoning is missing in two of the five samples, and Stage 6 reasoning is absent in three of the samples" (68, p. 461). These results, however, do not disprove Kohlberg's theory of the universality of moral development that is sequential and directed. They prove only that different cultures develop at different rates and that they may stop at different stages. However, such a significant cultural difference deserves attention.

Gorsuch and Barnes (33) have also attempted to assess cultural factors in moral reasoning. These researchers compared Black Caribs of British Honduras (ages ten through sixteen) with a United States population and reported that the development of moral reasoning by both groups is similar. There were also significant differences, however. For instance, only one of all the Black Carib subjects tested was reasoning at a level higher than stage two. Kohlberg's findings in the United States indicate that most subjects of the same age are usually beyond stage two. Cultural factors seem to be important in determining at least the age at which one acquires a given mode of moral reasoning.

One of the better review articles, by Garbarino and Bronfenbrenner (31), argues that moral judgments show significant cultural differences. Adapting Kohlberg's stage theory to their own measurement techniques, they theorize that cultures differ in the extent to which they help children develop desirable modes of moral thought. One of their most interesting notions is that in order to obtain higher levels of thinking about moral principles a culture must be pluralistic—its basic social agents must represent different expectations, sanctions, and rewards for members of the society. As parents, teachers, and school

pull the child in somewhat different directions, he is compelled to
think and work out problems that confront him. In so doing, the child
develops a superior ability to think about moral issues. The evidence
provided in support of this suggestion is the finding that families in
which both parents have strong but different identities or roles have
children who are rated higher on dimensions of responsibility and
independence of judgment. Families in which one parent dominates
are rated lower (14). In addition, Bronfenbrenner (11) finds that the
Soviet adolescents raised in a single social setting or a boarding
school differ from those with two social settings such as school and
family. Students living at home were less authority-oriented and
struck a balance between competing social agencies, in this case
school, peers, and parents.

However, these theorists believe that the different expectations
must be firmly based in a common, fundamental set of social and
political beliefs, for example, a commitment to peace, democracy,
constitutional nationality, or a religious ethic. They consider the
absence of some underlying set of fundamental principles to be
injurious.

Related research indicating cross-national differences of moral
thinking is provided by Bronfenbrenner and others (see 12, 13, 15,
93). With respect to the extent that children prefer statements
indicating a desire to "go along" with friends rather than obeying
legitimate authority, clear differences have been found among diverse cultures, including the United States, West Germany, Switzer-
land, Netherlands, Sweden, Japan, United Kingdom, Canada, Israel,
USSR, Czechoslovakia, Hungary, and Poland. These national differences are not differences in moral reasoning in precisely the sense
that we have used the term, but they do suggest that differences exist
between cultures regarding at least the one moral dimension, following authority.

We will review additional illustrations that suggest significant
differences among cultures in the way members reason about moral
questions (e.g., 61). Admittedly, much of the following data are
indirect, but their implications are nonetheless important.

Employing a non-Kohlbergian measurement researchers compared
American and Finnish children (10). They asked the subject to
mention good and bad behavior and also to name praise and blame
for the behavior. For example, "What would be a good thing which a
boy your age could do so that someone would praise you or be

pleased?" In this study, Finnish children at ten years of age were compared with the same age group in America. From these data, the researchers concluded that American children were more concerned with personal pleasure and personality characteristics, whereas the Finnish children were more concerned with personal achievement, adequacy, goodness of character, and so forth. Another finding was that the Finnish children were more often concerned with their parents' opinions than were the American children.

Devereux, et al. (23, 24) found that in Germany the family plays a more central and important role in child rearing and socialization than does the family in the United States. In the United States, the children spend more of their time with peers than with family members. However, the influence of the peer is even stronger in England. English children are even more ready than American children to transgress the behavior advocated by parents and other adult authorities (7). In contrast, children from the Soviet Union are very compliant with adult values, which even the peer groups uphold and promote (15). (These findings will be discussed in greater detail in chapter eight.)

Cultures also seem to vary in how much their members believe in punishment. Eleven- to thirteen-year-old Cubans propose more punishment or sanctions for others than do American children of the same age. Also, seven- or eight-year-old black children in rural Florida approve of less punishment than whites, but this trend reverses by late adolescence. This is thought to be due to personality changes in Negro youth, who are subjected to castelike discrimination through late adolescence, conditions which produce low self-esteem and anger. This anger produces passive aggression, reflected in a higher frequency of proposed punishment (101).

Such differences however, may be the consequence of socioeconomic factors, not of race. For example, Muir and Weinstein (83) conclude that middle-class people perceive obligation, service, or helping others in much the same way they perceive financial transactions. That is, they use economic or businesslike thinking to establish whether or not they should help others. In contrast, persons low on the socioeconomic scale tend to feel that social obligation should not be the critical factor in determining interpersonal behavior; rather, they believe in a more altruistic approach in which one gives when one is able and then expects others to do the same when they are in a position to help. They tend to disregard past favors, social debts, or obligations and instead to use the notion of mutual aid and one's current ability to help.

Light (75) draws the following conclusions about still another cultural difference found within the United States: rural and urban adolescent girls differ markedly in their attitudes. For example, rural girls are more likely to be influenced by family and religion; likewise, they are more influenced by peers. Rural girls continue to accept conventional ethical standards whereas urban girls are more receptive to new morality. Despite the fact that urban girls have more frequent contact with people of other races and ethnic backgrounds, both groups exhibit prejudice. Urban girls are more uncertain of their attitudes, which seems to be the consequence of the smaller degree of influence from family and church. Finally, rural girls place a greater value on education (75, pp. 226–27).

A major study by Rokeach (96) reports wide cultural differences in values, including values similar to those discussed above. Again, cultural, social, and economic differences in values do not necessarily indicate differences in moral reasoning, but the consistency of such findings strongly suggests that there is a close relationship. Rokeach provides persuasive evidence that differences in moral reasoning are indeed related to differences in values (94, 95, 96, 97, 98).

Another major cultural difference that seems to affect moral reasoning is the difference between what are called "guilt" and "shame" cultures (8, 77). Some societies control their members through shame, while others, such as Western society, use guilt. Shame cultures are said to be those in which people who are in authority usually exhort, threaten, or otherwise strive to arouse fear in order to obtain compliance from others. Compliance like this resembles moral action on Kohlberg's lower levels. Guilt cultures, on the other hand, are those in which authorities attempt to develop people's self-control by instilling in them strong feelings that will serve to govern their behavior. It is usually assumed that mature guilt cannot occur without the employment of some type of reasoning (49). Shame cultures are said to produce weaker consciences because people learn to rely on external sanctions to govern behavior rather than on internal controls. In addition, most shame cultures also have kinship, clan, or family extensions that allow the disciplinary role of the parent to be delegated among other people. The Samoan culture is said to be typical of the shame society, whereas mainland United States is said to be basically a strong guilt culture. Grinder and McMichael (37) found that there were numerous differences between these cultures in such areas as levels of guilt, resistance to temptation, acceptance of remorse, frequency of confessions, and use of restitution following transgressions. It was found that Samoans possessed fewer traits associated with guilty behavior than American Caucasian children of the same age, illustrating another difference in moral reasoning that is apparently due to cultural difference.[7]

It does appear that culture greatly influences moral judgments and reasoning, but the direct evidence for this is not as strong as many researchers would like. Most psychologists conclude, however, that each culture will possess certain dominant types of moral reasoning that arise because socialization patterns endorse a given mode of moral thought. Indeed many subtle factors may cause the preference for and persistence of a mode of thought in a given culture. Just what these factors are, of course, is an important subject yet to be sufficiently researched. An interesting and well-documented presentation of the subject can be found in Maria Ossowska's excellent short book *Social Determinants of Moral Ideas* (84).

SOME MISCELLANEOUS DIFFERENCES

Another type of cultural influence seems to appear every twenty years—a difference in moral thinking between one generation and another. Throughout the ages this difference has been seen as the falling away of the youth or the lack of respect of the youth for the aged. The perennial concern over the morals of the young is typified in a statement by Reverend Ives made one hundred years ago: "I cannot suppress the humiliating conviction that even Pagan Rome, in the corrupt age of Augustus, never witnessed a more rapid and frightful declension in morals nor witnessed among certain classes of the young a more utter disregard of honor, of truth, and piety, and even the commonest decencies of life" (48, p. 174).

Numerous explanations for this phenomenon have been advanced: (a) all young people deal with experiences that are unlike their parents' when they were the same age; (b) parental influence and authority is disintegrating; (c) adults and youth naturally differ because of their different age and experience. For example, Winston Churchill, a noted conservative, is quoted as saying that "an adolescent who is not a liberal has not a heart." Deep-seated psychological differences between different generations are sometimes explained as being due to unresolved Oedipal complexes, death wishes, or competition between children and parents (30). Psychoanalysts have proposed similar intrapsychic explanations, emphasizing different motivations at different ages. Erikson (26) proposes that the central problem during adolescence is to establish an identity, which explains the conflict between the adolescent's beliefs and the beliefs of others, particularly authorities. Apparently, though, such reasons are only a sampling of differences that give rise to variances in moral thought and ideas between generations; the bulk of differences can be attributed to the interaction of perhaps hundreds of more subtle social and cultural determinants (34).

Contrary to usual expectations, it was found in one study (116) that college students expressed value orientations very similar to those of students of previous years. Only in the area of sexual behavior was a definite shift toward a more liberal stance noted. This is surprising because in this investigation the range of moral acts was quite broad, including such things as "killing a person in defense of one's own life," "forging a check," "girls smoking cigarettes," and "advertising a medicine to cure a disease known to be incurable by such a remedy." This indicates that generational differences may be neither as deep, nor as broad, as many claim. Or, it might simply prove that even over the years, young people tend to resemble each other, but that generational differences stay just as marked: In short, that young people become more conservative as they grow older and—as parents—do not agree at all with young people.

While the authors know of no theories of moral reasoning that posit a significant sex difference in the development of moral reasoning, a number of studies (e.g., 70, 108) have shown such differences. It has been reported that when girls move from high school or college to motherhood, many of them remain at stage three while their male age mates move on to level four or other higher stages (66). This finding is not quite as strongly established in younger age groups, however (58). There seem to be at least two reasons to expect greater sex differences at older ages.[8] First, American culture emphasizes many stage three characteristics as more appropriate for girls—this would tend to move them into stage three somewhat earlier than boys and keep them in it longer. Second, males seem to engage in formal operational thinking sooner than girls, which would suggest that males would move into postconventional thinking sooner than girls. This would explain the evidence of greater sex differences at older, rather than younger, ages, as research results suggest.

SUMMARY

The experimental results presented in this chapter suggest that moral thinking is significantly related to several factors: cognitive development, age, cultural and socioeconomic factors, and religion. It is also apparent that rational persuasion can affect moral thinking and that an individual's behavior is very often closely related to his moral thought.

Obviously people differ in their moral thought; the crucial matter is knowing precisely *how* they differ. One of the major differences is between age groups, but perhaps the significant element in age differences is the cognitive ability to comprehend, understand, and engage in advanced thinking. An additional factor that apparently creates age differences, however, is social experience. Also, the study of differences in cultural socialization suggests that people differ in the mode of reasoning they employ. Although this area has not been researched sufficiently in a direct way, there is much indirect evidence suggesting that differences do exist.

A similar position regarding the existence of cultural differences has been advanced by a social psychologist, Robert Hogan (44, 45, 46). Hogan describes man as a rule-formulating and rule-following animal, which certainly implies that man engages in moral reasoning. He proposes that all social behavior occurs within new rule systems and that rule systems form a necessary and integral part of every community, even though the rule systems may differ greatly. By knowing about the nature of man as a rule-following animal and the existence of rule systems within each culture, we can explain the general outline of all social behavior. While other factors besides rule following can be employed to explain human behavior we concur that rule-following awareness in moral reasoning is an important and critical predictor of man's individual and social behavior. And this, of course, is close to a restatement of what Piaget suggested more than forty years ago.

NOTES

1. Throughout this chapter all references to Kohlberg's scale are to his early one.

2. If one were to include research on beliefs and acceptance of norms, then an entire body of evidence could be cited which demonstrates a relationship between thought processes and behavior. For further reading review chapters on social norms in J. Macaulay and L. Berkowitz, *Altruism and Helping Behavior* (New York: Academic, 1970).

3. We have been unable to obtain a full report of this data, however.

4. Thus, stage three subjects would be expected to imitate the significant others in their lives; consequently they might appear to behave in a manner consistent with stages two, four, or even five. But this is exactly what would be expected of a stage three individual, and thus the findings on such individuals need not be seen as inconsistent with the expected relationship between stage of reasoning and behavior.

5. Despite the lack of research this idea is compelling to many. A representative statement comes from J. Edgar Hoover: "Invariably when you analyze the reasons for such [criminal] actions, certain facts stand out stark and revealing—the faith of our fathers, the love of God, and the observance of His Commandments have either been thrust aside or they never existed in the heart of the individual transgressor. . . ." (20).

6. See Lickona (74) for a critical discussion of studies relating specifically to Piaget's theory of development.

7. For a general discussion of conscience see Johnson, Dokecki, and Mowrer (56).

8. We are indebted to Charles Blake Keasey for these points.

7 / Changing Moral Thinking: Direct Approaches

As was seen in chapter five, there are two points of view regarding the effect of training on moral reasoning. The first states that it is impossible directly to make genuine cognitive changes in moral reasoning through short education programs; the second view proposes that this is possible.

The first view is the conclusion of cognitive-developmentalists, who hold that moral reasoning is subject to the restrictions of the underlying and slowly maturing mental structures. They therefore conclude that a child cannot be taught the characteristics of a higher morality unless the child's basic mental characteristics are first altered. This implies the necessity of using indirect methods to facilitate moral development. Cognitive-developmentalists interpret immediate change reported in research as a superficial change in a child's verbal responses (or of content), and not a genuine change in his underlying moral thought structure. The behaviorists, on the other hand, feel that a change in a child's moral behavior, choices, or other characteristics is concrete evidence of a change in mental processes, evidence that must be accepted as legitimately scientific. Accordingly, they reject the necessity of changing an unidentified underlying thought process in order to change moral reasoning. Obviously this kind of theoretical distinction makes a great difference in one's choice of an education program for promoting moral maturity. Applied psychologists are interested in influencing moral development, but the approach they adopt for this purpose depends on the view they take regarding the possibility of directly teaching moral maturity. What, then, is the correct view?

133

To demonstrate that it is possible directly to train young children to reason about morality more maturely, we conducted a series of experiments in our laboratory. All of the experiments deal with those dimensions described by Piaget as being typical of children in the heteronomous stage of reasoning (see 10). Although the experiments seem to indicate that preschool children can be trained to make more mature judgments, some serious questions can be raised; these are treated following the discussion of the experiments.

Intentions

According to Piaget, one aspect of moral maturity is the realization or consideration of the intention underlying a given act. In contrast to this is objectivity, defined as focusing only on the consequences of the act to the exclusion of the actor's intentions.

In our laboratory (3,5) children were presented with a series of moral problems with associated reasoning and were asked to respond to a picture corresponding to each story. The following are two examples:

Sue's friend is visiting her. Sue puts her friend's bicycle in the driveway so that her friend will see it and will not forget it when she goes home. Sue goes back inside. Just then, a truck comes by and hits the bicycle and breaks a pedal.

Edith's friend won't let her ride her bike. So, Edith pushes her friend's bike over, and a pedal breaks off.

Two training procedures were employed with these stories. The following questions are typical of those asked in the discussion, or indirect, training technique:

(a) Which little girl left her friend's bicycle in the driveway because she didn't want her friend to forget it?
(b) Did she want the truck to hit the bicycle? Was this an accident?
(a) Which little girl pushed her friend's bicycle over?
(b) Did she do this on purpose?

The experimenter nodded or replied "yes" if the question was answered correctly. If not, another child was asked the same question until someone responded with the correct answer.

In the labeling, or direct training, group the same stories were presented, after which the experimenter asked, "Who was naughtier?" After the children had made their choices, the experimenter identified the naughtier person without explanation or discussion and simply rewarded the children who had made the correct choice. This was the extent of their training. Later, they were tested to determine if training produced a change.

In both of these training methods and in the control groups, a correct response had to imply consideration of the intention to do harm. The concern of the study was to see if direct training would affect consideration of this dimension. Both training groups became significantly more mature (as measured by intentionality) in their moral judgments than the control group. There was no significant difference in effectiveness between the two training procedures, which seemed to illustrate the favorable effect that training, both indirect and direct, has on the development of intentionality in the moral judgments of young children.

Sanctions

Piaget (13) proposes that the child's ability to judge the rightness or wrongness of an act depends upon any sanction administered by an adult. That is, a young child is described as being in a heteronomous stage of development when he has unquestioning respect for adults and their rules. If an adult rewards an act, then the child will simply judge the act to be good without consideration of other factors. Kohlberg (10) cites an example. Young children were asked to judge a helpful obedient act (attentively watching a baby brother while the mother is away) followed by punishment (the mother spanks the babysitting child). He says that many four-year-olds simply say that the obedient boy was bad because he got punished. In fact, they may even invent a misdeed to account for punishment; their response to such a story might be that the boy threw the baby on the floor and that is why he was spanked. In general, four-year-olds define the story action as good or bad according to the reward or punishment received rather than according to the more relevant features of the act. Conversely, older children tend to define right and wrong in terms of these more relevant features and show concern about the injustice of punishing good and rewarding evil.

Therefore an experiment in our laboratory (4) was designed to determine whether or not preschool children could be trained to disregard the sanction following an act when they evaluated the act on a good/bad dimension.

Large booklets containing illustrations of stories were presented to the children in a pretest, training sessions, and posttest. These stories depicted a child's act followed by a sanction. In each case the first story recounted a good act followed by punishment; the second, a bad act followed by punishment. Two such stories were:

1. A little child was practicing his violin. His mother became angry and spanked him. Was practicing the violin good or bad? Why was that good or bad? Why did his mother get angry and spank him?
2. A little child poured milk all over the table. His mother became angry and spanked him. Was pouring milk all over the table good or bad? Why was that good or bad? Why did his mother get angry and spank him?

Using training procedures (both indirect and direct) similar to those used in the previous experiment, we found that both training groups showed large gains between the pretest and the posttest, with almost no change taking place in the control group. This study was replicated, and the same results were found after a two-month delay. It would seem that direct training procedures are effective in developing mature moral thought.

Immanent Justice

According to Piaget (13), young children mistakenly believe in immanent justice, the idea that some misfortune will automatically follow any wrongdoing. A desirable training program, therefore, would help the child to perceive the difference between the chance negative events which follow an act and those negative events which lawfully result from behavior, strengthening a belief in naturalistic explanations and weakening belief in immanent justice. Such a change would indicate an increase in moral autonomy.

To test this possibility, children were trained as in our other experiments (7). The following is an example of a story with discussion questions:

A mother told her little girl not to play with the neighbor's dog. The little girl did not mind her mother. She went over and played with the dog anyway. Her mother never found out that she had played with the big dog. What happened to the little girl? What really happened was that the dog bit the little girl's hand. Why did the dog bite the girl's hand?

(a) If the little girl's mother had said it was all right to play with the dog, would she have been bitten anyway?
(b) Why do dogs bite children?
(c) Did the dog know that the little girl disobeyed her mother?

As a consequence of such training procedures as these, children learned to prefer naturalistic explanations over those implying a belief in immanent justice. Again, results seem to indicate that direct training can significantly effect the development of moral maturity.

Punishment

Young children view punishment as having only a punitive, as opposed to a restitutive, function. When young children are presented a story about another child who has done something wrong and are asked what a fair punishment for that child would be, the majority will suggest a rather severe punishment. Characteristically, the punishment suggested does not allow for the restitution or repair of damage. In contrast, older children will temper the punishment and propose a punishment that provides an opportunity for the transgressor to make restitution and learn from his error.

Two experiments were conducted to see if it is possible directly to change children's beliefs about punishment (6). Children were asked to pretend that they were the mommy or daddy and to make up a good or fair punishment for the child in each story presented them. An example story is:

Linda got mad at her brother when they were getting ready to eat lunch, so she poured salt into his soup. What would be a fair punishment for Linda?
(a) Make her give her soup to her brother.
(b) Send her to her room for three hours.

In one training procedure, after children identified the type of punishment they preferred, the experimenter identified the correct response (the restitutive punishment) and quietly rewarded the children who had chosen that response. In the other procedure, the experimenter simply engaged the children in a discussion of why they had chosen a given response. No attempt was made to identify or reward the correct choice.

Both training procedures were effective in leading children to prefer restitutive forms of punishment over more punitive measures. While the second training procedure suggests the efficacy of indirect methods in promoting moral maturity, the first procedure suggests the same for direct methods. Again, apparently, direct methods can be useful in promoting moral maturity.

Reciprocity

Piaget suggests that young children tend to ignore concepts of reciprocity and instead seek an authority figure in conflict situations. Reciprocity is defined as a fairness and equality of interaction wherein the participants act upon the basis of the Golden Rule. Reciprocity, perhaps a keystone in the development of the moral superstructure, is acquired as the child moves away from exact distributive and retributive equality of justice (such as "an eye for an eye and a tooth for a tooth") and toward a concept of fairness and justice based on the other person's needs and point of view (such as the Golden Rule). Forgiveness would be characteristic of mature reciprocity.

An experiment was performed to study the effects of direct training on developing such reciprocal judgments in prekindergarten children (8). In treatment A, a series of discussions was given in which the children acted out a conflict situation. Children then discussed their feelings about the situation, suggested possible solutions to the conflict, and then reenacted the situation using a mature response supplied by the trainer to resolve the conflict. Each child in this treatment had an opportunity to act out a role and verbalize the mature response of discussing the problem with the offending child to resolve the conflict.

Treatment B did not have a discussion. Each child was asked to indicate what he thought should be done to solve the problem. If he answered with a solution that included trying to solve the problem with the older children without physical or verbal aggression, he received a gold star by his name on a special chart. If he suggested trying to enlist the aid of an adult to help solve the problem, he received a silver star. If the child did not give an answer related to either of these, the trainer went to the next child, ignoring the inappropriate response.

The results of this study seemed to confirm the hypothesis that direct training is useful in moral development. Both treatment A and

B were shown to be effective ways to train children to use reciprocity in making moral judgments.

QUALIFICATIONS TO THE PRECEDING CONCLUSIONS

The experiments performed in our laboratories suggest that direct training can indeed influence maturity of moral reasoning. Each of the dimensions tested is associated with young children's moral reasoning, and the fact that these variables were significantly and positively affected through direct training argues that genuine changes in moral maturity may be produced through direct training procedures, and that sufficient maturation of underlying thought processes is already present—only adequate experience is needed.

Such a conclusion cannot be accepted without serious qualification, however; the question of true internalization or autonomy must still be considered. For instance, did the children who were taught to consider factors other than adult sanctions learn to do so precisely because of adult sanctions? Did they learn to consider the act itself simply because they were reinforced, positively sanctioned by the experimenter, for doing so? If so, then, nothing has been proved except that children judge good and bad, right and wrong primarily in terms of adult, or at least external, sanctions. If they learned to consider other factors *because* of adult sanctions (experimenter rewards and punishments, approval, disapproval, even those subtly disguised in discussion groups), then we are forced to admit that adult sanctions were used to prove that children can be trained not to consider adult sanctions. The very method is paradoxical.

In order to see how this difficulty arises, we must understand just what moral maturity is and what it is that moral development implies. At the outset, it should be noted that little disagreement exists over whether specific types of reasoning can be altered through direct training. There is little doubt that training procedures can effectively change a child's beliefs concerning such things as lying and stealing, or change his way of thinking, for example, from rule-deontology to act-utilitarianism. The more important question is whether such direct procedures can influence the child's moral maturity, not just his beliefs or ways of thinking. To answer this question, we must first understand what is meant by maturity. Generally, the concept is associated with autonomy or independence of thought.

Autonomy and Internalization

Of all theorists, Piaget (13) has had the greatest influence in emphasizing the importance of autonomy in moral thought. His theory that moral development is a progression from heteronomy to autonomy was presented in chapter five, where it was seen that the autonomous stage of moral development is characterized by independence from external controls. The individual in this stage of moral thought sees the need to evaluate objectively all moral pronouncements or commands and is not content to accept them merely because they originate from external or authoritative sources. At this stage, the individual's moral judgments come from within himself. This view, of course, is consistent with Kohlberg's theory, particularly as characterized by his recent model. The postconventional, level three person sees the individual as logically prior to society, and thus morality is a matter of individual choice and commitment, not merely the acceptance, or even internalization, of others' expectations and rules. The morally mature individual is independent: he has individuated himself from others' expectations and adopts his own principles instead. This is the essence of a moral autonomy.

A crucial feature of this autonomy is internalization—not the internalization of external moral principles, but the internalization of one's own moral standards or normative assumptions. Several authors, besides Piaget and Kohlberg, have discussed the importance of this feature in moral development (1, 2, 9, 12, 14).

For instance, Martin Hoffman (2) posits three levels of internalization. The most primitive is based on conditioned fear. For example, a child who is repeatedly punished for a particular behavior gradually becomes anxious when he thinks about the act. The child learns to avoid the behavior and thereby dispel the anxiety. Although this process might be defined as internalization, since the child will behave morally in the absence of the punishing person, Hoffman feels that this can only be a borderline morality because the child is motivated solely by external threat, not by evaluation of the behavior itself.

The second type of internalization occurs when an individual adopts standards out of respect for others. He believes in and abides by the standards not because of their content, but because they were given to him by individuals whom he respects.

When an individual views standards as worthwhile in and of themselves, he experiences the third level of internalization. The individual accepts the obligations of the rules as his own and acts to avoid self-condemnation, rather than the condemnation of others.

Herbert Kelman (9), a social psychologist, also suggests three processes in adults, which he calls compliance, identification, and internalization. These are analogous to Hoffman's three levels of internalization. Compliance occurs when the individual hopes either to gain rewards or to avoid punishment. The exact behavior induced is irrelevant, and the actor makes no attempt to evaluate its rightness or wrongness. When an individual changes his behavior because of the relationship to another person or group, identification may be said to occur. Again, motivation for the behavior comes from satisfaction in the relationship without regard to the content of the behavior. In this case too, the actor acts without questioning. Finally, internalization may be said to occur when a behavior change results from evaluation of the content of the behavior. The individual finds the behavior itself to be rewarding (i.e., Hoffman's definition of mature internalization).

Another prominent psychologist, Urie Bronfenbrenner (1), describes five types of moral judgment and behavior. These are:

1. *self-oriented*: in which the individual is motivated primarily by impulses of self-gratification without regard for the desires or expectations of others, except as objects of manipulation;
2. *authority-oriented*: in which the individual accepts parental strictures and values as immutable and generalizes this orientation to include moral standards imposed by other adults and authority figures;
3. *peer-oriented*: in which the individual is an adaptive conformist who goes along with the peer group—which is largely autonomous of adult authority and ultimately of all social authority—and in which behavior is guided by momentary shifts in group opinion and interests;
4. *collective-oriented*: in which the individual is committed to a set of enduring group goals which take precedence over individual desires, obligations, and interpersonal relationships;
5. *objectively oriented*: in which the individual's values are functionally autonomous—that is, having arisen through social interaction but are no longer dependent, on a day-to-day basis, upon social agents for their meaning and application—and in which the individual responds to situations on the basis of principles rather than on the basis of orientations toward social agents. [1, p. 71]

This sequence, while composed of five steps, is almost exactly the same as that of the other theorists presented. There seems to be consensus among many other behavioral scientists that the achievement of internalized values, beliefs, and reasoning is the most effective and desirable type of individual motivation. This internalization, of course, is closely related to the concept of autonomy that is stressed by Piaget and Kohlberg.

The Paradox

Virtually all researchers in moral development agree that the crucial aspect of moral maturity is autonomy—subjection to one's own, internalized law. However, to follow Piaget's thinking, certain elements of moral reasoning are related to this autonomy. They include: consideration of intentions, independence of sanctions, disbelief in immanent justice, preference of restitutive over mere punitive punishment, and reciprocity in social interaction. These were the elements examined in the previous experiments. However, theorists who build on this foundation often make a mistake. They assume that since these variables are frequently associated with moral autonomy, their presence must always indicate maturity—where moral autonomy is found these elements will always be, and where these elements are found moral autonomy will always be. However, the strong religionist may well surprise us with the extent of his belief in immanent justice (for example, the Roman Empire was destroyed by God because of its wickedness) and he might therefore be scored low in moral maturity, while on some independent measure of maturity he might score quite high. This is true for all but one of the related dimensions mentioned above. Each may frequently be associated with moral maturity, but it would be a mistake to take any of them as a definition of maturity.

Of all the related elements listed above, the only one that is a natural and necessary concomitant of moral autonomy is independence from adult, or external, sanctions. If one is to be morally autonomous, one must *necessarily* be independent of external sanctions in moral reasoning. All of the other elements are related to autonomy in some way, but none of them follows as a logical necessity as does this one. Instead, they appear to be merely beliefs, and, as mentioned earlier, there is no dispute as to whether beliefs can be readily changed. Mere change of beliefs, however, cannot prove that movement toward moral maturity has occurred. Thus, studies which show such changes cannot be used to infer actual moral growth.

Of all the elements of moral reasoning, independence of sanctions is the crucial one for establishing that actual moral growth has taken place. Yet this is the very principle that is violated in studies purporting to show the significance of training procedures in producing moral autonomy. This is why the conclusions derived from the previous experiments must be stated with drastic qualifications. Training procedures of the type presented there typically involve at least subtle adult sanctions (reinforcement or punishment), and the very fact that children respond to them so readily is evidence of their moral immaturity. This is a philosophical-methodological difficulty that haunts all such training studies. If a directive training procedure has been used, and if results show that the training procedure was effective in promoting the moral autonomy of the children (as measured by improvement in one or more of the above elements of moral maturity), then, paradoxically, that is itself evidence that moral autonomy has not been increased at all; instead, the effectiveness of such sanctions proves moral immaturity.

This poses a problem for all training studies in the area of moral development, because the very foundation of most of these studies is adult or some other external sanctioning. It is impossible to escape the paradox we have described. It is much like the wife who says she will make a "real man" of her husband: if she must *make* him she can never really think of him as a real man—the one condition precludes the other. It seems, then, that the very idea of direct training of moral autonomy is a logical contradiction. Certain related elements of moral maturity (i.e., beliefs, and types of normative reasoning) can be introduced through direct training, but this is always at the expense, or at least exhibits the lack, of moral autonomy itself.

Lickona (11) provides an excellent example of this problem. He states:

If you really wanted to violate Piaget's view of development, I thought, what would you do? You'd just tell the kid what was the right answer. So the "Didactic Rule Training Condition" consisted simply of telling the child that the malicious story character was naughtier, because intentions are more important than consequences in deciding who's naughtier. For example:

Child: John's naughtier because he broke more cups than Henry.

Experimenter: No, Henry is naughtier because he was going to do
                            something bad when he broke 1 cup. He wasn't
                            trying to help anyone. But John was trying to help
                            and he didn't mean to break the 8 cups. If somebody
                            is trying to do something good for someone else, he's
                            not naughty, even if he breaks something by accident
                            when he's trying to help. [11, pp. 7–8]

Following this didactic, rule-giving condition, Lickona obtained the
greatest change of any condition he employed: there was no subject
who did not make gain and all subjects finished with a predominantly
higher moral reasoning score. This, of course, could be interpreted as
evidence contradicting Piaget and supporting the idea that direct
training effectively increases moral maturity. But such a conclusion is
inappropriate. Would a morally autonomous and mature person
significantly alter his way of reasoning, as results show these children
did, simply because a man in a white coat—a virtual stranger—told
him to? Yet children are often said to have made significant gains in
moral maturity for doing precisely that. The only point proved by
such a finding is that the subjects are quite as immature in their moral
reasoning as Piaget would have predicted. Paradoxically, at least
from a direct training point of view, moral autonomy is exhibited only
when subjects refuse to respond blindly to an experimenter's direction. Apparently, the primary hope for effectively developing
moral autonomy lies in more indirect methods.

8 / Changing Moral Thinking: Social Interaction, Modeling, and Role Taking

In the preceding chapter we have seen that direct attempts at promoting moral autonomy present a fundamental problem. In this chapter we will discuss more indirect methods: modeling, social interaction, and role taking.

SOCIAL INTERACTION

The reader will recall from our discussion of Piaget (20) that if the child is to mature cognitively he must learn to differentiate his own perspective from others'. Piaget said this growth is complemented by the child's learning to reciprocate and to be aware of other's opinions. These skills normally are thought to develop out of situations characterized by reciprocity, equality, group consensus, mutual respect among peers, and the like. The child moves from the moral realism of adult authority (lower level) to the higher level of autonomy and a morality of cooperation. It would seem reasonable to conclude, therefore, that children who participate in forming rules will show greater flexibility in the use of rules and thus demonstrate greater moral maturity. (This would be true to the extent that they intend to change the rules, not to break them.) To test the truth of these ideas, researchers in one study (18) matched and paired kindergarten and first-grade children on relevant variables, and then divided them into two groups. One group was called the participating group, and the other, the nonparticipating group. The experimenter showed toys to each child in the participating group and said that he could make up a game to see who could win the most marbles.

She told him he could make up what had to be done to win a marble and it could be anything he wanted. "For example, we could try to drop something into something else (experimenter demonstrates dropping medium ball into cup). Or we could try to hit something with something (rolls small ball at jack). Or we could do all sorts of things." The task made up by the child was usually very similar to these examples. [18, p. 292]

Children in the nonparticipating group were simply taught the game by the experimenter. Later, a child's flexibility in changing rules was tested by having him answer questions like the following:

1. The child was asked whether it would be "fair" or "wrong" if two players agreed to play the game with a minor substitution of equipment: e.g., substituting the small ball for the large one or a marble for a jack.
2. The child was asked whether it would be "fair" or "wrong" if two players agreed to have 10 turns each rather than the usual number of turns.
3. The child was asked whether it would be "fair" or wrong" if two players agreed that they both could get closer, making the task easier. [18, pp. 294–95]

It was found that the children who were given the social experience of making up the rules did in fact show more flexibility in changing rules in the game than did the children who had not had the experience; the children in the participating group exhibited a greater degree of autonomy of thought. It was also found that first-grade subjects were more flexible than the kindergarten children.

In a more naturalistic setting, Keasey (14) interviewed boys and girls in the fifth- and sixth-grade using the Kohlberg test. The teachers and Keasey also measured the amount of social interaction of each child. It was found from these data that moral development was related positively to the amount of social participation, whether judged by peers or by teachers.

In order to increase the level of moral reasoning among first- and second-grade children, Lickona (16) also used a social interaction technique. The following conversation, about Fred who bumped over a can of paint while helping his father and Paul who deliberately dribbled a little bit of paint on the ground because he did not want to help his father, is quoted by Lickona:

Helen: Fred's naughtier. He shoulda looked where he was going.
Amy: I think Paul is naughtier. He just didn't want to help paint the table, that's why he spilled the paint on the ground.

(to E)   Which one of we are right—her or me?

E: . . . People have different opinions.

Amy: Helen, I think I'm right because that boy, he shouldn't spill that on the ground!

Helen: (to E) Maybe she's right.

E: You think that Amy is right? Remember, I want you to say what you really think.

Amy: I bet I'm right. Come *on*, Helen!

Helen: I think I'm right. I just think I'm right.

(Silence)

E: Helen, tell Amy why you think you're right.

Helen: Because the first boy shoulda still looked where he was goin', or he shoulda told his father that he didn't mean to spill the paint.

Amy: I think I'm right because . . . um . . . I gotta think up some more answers! (reasons) . . . He (Paul) was mad because his father asked him to help and he didn't want to and he spilled a drop of paint on *purposely*.

Helen: He shoulda looked where he was goin.

Amy: Helen, you keep on saying that!

Helen: Well, that's what I mean! [16, pp. 5–6]

It was found that 60 percent of the children who experienced this treatment moved to the higher levels of reasoning on a posttest. This is extremely high in comparison with the change ordinarily cited in the research literature. Furthermore, Lickona found that the changes came after discussion, so it was not just a matter of social approval; social interaction, itself, seemed to be the important variable.

Problems Associated With Peer-Group Change

A serious concern must be introduced here, however. While authors often assume a positive effect from the peer group and social interaction, this need not always be the case. Peer interaction, particularly in older age groups (Piaget, in stressing peer interaction, was speaking primarily of the ages five through nine), will often obstruct the process of discussion and compromise rather than promote it. Often the weight of peer opinion allows less, not more, freedom in selecting and considering various moral points of view; any group that dictates a limited range of thought or opinion is a hindrance rather than a help in facilitating the growth of moral reasoning.

For example, Bronfenbrenner's studies (5, 6, 7, 8, 11) show that surprising differences exist between children from the United States and the USSR. In regard to the opposition between adult and peer standards, Bronfenbrenner (6) found that in the United States, twelve-year-old children will provide different answers to moral dilemmas, depending on whether peers or adults will inspect their tests. If they are led to believe that parents will inspect their answers, they give more prosocial responses, but when they believe peers will inspect their answers, they give more antisocial answers. However, in the Soviet Union children score their resolutions toward the prosocial or positive end of the dimenson for both parents and peers.

In another study, Beloff and Temperley (3) found that twelve-year-old Scottish children are peer-oriented in their answers on this same test; they prefer answers that would seem undesirable in the context of the society's values. Also, the relatively adult-oriented, more socialized children are less popular. The researchers concluded that popular children are informal leaders in the school environment, and they provide a hidden curriculum for other pupils which contradicts the teacher-approved or culturally approved social values. This suggests that the power of the pupil to reinforce other students effectively may be greater than that of the teacher, and it may well be that peers actually contribute to lower values.

The power of peers is again illustrated in a study by Berkowitz and Walker (4). University students were tested to see if laws and peer opinions could influence their judgment of morality and social action. Three groups were formed. One group was told that laws existed, defining actions as legal or illegal. The second group was told that the peers approved or disapproved of the behavior, and a control group received no influence. The following indicate the type of problems posed:

A man who is drunk in a public place is acting in an immoral manner even if he is not disorderly.

A person is *not* in the wrong morally if he allows someone else to borrow his car without checking this individual's license.

The person who borrows money for the purpose of betting is not doing anything morally wrong even if he does not inform the lender why he wants the money.

The individual who sees another person attempting to commit suicide and does not try to stop him is acting immorally himself.

People should be willing to overlook failures in the manners and unpleasant habits of other people.

It is always important to finish anything that you have started.
I would never let a friend down when he expected something from me. [4, p. 416]

It was found that both knowledge of the law and knowledge of peer opinions led to greater shifts in judgment than was found in the control group. Moreover, peer opinion was found to cause a greater change than belief in the existence of legal sanction. It was further found that even highly authoritative or rigid subjects were more influenced by peers than by knowledge of the law. Thus, as Piaget hypothesized, the effect of social interaction, especially peer interaction, does seem to have a great impact on moral judgments. The specific direction of this impact, however—although partly due to age differences—may be a function of more subtle factors as well. This point will receive further attention later.

The peer group and Soviet methods of character development

The Soviet program of moral education relies extensively on peer group influence. While only a small percentage of children are raised in collective settings, 20 percent between ages three and six, and 5 percent of all school-age children (8, p. 17), the Soviet program nonetheless constitutes an experiment of massive proportions. The effectiveness of this experiment is reported by an eminent American psychologist, Urie Bronfenbrenner (8).

Moral education in the Soviet Union is indebted to the efforts of Anton Semyonovich Makarenko, whose many published works are based on practical experience with juvenile delinquents. In his work in rehabilitation, Makarenko developed group-oriented disciplinary techniques that are used to develop moral responsibility and social behavior. His success in rehabilitation won him favor with the Communist party and his work is now the official guideline in moral behavior for both parents and educators. When Makarenko writes for parents, he points out that the family is responsible for all aspects of individual development. Consider the following statement: "In delegating to you a certain measure of societal authority the Soviet State demands from you the correct upbringing of its future citizens. Particularly it relies on you to provide certain conditions arising naturally out of your union: namely, your parental love" (7, p. 551).

Thus, the parents become an arm of the state and are supplemented by other state agencies, the community, and schools. To see how the schools are used, consider the following account:

The bell has rung, but the teacher has not yet arrived. She has delayed deliberately in order to check how the class will conduct itself.

In the class all is quiet. After the noisy class break, it isn't so easy to mobilize yourself and to quell the restlessness within you! Two monitors at the desk silently observe the class. On their faces is reflected the full importance and seriousness of the job they are performing. But there is no need for them to make any reprimands: the youngsters with pleasure and pride maintain scrupulous discipline; they are proud of the fact that their class conducts itself in a manner that merits the confidence of the teacher. And when the teacher enters and quietly says be seated, all understand that she deliberately refrains from praising them for the quiet and order, since in their class it could not be otherwise.

During the lesson, the teacher gives an exceptional amount of attention to collective competition between "links." (The links are the smallest unit of the Communist youth organization at this age level). Throughout the entire lesson the youngsters are constantly hearing which link has best prepared its lesson, which link has done the best at numbers, which is the most disciplined, which has turned in the best work.

The best link not only gets a verbal positive evaluation but receives the right to leave the classroom first during the break and to have its notebooks checked before the others. As a result the links receive the benefit of collective education, common responsibility, and mutual aid.

"What are you fooling around for? You're holding up the whole link," whispers Kolya to his neighbor during the preparation period for the lesson. And during the break he teaches her how better to organize her books and pads in her knapsack.

"Count more carefully," says Olya to her girl friend. "See, on account of you our link got behind today. You come to me and we'll count together at home." [7, p. 553]

The problem of discipline in the Soviet school is largely solved through peer control. The peer groups are organized with adult leadership, but they soon become somewhat autonomous in setting standards, developing discipline, and enforcing proper behavior. Often, the problem of discipline disappears when emphasis is placed on competition between links, or groups of students, because the criteria for success in the competition include behavioral and attitudinal elements that reflect discipline and proper morality. Rewards are given to successful classes or links. This positive approach, however, also involves the negative feature of group criticism:

The feature of Soviet socialization practices which clashes most sharply with the American pattern is the Russian's widespread resort to the procedure of criticizing others and one's self in public. The practice is common throughout all levels of Soviet society from school, farm, and factory to highest echelons of the party. Thus by being taught these techniques in early childhood, Soviet youth are being prepared in patterns of response that will be expected and even required of them throughout their life spans. [7, p. 561]

Later, other elements are added to the collective discipline and social organization. For example, students learn to criticize others and themselves publicly, and, if necessary, they can be expelled from the link. Because the family is also a group and is expected to work closely with the school, its influence can also be relied upon in helping the child develop cooperative skills.

In "The Changing Soviet Family" (5), Bronfenbrenner discusses the instructional methods that are used to accomplish the goals of self-reliance, discipline, and collective responsibility in the students. For instance, each child entering the school is given specific training in developing personal self-reliance, such as toilet training, standing in a crib, or dressing himself. Particular stress is given to language training, which is accomplished by very close attention to the children's vocal behavior. Collective responsibility is taught in part by an early emphasis on sharing. Positive examples of sharing are frequently shown to children. Games which require cooperation among the group are used rather than the competitive games emphasizing individual achievement which are typical of American life. To develop group identification, there is instruction in group behavior and in public criticism in the collective schools.

However, as already mentioned, the group is not simply a peer group. The importance of adults in the peer collective is not to be understated. Bronfenbrenner points out that while the collective is only an extension of adult society, reward and punishment toward the group occur in close correspondence with the wishes of the adults or the communistic society. It is, in fact, the adult society which rewards the individual or collective links, and so it is to the advantage of an individual child and the peer group to work for the benefit of society. Here the adult society is closely informed and works with the peer groups. This may be the reason why the peer groups are so effective in promoting specified types of moral reasoning.

Soviet youth and moral autonomy

The reported effectiveness of the Soviet program is congruent with other evidence of the general social and behavioral maturity of Soviet youth. However, the following passage suggests the system's weakness in developing autonomous moral thinking.

The results showed that Soviet youngsters placed stronger emphasis than any other group on overt propriety, such as being clean, orderly, and well-mannered, but gave less weight than the subjects from the other countries to telling the truth and seeking intellectual understanding.

This result is, of course, not incompatible with the other data we have reported highlighting the obedience of Russian children. Indeed, another way of describing our findings as a whole is to say that, from a cross-cultural perspective, Soviet children, in the process of growing up, are confronted with fewer divergent views both within and outside the family and, in consequence, conform more completely to a more homogeneous set of standards. [8, p. 81]

Effects of Peer Interaction: Conclusion

Thus, it may be that while Soviet youth exhibit a great deal of propriety and obedience to societal norms, they are not really morally autonomous or mature, despite extensive interaction with peers. Apparently, therefore, it is not peer interaction per se that is the crucial element in moral development, but whether that interaction is in fact free and open. Piaget (20) explicitly recognized this point. Clearly, adolescent and even younger peer pressure can restrict an individual's range of thought and thus hinder his moral development. In such cases, the influence of peer interaction is largely negative. However, in those cases where much of the interaction is directed toward mutual problem-solving and compromise, the results can be positive. The value of peer interaction is the potential it holds for promoting a feeling of equality among participants, thus fostering open discussion and active search for agreement. Social interaction can indeed play a significant role in the development of moral autonomy, but to do so, that interaction must have other characteristics, such as freedom and openness, as well.

MODELING

One of the most time-honored and highly respected methods of influencing others is that of setting an example. Psychologists, as well as the general public, seem to be intrigued with modeling as a mode of learning, as the large number of research reports attests. There is available evidence that modeling does have an impact on moral reasoning (e.g., 2, 7, 13, 21). While other studies could be cited to show a general impact of modeling on opinions or beliefs, it is not entirely clear what actually produces these changes. For example, do the models cause confusion, resulting in a shift of opinion? Do they illustrate ways of obtaining rewards or status? Do they only affect surface-level opinions, or do they change the underlying cognitive processes—the manner in which a person actually reasons? Is the effect long-lasting or simply a superficial act of conformity? One of the clearest statements of this complexity is given by the reviewers in the 1971 *Annual Review of Psychology.* "Modeling is implicated as a *process* in the development of children's moral thinking even though the *extent* to which modeling is involved in the development of moral judgments and the nature of its interaction with other aspects of a child's cognitive functioning are less clear" (12, p. 374; see also 10).

Keasey (13), attempting to clarify the general findings, used three modeling conditions with fifth- and sixth-grade children. He varied opinions of the models, sometimes with and sometimes without reasoning, sometimes at the subject's own level of moral development or one stage above, while considering the effects over time. After analyzing this complex experiment Keasey concluded that the changes in moral reasoning could be explained only partially by the effects of modeling. He states:

However, a modeling interpretation cannot account for the significant increase in higher stage reasoning evidenced by these two groups on the 2-week posttest. First of all, subjects in neither of these two groups (same stage and opinion only) had an opportunity to observe models using higher stage reasoning. Second, since there is no link between moral opinions and stage of reasoning in Kohlberg's system as there is within Piaget's, it is not likely that subjects could have detected any underlying moral orientation by hearing the models give only opinions or reasoning at the subject's own stage. . . .

It could be argued that the relative equilibrium of subjects exposed to these two reasoning conditions was disrupted. In fact, it appears that disequilibrium can be induced by a variety of conflict situations. This conclusion is supported by the fact that all three of the experimental paradigms used previously seemed to induce sizeable amounts of upward reasoning change. Once disequilibrium has been induced, the upward reasoning change evidenced by these two groups may be accounted for by either of two processes. [13, p. 35]

In interpreting these findings, a general conclusion is that modeling is surprisingly complex and at the present time is not completely understood. It appears that discrepant or novel behavior on the part of the model produces disequilibrium or in other ways stimulates an observer who is ready to learn. It is also plausible that the model serves an important function in providing information for the learner who is motivated. In many cases, the model may provide the first coherent and integrated logical statement representing a moral justification. In this case, the model is not a necessary element but is one of the many possible means whereby a child obtains information of a complex nature. The model may also provide information about the appropriateness of certain verbal statements, give indications as to social reinforcements, and/or exert social pressure. A reasonable conclusion might be that the most meaningful role that models could play in the development of moral judgments is providing content, information, exemplary reasoning, and motivation by producing disequilibrium. It should be noted with Keasey, however, that such modeling is not a necessary condition for inducing such moral changes; significant movement can occur where modeling has little or no influence.

ROLE TAKING

Role taking is another complex factor in the development of moral reasoning. It can refer to a conceptual ability or to a training methodology. In most cases, however, the first meaning, namely, conceptual ability, is implied. This is the case in Kohlberg's recent addition to his general theory. He considers role taking to be parallel to his six familiar stages in the development of moral thinking (15). Similarly, a psychologist-educator who for many years has stressed the importance of role taking has recently published an excellent chapter describing the relationship between role taking and moral thought (25). His integration, regarding Kohlberg's first four stages, is presented in table 5.

Other researchers in the area of moral reasoning have also hypothesized that the level of moral development is positively correlated with role-taking ability; one's moral maturity should be associated with his ability to understand another's point of view. Campagna and Harter (9), for instance, compared sociopathic children with normal children in moral reasoning and found the normal children to be significantly more mature (using Kohlberg's scale). These researchers suggested that one reason for the finding was that sociopathic children come from families and environments that restrict role-taking opportunities: parents of these children were inconsistent in disciplining and in fulfilling the needs of their children, and they often acted out their own hostilities by victimizing them. These results lend support to the hypothesis that the ability to role-play is important to the attainment of moral maturity.

Another study was performed in which children were first measured in their role-taking ability (24). Then the experimenter showed the subject two boxes. On one box was printed "10¢" and on the other "5¢." The coins, a dime and a nickel, were placed in the respective boxes. The experimenter told the subject that in a few minutes someone else was going to come and choose one box, and take the money from it. The child's task was to remove the money from either the dime or the nickel box, whichever one he expected the other to choose, and thereby trick him. The important thing for the child to remember was that the other person knew that he was going to trick him. Therefore, the child had to predict which box would be chosen. After he removed the money from the box, the child was asked why he thought the other would choose the box.

The subject's responses were analyzed and scored at one of three categories, reflecting three assumed levels of role-taking ability. The first level was characterized by an inability of the child to offer a rationale for the choice he felt the other person would make. Such randomness indicates the child is not able to put himself in another person's position and role-play. Level two was characterized by the child's ability to offer a motive for his choice, but an inability to take into account the fact that the other person would also be aware of his motives. The child at the third level was able to impute motives to the other person; he was likely to say, for instance, "He will think I will take the dime box and so he will switch to the nickel, so maybe I better take the nickel box." Such reasoning represents a high level of

TABLE 5. PARALLEL STRUCTURED RELATIONS BETWEEN SOCIAL ROLE-TAKING AND MORAL JUDGMENT STAGES

Social Role-Taking Stage	Moral Judgment Stage
Stage 0 EGOCENTRIC VIEWPOINT (Age Range 3-6) Child has a sense of differentiation of self and other but fails to distinguish between the social perspective (thoughts, feelings) of other and self. Child can label other's overt feelings but does not see the cause-and-effect relation of reasons to social actions.	Stage 0 PREMORAL STAGE Judgments of right and wrong are based on good or bad consequences and not on intentions. Moral choices derive from the subject's wishes that good things happen to self. Child's reasons for his choices simply assert the choices, rather than attempting to justify them.
Stage 1 SOCIAL-INFORMATIONAL ROLE TAKING (Age Range 6–8) Child is aware that other has a social perspective based on other's own reasoning, which may or may not be similar to child's. However, child tends to focus on one perspective rather than coordinating viewpoints.	Stage 1 PUNISHMENT AND OBEDIENCE ORIENTATION Child focuses on one perspective, that of the authority or the powerful. However, child understands that good actions are based on good intentions. Beginning sense of fairness as equality of acts.
Stage 2 SELF-REFLECTIVE ROLE TAKING (Age Range 8–10) Child is conscious that each individual is aware of the other's perspective and that this awareness influences self and other's view of each other. Putting self in other's place is a way of judging his intentions, purposes, and actions. Child can form a coordinated chain of perspectives, but cannot yet abstract from this process to the level of simultaneous mutuality.	Stage 2 INSTRUMENTAL ORIENTATION Moral reciprocity is conceived as the equal exchange of the intent of two persons in relations to one another. If someone has a mean intention toward self, it is right for self to act in kind. Right defined as what is valued by self.

role-taking ability which is absent in children at the other two levels. Consistent with the hypothesis, it was found among eight-, nine-, and ten-year-old boys and girls that development of these role-taking skills was related to the Kohlberg-type moral judgment measure.

In a more recent study, Moir (19) confirmed this hypothesis. He correlated the scores of forty eleven-year-old girls on Kohlberg's scale

TABLE 5. CONTINUED.

Social Role-Taking Stage	*Moral Judgment Stage*
Stage 3 MUTUAL ROLE TAKING (Age Range 10–12) Child realizes that both self and other can view each other mutually and simultaneously as subjects. Child can step outside the two-person dyad and view the interaction from a third-person perspective.	Stage 3 ORIENTATION TO MAINTAINING MUTUAL EXPECTATIONS Right is defined as the Golden Rule: Do unto others as you would have others do unto you. Child considers all points of view and reflects on each person's motives in an effort to reach agreement among all participants.
Stage 4 SOCIAL AND CONVENTIONAL SYSTEM ROLE-TAKING (Age Range 12–15+) Person realizes mutual perspective taking does not always lead to complete understanding. Social conventions are seen as necessary because they are understood by all members of the group (the generalized other) regardless of their position, role, or experience.	Stage 4 ORIENTATION TO SOCIETY'S PERSPECTIVE Right is defined in terms of the perspective of the generalized other or the majority. Person considers consequences of actions for the group or society. Orientation to maintenance of social morality and social order.

SOURCE: 25, p. 309.

of moral development with their scores on nonmoral role-taking tests. The results of his study showed that much of the variance in the moral maturity of the subjects could be accounted for by measures of role-taking ability.

In another study (1), psychology students role-played moral dilemmas against opponents who used advanced, one-stage-higher, moral reasoning. Role-playing subjects later showed advancement in their reasoning. The author stated:

This study provides clear evidence of the effectiveness of actual role playing in the context of a moral dilemma for producing both immediate and relatively long-term changes in the maturity of moral judgment. . . . [It] has demonstrated the efficacy of active participation in the resolution of a moral dilemma for inducing change in the maturity of one's moral judgment. Role playing, particularly in combination with other previously demonstrated techniques for producing structural change, should provide both researchers and educators with a valuable method for the study and promotion of prosocial styles of thinking. [1, p. 322]

Recent evidence suggests that the ability to play a role, to see things from another person's point of view, is an important factor in the development of moral maturity.

While enacting a role can lead to a change in moral reasoning it may not necessarily be more effective than other influences. Is there something unique in role playing that produces more change? One team of researchers found that they could produce change by having eleven- to twelve-year-old children play the role of someone giving moral advice (17). However, the amount of change was no greater for these role-playing subjects than it was for subjects who simply heard moral reasoning different from their own. Most change occurred when the advice was two stages, rather than one stage, higher than their own previously measured reasoning. While there are some concerns about relying heavily on this single study, it could be interpreted to support a concept we propose in chapter nine: the significant cause for change is the disequilibrium that results when persons encounter information discrepant from their own thinking. Role playing or modeling may be effective primarily as a means of illustrating or communicating such discrepancies.

It appears that role taking is an important element in cognitive and personal development and perhaps a significant factor in mature moral development as well. Unfortunately there appears to be little research demonstrating how to increase or influence requisite role-taking skill (although Selman [22, 23] has developed some initial intervention programs). This, then, should provide valuable direction for future research in moral development.

CONCLUSION

In many respects, the material presented in this chapter is subject to the same limitations as that in the previous chapter. It will be remembered that there is a serious difficulty with the notion of using direct training techniques to increase moral maturity in children: the technique used to improve moral maturity is the very one that precludes it. As long as children are so malleable and dependent on adults or other external sanctions, then they are held to be neither morally autonomous nor mature. It seems, then, as stated earlier, that the notion of direct training of moral autonomy is a logical contradiction. Elements related to moral autonomy can be introduced through direct training, but maturity itself seems to defy such training.

This finding raises certain questions about topics discussed in this chapter. Modeling, for instance, has been shown to be effective, though not necessary, in altering subjects' behavior (and by inference, their reasoning), but it is doubtful whether such studies have shown just how to increase moral development per se. Modeling studies often encounter the same difficulties as the direct training procedures: the very success of simple modeling behavior, whether by adult or peer, is evidence of the subject's dependence on others and his lack of an internalized set of self-chosen moral principles. In fact, research on modeling (e.g., 1) clearly shows that the model's effectiveness is closely related to sanctions for either the model or the subject. That such behaviors are external in origin is sufficient to establish that they are similar by definition to Piaget's heteronomy and concomitant immaturity of moral reasoning. Perhaps the needed study in this field would involve observation of a number of models, each of whose moral principles is clear to the subjects and who were seen acting autonomously. The autonomy, then, rather than a specific type of reasoning, would be imitated.

Regarding the Soviet method, it appears that except for their emphasis on parental love, the techniques used represent direct training techniques. These, as we have seen, can be extremely effective in promoting various elements and types of reasoning, but they are antithetical to promoting maturity or autonomy. In almost every phase of life there is direct adult and social pressure; even the influence of peer groups is an arm of direct social forces. Enough has been said on the paradoxical and self-defeating nature of training moral maturity to see that it is exemplified in the Soviet system.

It appears that both modeling techniques and Soviet methods of moral education are to some extent inadequate in fostering individuals' moral autonomy. Conversely, the concepts of productive social interaction and increased role-taking ability have been shown to be useful. In the next chapter we present a further discussion of social interaction and another technique that has been shown to influence moral thinking.

9/Social Interaction: Disequilibrium and the Role of the Family

Social interaction seems to be most free of the problems common to the direct training procedures. Piaget explained that social (i.e., peer) interaction is a superior experience because of the absence of adult authority. In such interaction children must solve problems among themselves, and these experiences result in improved reasoning. This interaction is a state in which all of the participants are considered more or less equal, so there is no recourse to a final authority. The child also learns that his own ideas are as valuable and important as others' and that compromise—the abandonment of formerly strict, but sometimes trivial rules—is a necessary and acceptable way of solving problems. In this way, he comes to learn that rules and standards are often products of social compromise and that he, individually, can play an active part in changing or forming them. No longer must he accept adult mores as eternal and unchangeable; he comes instead to see them as socially accepted standards of conduct that can change over time. From this perspective, the child develops the realization that morality comes from within and that one's principles can no longer merely be accepted from an outside authority. They must be examined and fully internalized for their adoption to be justified in a complete sense. The individual who reaches this point is morally autonomous, and a primary vehicle for his growth seems to be active social interaction.

DISEQUILIBRIUM

One way of explaining this mechanism has been called the "disequilibrium hypothesis." To introduce this concept we turn to the

160

work of two social psychologists, Sherif (39) and Asch (7), who observed that a person's judgments about a factual observation can be altered by having a group express contrary opinions. It was found that people frequently change their evaluations to agree with the group's opposing point of view. One can explain the change in two ways, by conformity to group pressure or by mental conflict resulting from a discrepancy between what one saw and what others were seeing. Similarly, some researchers have held that when various disagreeing opinions or perspectives are presented on an issue, a person will tend to reduce disagreements between his own opinions and those of others. This disequilibrium, or conflict, is often resolved by the person's changing his own opinions and even his method of reasoning. If this is the case, presentation of different moral opinions and reasoning should result in changes of moral thinking. A person, through repeated exposures to different levels of moral reasoning and opinion, should feel mental discomfort and move toward more advanced thinking. This should occur naturally without any other accompanying inducements.

To test this hypothesis, Keasey exposed pre-adolescent boys and girls who were reasoning at Kohlberg's first three stages to higher levels of reasoning (29). A dilemma was first presented:

In Europe, a woman was near death from a special kind of cancer. There was one drug that the doctors thought might save her. It was a form of radium that a druggist in the same town had recently discovered. The drug was expensive to make, but the druggist was charging ten times what the drug cost him to make. He paid $200 for the radium and charges $2,000 for a small dose of the drug. The sick woman's husband, Heinz, went to everyone he knew to borrow the money, but he could only get together about $1,000 which is half of what it cost. He told the druggist that his wife was dying, and asked him to sell it cheaper or let him pay later. But the druggist said, "No, I discovered the drug and I'm going to make money from it." So Heinz got desperate and broke into the man's store to steal the drug for his wife. Should Heinz have done that?

Subjects were later exposed to the following arguments to see if their reasoning would change if presented with reasoning at the same stage (two), or one stage higher (three). The following is an example of such reasoning:

(Same stage reasoning, Stage 2 con) Don't steal the drug for your wife. She probably wouldn't steal it to save your life so why should you risk your life for her? You can easily find another wife. The druggist has a right to sell the drug for what he wants.

(Same stage reasoning, Stage 2 pro) You should steal the drug because you need it. Your wife will do a lot for you; you should do something for her. Where would you be if she dies?

(Plus one reasoning, Stage 3 con) You should not steal the drug. You can go to the police or to a doctor and they will help you get it. Anyway it is not your responsibility, it is the druggist's responsibility. He is only being selfish and he should let you have the drug.

(Plus one reasoning, Stage 3 pro) It is your duty to steal the drug because you love your wife and are her husband. The druggist is supposed to help people with his drugs and he certainly isn't doing that by charging too much for it. Stealing is not as bad as the druggist's meanness. [29, p. 32]

Note that a person could encounter reasoning with the same opinion but different reasoning, or a different opinion and the same reasoning. A number of similar dilemmas accompanied by opinion and reasoning statements were presented. It was found from these experiments that an opinion change as to what should be done occurred more frequently when it was justified by reasoning one stage higher. It was found that exposure to reasoning one stage higher had an immediate one-day effect, but after two weeks, exposure to the same level of reasoning, or even to no reasoning at all (only opinions), also resulted in as much increase in moral reasoning. Thus, the conflict itself, as much as the stage differences in reasoning, accounted for the upward movement. Keasey concluded:

It could be argued that the relative equilibrium of subjects exposed to these two reasoning conditions was disrupted. In fact, it appears that disequilibrium can be induced by a variety of conflict situations. This conclusion is supported by the fact that all three of the experimental paradigms used previously seemed to induce sizeable amounts of upward reasoning change. [29, p. 35]

Other researchers have also mentioned that exposure to higher levels of reasoning is sufficient to increase moral reasoning (12, 42). One such study (41) using seventh-grade boys found that moral reasoning could be facilitated by exposure to moral reasoning one stage higher and that the most progress was made by those at the lower levels of moral reasoning. But another finding, similar to Keasey's, was that subjects who were given only a pretest but no exposure to higher reasoning also changed. The researchers suggested that mere exposure to the problem or question was sufficient to initiate movement toward higher reasoning. They stated:

One inference from this finding is that the pretest interview is a powerful manipulation for subjects at a low level of moral judgment. In attempting to match theory to this finding, one must look closely at the nature of the interview itself. Dilemma situations are presented to the child. The task of the interviewer is to probe the child's reasoning in an effort to obtain scorable responses. In completing this task the interviewer explores areas the subject might otherwise overlook or actively attempt to avoid. Therefore, it seems reasonable to conclude that children at low levels of moral judgment would find the interview situation unique. In addition, the demand upon the child to articulate his reasons and motives for judging specific conflicts might itself be a novel experience for Level I subjects. [41, p. 242]

These studies indicate that exposure to moral dilemmas and different types of reasoning alone may result in an increase in moral maturity. Such results, of course, are open to all of the questions that have been raised about Kohlberg's early model (30) (these studies were based on it) but they still provide valuable research data, and they escape the philosophical and practical problems encountered in the use of direct training techniques. In fact, presentation of dilemmas and different types of reasoning would induce the process of introspection and moral examination, and it seems that such a process would result in increased maturity even as measured by criteria other than Kohlberg's. This would be true because rather than reinforcing a specific response, this type of experimental condition induces a process, and it is this process that leads to maturity. In other words, it appears that introducing an element of disequilibrium into a person's moral thinking is the best way of increasing his moral maturity.

From this conclusion, it is expected that the individual who is active in examining himself and his world and who eagerly seeks and digests knowledge will be far more likely to exhibit moral maturity than one who is lethargic and uninvolved. The person who refuses to hear all sides of an issue and the person who refuses to hear anything are neither open enough to new information nor to new ideas to experience any significant moral growth. But he who is active and concerned, who processes a great deal of information and is open to new ideas, will be more self-aware and will become far more morally mature. He has undergone, or is undergoing, the process of moral self-examination, spawned by encounters with new information and new ideas, and he can hardly help but emerge with a more solid foundation and justification for his moral assumptions, in short, with greater moral maturity.

One more example will help to illustrate this point. A study (6) was performed to test the effects of role playing on moral reasoning (as measured by Kohlberg). In this study, subjects were paired off and each member of the pair was assigned a role to play in a moral dilemma in which they were pitted against each other. One was to play Heinz and the other was to play the druggist as in the dilemma on p. 161. Each subject was assigned the task of convincing the other person, using the best reasoning possible, that his own position was right. All subjects were given a pretest and both an immediate and a delayed posttest. Results of the study showed that subjects who had argued with opponents who used higher levels of reasoning made significant upward change on both posttests, indicating that mere exposure to better reasoning causing disequilibrium is sufficient to impel some degree of moral growth.

The finding that there was no change for subjects who had argued with opponents using lower levels of reasoning may be explained by the fact that they were exposed to nothing new or that they found the lower level reasoning objectionable or unappealing. There was likely no disequilibrium for those subjects encountering reasoning at a lower level. In any case, this study does seem to support the disequilibrium hypothesis and to argue for the role of openness and active social interaction in promoting moral maturity.

THE ROLE OF THE FAMILY

Active social interaction is basic to moral growth; it introduces disequilibrium into the child's moral thought and provides the child with the requisite sense of equality. It also escapes the philosophical problems (at least our objections to them) encountered with direct training attempts. The primary difficulty with seeing peer interaction as the foundation of moral development, however, is that the peer group frequently becomes as authoritarian and tyrannical in its effect on an individual's thought as Piaget claimed adult authority could be. In the previous chapter we discussed a number of studies that illustrate the tremendous impact that peer influence has on an individual's moral reasoning. Children and even college-age students were significantly swayed in their thinking merely by what they thought their peers believed. It is indisputable that peer pressure holds a strong and pervasive influence over individuals' thoughts and actions; the chances that moral growth will occur under these conditions are not much better than they are under conditions of strict adult authority. It appears, however, that moral autonomy is enhanced by peer interaction which fosters open discussion, equality, and mutual resolution of problems—but there have been few generations, if any, possessing the ability to fulfill these conditions for very long.

What, then, is the answer? First, it must be recalled that the critical element in Piaget's explanation of moral growth is the experiencing of a sense of equality and reciprocity. These elements, not the peer interaction itself, produce moral maturity. If the desired elements of social interaction are present and if a problem is encountered, then the natural course of events should lead to cognitive equilibrium. Piaget added the notion of peer interaction because in his experience this is the primary situation in which the child experiences these qualities. There is no prima facie reason, however, why these same qualities of mutual respect and equality cannot be established in other social encounters, such as in family or school contexts. Indeed, Piaget (34) himself recognized the importance of these qualities in family interaction. Again, the concept of peer interaction is largely incidental. The critical element is interaction with anyone on the basis of mutual respect, and this certainly can include the child's family.

The other probable alternative is the school system. Although much can be accomplished through effective classroom experiences, it still cannot duplicate the moment-to-moment immediacy of family decision-making nor construct the profound in-depth network of interpersonal relationships with which morality is so concerned. For these reasons, it seems that, wherever it is possible, efforts to promote children's moral autonomy should be undertaken by the family.

The remainder of this chapter outlines family conditions that appear to be conducive to moral growth. However, since there is little research directly examining the relationship between family interaction and the aspects of moral development described by Piaget and Kohlberg, little experimental material will be cited. The points outlined are simply general and nontechnical principles that can be loosely derived from the research results already discussed.

General Family Conditions

Most behavioral scientists in psychology, pediatrics, psychiatry, and sociology have concluded that affectionate and accepting relationships among family members are necessary to foster a sense of security and healthy interdependence among individual members. One family therapist (4), for instance, has recently written of the need to promote horizontal, or level, rather than vertical interaction—building a relationship based on mutual respect, love, and cooperation, rather than on distance, attempts to hurt, and competitiveness. He states:

[One] characteristic of people who function horizontally is their mutual respect for one another. Their relationships are free from demeaning critical comments. Each is secure in his belonging and is therefore free to risk learning new ideas. He progresses quickly for he is freed from fear of failure. . . . Love is not tied to success or failure, it is ever present.

In the horizontal relationship, love and affection tend to be expressed freely, with little reserve, for there is no fear of rejection. Trust in one another encompasses those relating horizontally. [4, p. 28–29]

This type of family atmosphere promotes moral maturity among individual members in two ways. First, it establishes the sense of mutual respect and equality that seems to be necessary if heteronomous moral thought is to be abandoned. In such a family, decision making is a family function in which all members' opinions, even those of children, are accorded respect. Here, as well as in peer interaction, the child will learn the give-and-take of problem solving, and he will learn that rules must be derived as well as obeyed. In the process of such horizontal interaction, the child will likely learn more than he would from his association with peers, because he is not threatened with the possibility of rejection. This dimension, combined with the other features of horizontal interaction, insures the continued enjoyment of the equality and respect necessary for effective moral growth.

Second, horizontal interaction establishes the type of family atmosphere in which effective teaching can take place. The learning of given moral concepts can occur far more easily in a home in which the children have no desire or reason for summarily dismissing whatever their parents say. Horizontal interaction minimizes such blind anticonformity and thus increases the general effectiveness of parental teachings. Horizontal interaction as a general family condition appears to be an excellent framework within which proper moral development can occur.

Child-Rearing Techniques

Mutual respect and equality thus seem to be important factors in effective family relationships. In searching for a general philosophy of child rearing that also reflects these concerns, we have tentatively borrowed much from the framework arising out of Adlerian psychology (1, 2, 3, 5, 13). This theory has been adapted for family interaction analyses by Rudolf Dreikurs (14, 15, 16, 17). Indeed, it was out of this general approach that Allred (4) proposed his horizontal-vertical interactional framework. This theoretical position stresses that man's behavior is purposeful, that his primary goal in life is to achieve a sense of belonging with significant others, and that he is free and possesses creative power of self-direction.

With regard to the raising of children, this approach emphasizes the equality and respect due children as human beings. This emphasis has a significant effect on the specific techniques used to raise children. For instance, the notions of rewarding good behavior and punishing bad behavior are discarded as offensive to the self-respect of the child. Concerning punishment, it is said: "Parents can no longer assume the role of the 'authority.' Authority implies dominance: one individual having power over another. There can be no such dominance among equals. Dominance—force, power—must be replaced with egalitarian techniques of influence" (17, p. 69). And concerning reward it is said:

The system of rewarding children for good behavior is as detrimental to their outlook as the system of punishment. The same lack of respect is shown. We "reward" our inferiors for favors or for good deeds. In a system of mutual respect among equals, a job is done because it needs doing, and the satisfaction comes from the harmony of two people doing a job together. . . . [17, p. 72]

It is on the basis of respecting the child's equality that these theorists discard rewards and punishments as child-rearing methods. These methods are seen as instruments of superior position which communicate to the child his inferiority in an adult's eyes. This reintroduces the concept of the adult authoritarian that characterizes heteronomous morality. Such authoritarianism undermines that sense of reciprocity and equality that seems to be necessary for promoting development toward autonomy in moral thought. With respect to moral development, then, a system not heavily based on either rewards or punishments seems to be desirable.

But what do these psychologists offer instead? The primary method suggested in place of a system of rewards and punishments is the use of natural and logical consequences. For instance, a child who persists in losing his toys simply goes without toys; he suffers the natural consequences of his own behavior. There is no attempt to punish the child for his carelessness. The rationale is to let him assume responsibility for his own actions. In this way the child learns to accept responsibility, and yet he escapes the position of "the inferior punished by the superior."

The use of logical consequences is simply the structuring of circum-stances so that the child experiences the logical consequences of his actions when there are no natural ones. For example, when a child is late to school, the parents might put him to bed early that night on the logical assumption that if he is too tired to arrive at school on time, then he must need more rest (4, p. 86). This is a reasonable assumption, and it follows logically from the misbehavior.

In using these natural and logical consequences, Adlerian psy-chologists stress, parents need to adopt a matter-of-fact attitude. There is no difference, they point out, between direct punishment and a logical consequence that is employed angrily. Therefore, these theorists emphasize that to maintain the benefits of a child's being oriented to consequences, parents should keep their interaction with the child calm and caring rather than angry or spiteful. In this way, it is asserted, discipline can be appropriately strict without incurring the disadvantages associated with punishment.

In identifying children who were more morally mature (although by criteria other than Kohlberg's) Hoffman also identified a critical disciplining technique associated with this maturity. He calls the process "induction," here described by Saltzstein:

Induction primarily involves pointing out to a transgressor the consequences of his behavior for other persons (the parents themselves or some third party). This technique contrasts with power assertion, defined as physical punishment or any other exercise of physical or material power over the child (such as threatening loss of privileges and physically forcing the child to do or not do something), and with *love withdrawal*, defined as nonphysical expression of anger or withdrawal of love (such as the parent's telling the child that she doesn't love him or is angry with him, or her walking away in disgust).

. . . Hoffman and Saltzstein [27] found that higher scores on the various indices of morality generally were negatively associated with use of power assertion, positively associated with use of induction, and unassociated with use of love withdrawal. The same results were obtained regardless of whether the child, parent, teacher, or peers was the source of information for the moral index, or whether the mother or the child reported the mother's discipline. The authors explained the "superiority" of induction over power assertion in terms of the nonaggressive model that induction provided, and the opportunity it afforded for learning and role taking. [37, p. 254]

The use of these child-rearing techniques appears to retain the child's self-respect and his sense of equality with his parents, while at the same time teaching him responsibility. These factors combine to create the conditions that are necessary for effective moral growth. Thus, based on his review of the literature, Saltzstein hypothesizes that

frequent use of power assertion, especially physical punishment, retards the development of any kind of internal morality. Psychological techniques, especially pointing out the consequences of actions for others, facilitate the development of internal morality. Reasoning is conducive to the development of an altruistic or humanistic morality, that is, one based primarily on consideration for others. Love withdrawal is conducive to the development of a conformist or conventional morality, that is, one based on rigid conformity to rules for their own sake or in deference to authority. [37, p. 259]

In sum, though much research remains to be done, the following dimensions of parent-child interaction are shown in the literature to be facilitative of moral development: dialogue about moral issues (28, 40); inductive reasoning (26); mutual respect and cooperation between parent and child (34); consistency and trust (33); and affection and warmth (10, 11, 36).

Separation-Individuation

Although it is often useful to ignore the larger context in which moral development occurs (in order to study it more closely), it is

often equally useful not to do so. That is, while the goal of moral
development in particular is autonomy in moral thought, one of the
major goals of the whole adolescent period is individuation, or
separation, from one's strict identification-attachment to his parents
(18, 19, 20, 21, 22, 31, 35)—and it may be useful to study the former in
terms of the latter. Individuation, held to be the most serious
dilemma the adolescent and his family must face, is the process by
which the individual establishes his own identity as a separate
person, rather than continuing his strict conformity and attachment
to his parents. The goal of individuation, as in moral development, is
autonomy. It seems to follow that whatever measures parents take
toward promoting individuation will likewise be helpful in promoting
moral maturity.

The importance of individuation is clearly illustrated in the work of
several family researchers. Many writers in this field have described
patterns of family interaction that produce disturbed children, and
the essence of all of them is the attachment of the child to his family in
such a way that it is impossible for him to individuate. This impos-
sibility, apparently, is the cause of severe disturbances in the child's
mental and emotional life. In less severe forms it is likely manifest as
an obstruction of the child's mature moral development.

One family researcher, Bowen (9), has postulated the process of
"triangulation" as one way in which this type of bonding occurs.
Bowen states that triangulation occurs when a dyadic system encompasses a third member merely in order to maintain its own interaction
patterns. Thus parents will use their child in a way that maintains
their own homeostatic balance. He becomes an integral part of their
system and is expected to maintain it. This process results in a
bonding or emotional "togetherness" that Bowen calls an "undifferentiated family-ego mass." In such a system the child is not an
individual but merely a means of perpetuating a given homeostatic
system. He thus cannot be allowed to abandon the system by
realizing himself as other than merely a cog in the wheel—by
individuating himself. He must, instead, be forced to remain an
integral part of this system. Therefore, much of the family's interaction will be directed toward insuring that this is so. The child cannot
separate himself and, as Bowen (9) contends, he develops disturbed
patterns of behavior.

Other family researchers, largely of the Palo Alto group, have also written on the pathological nature of much family interaction and bonding (8, 23, 24, 25, 38, 43). These researchers agree that the bonding of children in many pathological families is the result of "double bind" or two-level communication. For example, a child affectionately hugs his mother and she stiffens, showing her disapproval; then, when he withdraws, she chastizes him by saying, "Don't you love me anymore?" (8). The child has received two conflicting messages about the same bit of behavior—what can he do? If his life is filled with such incoherent and puzzling communication patterns, he has little choice but to opt out of the situation entirely and adopt behaviors commonly labeled schizophrenic. The important point to be observed in such cases is that apparently the child is forced to respond in precisely the manner that his parents wish him to in order to maintain the family system; his behavior serves a function in maintaining the family as it is (23). The child's action in withdrawing or manifesting other disturbed behavior actually preserves the family's homeostatic balance, and to the extent he fulfills these expectations he becomes more integral to the family system and thus more tightly bonded to it. He is thus prevented from attaining individuation.

Minuchin (32) speaks of "enmeshment" and Wynne et al. (44) of "pseudomutuality" in roughly the same manner that undifferentiated family-ego mass and homeostatic balance are described. They all share the quality of pathological family interaction that effectively (but pathologically) binds the child to his parents and prevents his realizing his own individuality. In each of these conceptions of family interaction a prominent place is given to the family's obsession with the child as a part of the family system, an obsession that exists at the expense of the child's own uniqueness and individuality. This is why major proponents of the various attachment theories stress the need for individuation; when it is not allowed to take place disturbed child behavior is the result.

Obviously the child's individuation-separation from his parents in contrast to his early attachment to them is crucial. A striking feature of family researchers' analyses of pathological family interaction patterns is the frequency of their finding that individuation cannot occur. The family's emphasis is upon the individual as a mechanism of the system rather than as an individual person with individual needs. This, it is thought, is the antecedent of much emotional disturbance in the lives of children. It is likely to be associated with the obstruction of moral development as well.

General Hypotheses

With this discussion of individuation in mind, we can derive a number of general, nontechnical hypotheses about effective family interaction which, if followed, should aid the individuation process of children and also facilitate their growth toward moral autonomy.

One such hypothesis, or guideline, is that the parents should allow the child to be exposed to a wide range of information and experience. An infant is dependent on adults because of his almost total lack of both physical and mental skills, and he becomes progressively less dependent on them as he gradually develops these abilities. Because these skills are obtained through exposure to new information and new experience, the child's individuation depends on the parents' allowing and encouraging such exposure. The child who is one-sided in either his information about life or his experience with it is seriously hampered. Accordingly, his becoming autonomous and inner directed in any meaningful sense is likewise retarded.

A corollary guideline is that the whole family should be exposed to a wide range of information and experience. As the child begins to individuate and assert his differentness and individuality, he must be encouraged in this process by the continued respect and acceptance of his family. This continued acceptance is facilitated if other family members are also open to new information and change. If this is the case, the parents can accept more easily the changes introduced by their child's growth. If a family is not open to new information and change, then the child's differentness and assertions of independence—certainly a very powerful form of information and change—will be prohibited along with all other forms of deviation. This can only result in suppression of individual growth or in the child's overt or covert rebellion, neither of which leads to individual autonomy. Horizontal interaction remains a necessary condition in the development of moral autonomy, a condition facilitated by the entire family's exposure to change.

Third, much seems to be gained if parents emphasize the positive differences between themselves and their children. For instance, the child can have knowledge, as well as experiences, that the parents themselves do not have. Parents who desire individuation for their children appreciate and encourage each child's differentness both from each other and from themselves. This attitude focuses on the family member as an individual rather than as merely one of the family. It maintains his individual self-respect and sense of equality with others. This, again, appears to be positively associated with individuation and moral growth.

Finally, parents can move, as much as appropriately possible, from explicit to implicit rules in the home. That is, a child in the process of being different will be more responsive to rules that are simply assumed than to those that are carved in stone and handed down. The first step for accomplishing this is to emotionally bond the child to the family and then model the desired behavior. This is done essentially by building the child's self-esteem and sense of love and belonging through horizontal family interaction. In this atmosphere appropriate discipline can be maintained while the child is simultaneously allowed a significant degree of autonomy.

These general guidelines are obviously incomplete but are presented as examples of ways to facilitate individuation, and by inference they are assumed to facilitate moral development as well. Furthermore, these suggestions avoid the authoritative, rejecting atmosphere into which peer interaction, at one point or another, often deteriorates. Having created these favorable conditions, it is then more likely that the family will effectively stimulate morality.

STIMULATING MORAL MATURITY

Once these conditions are created, the parent's primary task in promoting the child's moral growth is to be morally mature himself. Essentially this means that the parent is able to identify his normative principles, his basic moral assumptions, and also to meaningfully justify them. We stated in the introduction that normative assumptions can usually be identified only by reasoning logically from the specific judgments one makes. For instance, if one makes several moral judgments such as "all war is evil," "capital punishment is wrong," "we should not eat meat," we may infer that one of the speaker's basic moral assumptions is that all life is sacred—whatever fosters life is good and whatever obstructs it is bad. The point is that the person making such ethical judgments should also know on what principles he is operating; he must have a reason for making the assertions he does.

This is essential if the moral autonomy of children is to be promoted. Parents and educators cannot be content merely to spout specific ethical opinions, for the issue of moral reasoning lies deeper than that; it lies at the level of moral assumptions. The child must confront these basic assumptions. The child who hears "the Viet Nam war was wrong" is not confronted with a clear moral issue that he can examine meaningfully. But if he also hears that "life is inherently sacred and can never justifiably be taken," then he is presented with a straightforward moral assumption; the issue is more clearly and simply defined. The child can therefore understand and examine the normative and metaethical elements. No such opportunity is afforded if he hears only specific statements. The importance of parents' being morally mature, knowing the normative principles on which they base their particular judgments, is clear: If parents know their normative principles, they can present them to children for the child's intelligent examination. Whether he rejects them or accepts them, the child is still confronted with a moral argument he can examine, and this process leads to his own moral autonomy.

The second task of parents is justification of the basic moral assumptions they have proposed. The parent is responsible for the ethical assumptions he holds, and he can demonstrate the fact by meaningfully justifying them. The parent can foster the child's search for a method of justification by knowing and presenting his own.

In summary, the method by which a child's moral maturity is actively stimulated is active discussion of fundamental aspects of morality that presents the child with moral possibilities and induces him to search for others. Such a process leads to moral autonomy.

SUMMARY

In earlier chapters we arrived at the conclusions that (a) attempts at direct training of moral autonomy are self-contradictory and hence undesirable, and (b) that social interaction (with mutual respect and equality), as an indirect method, is perhaps the primary condition free of contradiction and conducive to effective moral growth. The most critical and significant aspect of this exposure to moral dilemmas, or differing opinions, is perhaps best obtained in the family. Moral maturity is enhanced, first, by creating a general condition of horizontal, cooperative interaction, and second, by the parents' own autonomy and discussion of fundamental aspects of morality. These conditions will promote the child's moral development, and for that reason, are important to all persons concerned with the development of moral maturity.

III

PSYCHOLOGICAL-PHILOSOPHICAL
INTEGRATION: CONTENT AND
STRUCTURE IN MORAL THOUGHT

10 / A Psychological-Philosophical Component Model of Moral Thought

Thus far, in the first two parts, we have presented a wide range of thought about moral reasoning. Part one focused on the philosopher's contribution to the study of morality and moral thought, and part two emphasized the psychologist's contribution. The purpose of this section, and particularly of this chapter, is to illustrate how the results of both of these approaches can be combined to solve a particular problem in the study of moral thinking. This, then, will help provide a framework for a more efficient approach to the study of moral reasoning than has previously been available.

THE PROBLEM OF CONTENT AND STRUCTURE IN MORAL THOUGHT

As briefly mentioned in the introduction and again in chapter five, there are two basic elements involved in the process of moral reasoning: content and structure. Content refers to the actual moral beliefs that one holds, for example, "life is sacred," "laws are good," "pain is bad," and so on. Structure refers to the cognitive makeup, or the qualitative modes of thought, that lie behind those particular beliefs. The questions asked in this area include, Are the particular moral beliefs autonomously or heteronomously adhered to? Are the espoused ethical principles universal and self-chosen or are they narrow and inherited? What is the individual's social perspective? and so on. It is important to see that although content and structure are closely related elements of moral reasoning, they are nevertheless

179

separate. This, however, is a crucial distinction that has been recognized only recently. In order to understand its importance it may be helpful to document the problems that arise when it is not carefully made.

In chapter five it was noted that Kohlberg has recently improved, fundamentally, the stage model (7) that had guided research and theorizing for more than fifteen years. His reason for doing so was the recognition that that model inappropriately conflated elements of structure with content, thus obscuring the data it was intended to produce concerning structure alone. Much of the criticism of that early model was due to this conflation. For instance, in one review article, the authors concluded:

> Not only did the data fail to show that people go through stages in a preset order, but it also failed to demonstrate that people go through each of the distinct stages at all. Furthermore, there is no support for the view that each new stage is a reintegration of the previous one and therefore qualitatively different. . . .
>
> Not only is there no clear-cut evidence supporting the assumptions of invariance of stages and their hierarchical nature, but there is also evidence suggesting that these assumptions may be incorrect. Several researchers have demonstrated that different types of moral reasoning may also be learned. . . .
>
> In view of these many problems, it is difficult to make a definitive statement about the utility of Kohlberg's cognitive-developmental model of moral development. [9, p. 469]

Similarly, in Lickona's words, Mischel and Mischel (14) suggest that "a large part of what cognitive-developmentalists consider structural changes in moral reasoning may instead be a shift to a different 'style' of verbal justification for which the individual expects to be reinforced by his new social reference group" (10, pp. 13–14). A similar point is made by Simpson (16). Lickona refers to Simpson's contention that "moral autonomy can be 'the result of group values and training' and that principled moral reasoners 'can probably even identify the groups in which they learned to reason abstractly about morality and to employ the kind of *terminology* which admits them to elevated ethical status' on Kohlberg's scale" (10, p. 14).

Although these are significant criticisms, they can all be substantially accounted for by recognizing the extent to which content elements were involved in Kohlberg's early model. Kohlberg himself says:

Our aspect scoring was based not on "structure", but on certain statistical but probablistic associations between structure and content. For example, a social system perspective tends to yield moral judgments whose content is law and order. One can, however, have this content at stage three without the social system perspective, or one can have the social system perspective without this content. [6, p. 43]

Given Kohlberg's example, all these criticisms make a similar point: if moral stages are characterized primarily by attitudes, for example, an adherence to law and order, then how are such stages to be distinguished from mere learned ways of speaking, and how can they then be spoken of as following an invariant order of progression? Kohlberg here admits that a stage three individual may have a law-and-order content while one can be stage four without having that content. But in the earlier model, in practice, stage four was defined by a law-and-order orientation. Thus, there tended to be some obscuring of basic structural elements, because the content, law and order, came to be the primary defining characteristic of the stage. In that case there was no discrimination possible between a stage three person who had the content and a stage four person who did not. Because actual stage-typing was so closely tied to such elements of content, the more subtle structural dimension was often obscured.

An example of this obfuscation may be seen in Kohlberg's 1971 dismissal of Jeremy Bentham as being at stage two in his moral thinking (5, p. 222). This occurred at a time when stage two was defined as a "naively hedonistic orientation," and Bentham, clearly a quantitative hedonist, might well be seen by some to fit that description. But is such a description based on consideration of structure or of content? It might be asked, for instance, if Bentham's reasoning is really at the same stage of moral development as that of the eight- or ten-year-old who is also classified as being at stage two. Are they really fundamentally the same?

Furthermore, it may well be that Bentham could fit Kohlberg's more recent stage six. This stage is characterized by the recognition of persons as ends in themselves, by a belief in universal moral principles and a commitment to them, and by a belief in equality and universal principles of justice. But perhaps these are the very conditions Bentham attempted to fulfill in proposing his quantitative hedonistic utilitarianism and in issuing such dictums as "everyone to count for one and no one for more than one." Why could this not be a self-chosen ethical principle according to which universal justice is sought, with each person being seen, and treated, as an end in himself? Prima facie, there is no clear reason why Bentham could not be considered at stage six, or close to it, in Kohlberg's recent model, and this itself is evidence of the extent to which the earlier model was confused with content. Hedonism per se cannot become the definition of a stage because it is not a structural dimension. It is not one's *belief* in hedonism, but the *nature* of one's belief in hedonism, that defines one as being at a certain stage. For the young child, a hedonistic orientation develops out of an egocentric, individualistic social perspective, whereas for Bentham it likely developed out of a prior-to-society, "moral point of view," social perspective. This difference in the structural dimension was at least partially obscured in the earlier model and caused the confusion typified by the example of Bentham.

There is good reason to suppose, therefore, that these criticisms are due, not to problems with the theory of stage-wise moral development itself, but to this confusion of content and structure in Kohlberg's early model. It is not difficult, for instance, to demonstrate that the content of children's moral thinking can be easily changed. This is clear from evidence presented in chapter seven. Nor would it be expected that changes in moral content or beliefs would follow any invariant or universal pattern of development. Such elements are learned, and with respect to development, they are highly capricious and disordered. It may well be that such capriciousness accounts for the inconsistencies in Kohlberg's early model. It also probably accounts for many of the research differences that have been found, including those noted in chapter six. But there is no evidence that development of moral structure itself is inconsistent or capricious, only that Kohlberg initially may have described it inadequately. If inconsistencies are the consequence of that sort of flaw, then no damage is done to the theory itself; the only task is to achieve greater clarity in our use of the theory in order to avoid similar errors in the future. Kohlberg has greatly improved his description of the stage model of moral development; this recent model appears to have avoided the content-structure confusion of the earlier one and thus will likely yield more consistent results in the future.

TOWARD ASSESSMENT OF CONTENT IN MORAL THINKING

It is clear that the distinction between content and structure is important in the study of moral reasoning. Recently this distinction has been made primarily to permit a better focus upon structure. Indeed, as we have seen, Kohlberg's most recent presentation of his model is an example of attempts to allow full examination of elements which are presumed to be developmental in an invariant and universal fashion.

Although a clear focus upon the structure of moral thought is certainly important, content is also important. Obviously, just what an individual's assumptions *are* is important, and those assumptions are clearly worthy of study in their own right. What is needed, then, is an instrument that can allow a systematic assessment of the content of moral thinking. The results obtained could then be combined with results from the structural area to enhance our understanding of the entire moral reasoning process.

When the "content" of moral thinking is spoken of, however, there is often a tendency to lapse into discussions of "descriptive" ethics or of particular judgments and beliefs. For instance, we might say that the statement "The Viet Nam War was wrong" exhibits a content element of moral reasoning; a particular moral belief is expressed, and there is no indication of the structure underlying it, so it must be what is meant by content. Similarly, if one says, "Heinz should steal to save his wife," or "the Spanish Inquisition was wrong," or "capital punishment is right," then these also express particular moral beliefs and are thus expressions of content.

But there is a deeper and more interesting level of the content in moral thinking—the basic normative assumptions which one holds, and which tie the particular judgments together. For instance, it may be interesting to know that a person believes (*a*) that stealing to save the life of one's wife is wrong, while (*b*) that to kill one's "vegetable" child is right, but it is far more interesting to understand the normative base that allows him to make both of these particular judgments. Knowing that he holds these specific beliefs is of less importance than understanding why he holds them, and this requires an inquiry into his basic normative assumptions.[1] Theoretically, once a person's underlying moral base is understood, most of his particular judgments can be predicted.

CATEGORIES OF NORMATIVE ETHICS

Identification of such normative foundations, of course, is one of the primary contributions of philosophy to the study of moral reasoning. This was seen in part one. Since these categories of normative ethics are also the most important content dimension in the study of moral thought, they will be reviewed here.

Teleological Reasoning

In this system of reasoning, the concern is solely with consequences. The teleologist first has a definition of the good and then defines as right anything leading to it. The several ways that people define the good sorts them into the following three general categories:

Qualitative Hedonist:

This person, as a monist, defines pleasure as the sole good but asserts that quality of pleasure is more important than mere quantity. He usually prefers mental or spiritual pleasures over physical pleasures. Examples include Epicurus and John Stuart Mill.

Quantitative Hedonist:

This person, also a monist, defines pleasure as the sole good but claims that all pleasure is of the same nature and therefore that quantity of pleasure is the only important factor. Mental and spiritual pleasures offer no more to him than physical ones. Quantitative hedonism is thus usually associated with pursuit of physical pleasures. Jeremy Bentham is the most prominent example.

Nonhedonist:

This person, if a monist, defines something other than pleasure as the sole good. For example, Aristotle so valued happiness (as distinct from pleasure) and Nietzsche so valued power. This category also includes all pluralists, i.e., those who assert that two or more things constitute the good. Examples of pluralists are Plato and Ross.

The person who is teleological in his moral reasoning generally has one of the above values as his definition of the good. The teleologist can also be classified as one of the following, depending on the nature of his other beliefs:

Egoist:

This person is concerned with achieving his definition of the good primarily for himself. In his moral decisions, he will do that which will produce the desired consequences for himself without concern for its effect on others. Stirner was a so-called crude egoist, while Plato was an "enlightened" egoist. (Their respective definitions of the good are primarily responsible for this distinction.)

Rule-Utilitarian:

This person is concerned simply with maximizing the good, as he has defined it. He does so by adopting and endorsing various rules which, if strictly followed, will lead to that desired result.

Act-Utilitarian:

This person is also concerned with maximizing the good. However, he approaches each situation independently; he does not subscribe to any strict rules but evaluates each situation on its own merits and projected consequences.

Deontological Reasoning

In deontological reasoning, the individual considers the nature of the act itself, as well as its consequences, in determining rightness. Pure deontologists do not consider consequences at all in making moral judgments, while mixed deontologists will give consequences considerable attention. In either case, and contrary to the teleologist, the deontologist considers the act itself an important aspect of making moral judgments. The types of deontologists may be described as follows:

Pure Rule-Deontologist:

This person considers only the nature of the act itself in determining morality; consequences are irrelevant. Also, the morality of a given act is determined by its conformity to a rule or set of rules. Examples include Kant and Cudworth.

Mixed Rule-Deontologist:

This person also determines the rightness of a given act by its conformity to a rule or a set of rules. However, his rule or rules also include consideration of consequences. Thus, both consequences and specified features of an act are involved in the question of morality. The most prominent example is W. D. Ross.

Pure Act-Deontologist:

This person considers only the nature of the act itself in determining morality; consequences are irrelevant. However, he also has no general rules to which he adheres. Each act must be examined on its own merits, apparently leading to a type of existential choice or invention. Sartre may be an example.

Mixed Act-Deontologist:

This person examines each act without reference to any strict rules. He also includes consideration of both consequences and certain features of an act in the determination of moral rightness. Examples include E. F. Carritt and Garner and Rosen.

THE MORAL CONTENT TEST

These ethical categories, and their combinations, are probably all the normative foundations that are possible. Thus, the goal of any test of moral content must be to identify as far as possible these elements or components in a given individual's moral thinking. We have constructed an instrument for doing this, called the Moral Content Test (MCT). The format of the test closely follows that developed by Rest (15), but because his is a measurement of structure, and this is a measurement of content, the actual substance of the test is far different. The test is reproduced here in full, to be read or actually taken; a more complete discussion of it is found in the appendix.

Social Issues

Name _____ ___ Female

Age _____ ___ Male

School_____

In this questionnaire you will be asked to give your opinions about several problems. First you will be asked to read a story and give your opinion about what should be done. Then you will turn the page and rate several types of reasoning as to how important they were in making your decision. Levels of importance range from VERY important to NOT AT ALL important.

There are no right or wrong answers. This test is aimed only at understanding your opinions.

In rating statements for their importance, read them carefully. Mark any statements that are irrelevant or make no sense to you as NOT AT ALL important.

The Drug

Suppose . . .

Your closest loved one (e.g., mother, father, spouse) was near death from a special kind of cancer. There was one drug that the doctors thought might save him/her. It was a form of radium that a druggist in your town had recently discovered. The drug was expensive to make, but the druggist was charging ten times what the drug cost to make. You went to everyone you knew to borrow the money, but you could only get together about $1,000, which is half of the cost. You told the druggist that your loved one was dying, and asked him to sell it for less or let you pay later. But the druggist said, "No, I discovered the drug and I'm going to make money from it." You tried every possible way to get the money, and when that failed you tried every legal way to get the drug without paying the full amount of money. Nothing worked so you got desperate and began to think about breaking into the man's store to steal the drug for your loved one.

Should you steal the drug? (Check one)

_____ I should steal it

_____ I can't decide

_____ I should not steal it

REASONING ABOUT "THE DRUG"

On the left-hand side of the page check one of the spaces by each question to indicate its importance in the decision you made about whether or not to steal the drug. In other words, how important was each of these items in making your decision?

The column headers (angled) read, left to right: Very important / Quite important / To some extent important / Not very important / Not at all important

Very important	Quite important	To some extent important	Not very important	Not at all important	
					1. If you let him/her die will you have someone to take care of you and provide for your physical needs? Or, if you steal, is it worth risking the discomfort of going to jail yourself? (Of these two statements, respond in the left-hand margin only to the one which was the more important in making your decision.)
					2. Sometimes in the past you've had to go downtown yourself.
					3. Stealing is simply wrong, regardless of the results.
					4. If everyone stole when he wanted to, society would be so chaotic that there could be no happiness or peace of mind for anyone.
					5. In some cases stealing is justified because it allows an individual (in this case your loved one) to live and continue enjoying the companionship of loved ones and to fulfill his purpose in life.
					6. Will your decision, whatever it may be, lead to some abstract goal for yourself (e.g., salvation, honor, fame, self-actualization, respectability, etc.)?
					7. In this case it is just right to steal.
					8. If everyone stole when he wanted to, society would crumble and wouldn't be able to meet the physical needs of its members.
					9. In some cases stealing is justified because it allows another person (in this case your loved one) to overcome physical pain and suffering.
					10. In this case it is just wrong to steal.

From the list of items above, select the four that were the *most* important in making your decision about whether or not to steal the drug (do *not* list any items that you rated NOT AT ALL important; leave a blank instead):

Most important   _____
Second most important   _____
Third most important   _____
Fourth most important   _____

The Deserter

Suppose . . .

Your country was involved in a war a few years ago and during the war many soldiers deserted. Since the war ended your country has had a law that all such deserters, if caught, must go to prison and serve long sentences. Recently you saw a man whom you know to be a deserter and who is the father of two children. By checking up on him you have found that he has been a model citizen in every way and everyone in his town is very fond of him. The law says that anyone seeing a deserter must turn him in.

Should you obey the law and turn him in? (Check one)

_____ I should turn him in

_____ I can't decide

_____ I should not turn him in

REASONING ABOUT "THE DESERTER"

On the left-hand side of the page check one of the spaces by each question to indicate its importance in the decision you made about whether or not to turn the deserter in. In other words, how important was each of these items in making your decision?

Very important	Quite important	To some extent important	Not very important	Not at all important	
					1. In some cases the subjectiveness of living is less tenuous than the objectivity of life.
					2. In this case it is just right to break the law and not turn him in.
					3. Will your decision, whatever it may be, lead to some abstract goal for yourself (e.g., salvation, honor, fame, self-actualization, respectability, etc.)?
					4. If everyone broke the law when he wanted to, society would fall apart and wouldn't be able to meet the needs of its members. There would be a lot of physical pain and suffering for everyone.
					5. In some cases breaking the law is justified because it allows an individual (in this case the deserter) to avoid unnecessary physical suffering.
					6. In this case it is just wrong to break the law.
					7. Will you go to jail for not turning him in?
					8. If everyone broke the law when he wanted to, there would be only chaos and no one could have peace of mind or security.
					9. Sometimes breaking the law is justified because it leads to greater peace and tranquility for everyone involved. Making a good man go to jail does not increase peace or tranquility and is not best for society.
					10. Breaking the law is not right, regardless of the results. The law should be obeyed.

From the list of questions above, select the four that were the *most* important in making your decision about whether or not to obey the law and turn the deserter in (do *not* list any items that you rated NOT AT ALL important; leave a blank instead):

Most important _____
Second most important _____
Third most important _____
Fourth most important _____

The Dying Loved One

Suppose . . .

Your closest loved one is dying from an incurable disease. He/she is in a tremendous amount of pain and is expected to die in a matter of weeks. Your loved one is too sick to be able to give permission that he/she be administered a drug that will make him/her die sooner, but under the laws of your state you are able to give such permission. You know that he/she is in a great deal of pain and that he/she will die soon anyway.

Should you give your permission? (Check one)

_____ I should give permission

_____ I can't decide

_____ I should not give permission

REASONING ABOUT "THE DYING LOVED ONE"

On the left-hand side of the page check one of the spaces by each question to indicate its importance in the decision you made about whether or not to give your permission to have your loved one die sooner. In other words, how important was each of these items in making your decision?

Very important	Quite important	To some extent important	Not very important	Not at all important	
					1. It is not right to take someone's life. Killing is wrong, regardless of the results.
					2. In some cases killing is right because it reduces suffering and pain.
					3. What if everyone killed when he wanted to? Society would absolutely fall apart and everyone would experience great pain and physical suffering.
					4. Are you a member of the local rotary club or do you have a friend who is?
					5. In this case it is just right to allow killing.
					6. Will you have someone to care for you and provide for your physical needs?
					7. If everyone killed when he wanted to there would be no peace and no one could be happy.
					8. In some cases killing is right because it brings peace of mind and comfort to those close to the dying person.
					9. In this case, it is just wrong to kill.
					10. Will your decision, whatever it may be, lead to some abstract goal for yourself (e.g., salvation, honor, fame, self-actualization, respectability, etc.)?

From the list of questions above, select the four that were the *most* important in making your decision about whether or not to give your permission (do *not* list any items that you rated NOT AT ALL important; leave a blank instead):

        Most important   _____
        Second most important   _____
        Third most important   _____
        Fourth most important   _____

The Taxes

Suppose . . .

You are the breadwinner of a large family and the time of year has come when you are required by law to pay taxes to the government. Two things, however, make it hard for you to pay your taxes. First, a certain amount of your taxes goes to a government program you abhor, or dislike very, very much, because you think it is immoral. It bothers you very much that your money goes for this program. Second, having a large family, you need all the money you can get and your taxes are really more than you can afford to pay. Your family is already going hungry and, due to some detail, you are not able to get welfare. You have tried everything and cannot get help anywhere. You know a way in which you can lie about the amount of taxes you have to pay without getting caught. This would allow you to save the money that your family needs so much, and also, not as much of your money would go for the program you think is immoral. Furthermore, with so many millions of people paying taxes, the government would never miss the money you don't pay. You start to think about lying about your taxes.

Should you lie about your taxes? (Check one)

_____ I should lie

_____ I can't decide

_____ I should not lie

REASONING ABOUT "THE TAXES"

On the left-hand side of the page check one of the spaces by each question to indicate its importance in the decision you made about whether or not to lie about your taxes. In other words, how important was each of these items in making your decision?

Very important	Quite important	To some extent important	Not very important	Not at all important	
					1. If everyone lied when he wanted to, no one would be able to trust anyone else so no one could really be happy or have peace of mind.
					2. In some cases lying is beneficial because it leads to more favorable conditions (i.e., money, food, clothes) for the people who need them, in this case your own family.
					3. Will your decision, whatever it may be, lead to some abstract goal for yourself (e.g., salvation, honor, fame, self-actualization, respectability, etc.)?
					4. Is it worth the risk of suffering the discomfort of going to jail?
					5. In this case it is just right to lie.
					6. If everyone lied when he wanted to, society would crumble and everyone, not just one family, would end up in poverty and physical suffering.
					7. What if everyone proved the substantiality of taxation to be more transient than the cessation of essence?
					8. Such dishonesty as lying is simply wrong, regardless of the results.
					9. In this case it is just wrong to lie.
					10. Sometimes lying is beneficial because it leads to better overall conditions—greater peace of mind and tranquility for those involved, in this case your family.

From the list of items above, select the four that were the *most* important in making your decision about whether or not to lie about your taxes (do *not* list any items that you rated NOT AT ALL important; leave a blank instead):

Most important   _____
Second most important   _____
Third most important   _____
Fourth most important   _____

The Mine Shaft

Suppose . . .

You and two other people are trapped underground in a deep mine shaft. You know that rescue operations will take three or four days, but the air supply will not last all three of you for that long. Two of you, however, could probably live long enough on the available air—but that means one of you must die for the other two to live. You begin to think about killing one among you in order that two may live and return to their families.

Should one of you be killed to allow the others to live? (Check one)

_____ One should be killed

_____ I can't decide

_____ One should not be killed

Very important
Quite important
To some extent important
Not very important
Not at all important

REASONING ABOUT "THE MINE SHAFT"

On the left-hand side of the page check one of the spaces by each question to indicate its importance in the decision you made about whether or not one of you should be killed. In other words, how important was each of these items in making your decision?

					1. In this case it is just wrong to kill.
					2. In this case killing is justified because only one person suffers physically rather than all three. It is really a kind of self-defense for the two that live.
					3. Will you be one of the ones to live and thus avoid the pain of dying?
					4. What if everyone killed when he wanted to? Society would collapse and wouldn't be able to meet the needs of its members. There would be greater pain and physical suffering for everyone.
					5. In some cases killing is right because more people are then enabled to continue living and fulfilling their purpose in life.
					6. In this case it is just right to kill one of the people.
					7. If everyone killed when he wanted to, there would be no security and no one could have peace of mind.
					8. It is not right to take someone's life. Killing is wrong, regardless of the results.
					9. Sometimes it just doesn't pay to get up in the morning and that should be kept in mind.
					10. Will your decision, whatever it may be, lead to some abstract goal for yourself (e.g., salvation, honor, fame, self-actualization, respectability, etc.)?

From the list of questions above, select the four that were the *most* important in making your decision about whether or not one of you should be killed (do *not* list any items that you rated NOT AT ALL important; leave a blank instead):

Most important   _____
Second most important   _____
Third most important   _____
Fourth most important   _____

For each dilemma the test specifically taps the following content elements:

> hedonistic egoism
> nonhedonistic egoism
> hedonistic rule-utilitarianism
> nonhedonistic rule-utilitarianism
> hedonistic act-utilitarianism
> nonhedonistic act-utilitarianism
> rule-deontology
> act-deontology

It is around these basic categories that the statements following each dilemma are formed. However, with these items the test also yields data on the following, more general, categories:

> egoism
> hedonism
> rule-utilitarianism
> act-utilitarianism
> utilitarianism
> deontology
> rule orientation in general
> act orientation in general

The test can also, of course, yield a total teleology-versus-deontology score. Furthermore, the results can be manipulated to yield data about the complex mixed deontological forms of reasoning—whether they are pure rule, mixed rule, pure act, or mixed act. Almost all subjects tested thus far combine deontological and teleological elements into a mixed deontology, and the test can be useful in spotting these trends, e.g., the relative amounts of deontology and teleology, the particular type of teleology, and so on.

Further details concerning the test and its administration can be found in the appendix.

A MODEL OF THE PSYCHOLOGICAL-PHILOSOPHICAL COMPONENTS OF MORAL THOUGHT

The instrument described above is more than a test of moral content, however; it also suggests a fundamental model or way of looking at the content of moral reasoning. As such it does more than test; it also orders our thinking, providing definitions and parameters for the study of this crucial dimension of moral thought. Thus it is the foundation of a model for the psychological-philosophical components of moral thinking.

Using the categories of moral philosophy, this model describes components of moral thinking normally occurring in the postadolescent years (although they can be fruitfully used with younger children as well). This model of moral thought does not compete with either Piaget's or Kohlberg's; rather, it builds upon their theories. The psychological-philosophical model elaborates the content occurring within the structural stages described by Piaget and Kohlberg.

Motivational Trends

In order to understand the relationship between moral thought occurring in the autonomous stage and the preceding stages of thought, one needs an understanding of age differences. The stages of moral reasoning described by Piaget and Kohlberg may be seen as part of a basic motivational development that resuls from a complex blend of environmental and maturational elements, a process that extends into the postadolescent years. These elements include changes in cognitive style, general intelligence, prevalence of reasoning in environment, and the like.

Both Piaget and Kohlberg are aware that cognitive functioning is related to general motivation. Piaget's concern is pointed out by Theodore Mischel (13). In the following quotation the word *affect* refers to basic motivation:

In sum, Piaget finds that "there is egocentric thought just as there is egocentric affectivity, and there is socialized thought adapted to reality just as there is socialized affectivity adapted to reality" . . . in tracing the development of the former we also trace the development of the latter. We must, therefore, so Piaget contends, rid ourselves of the "romantic prejudice which makes us suppose [that affects are] immediate givens," and recognize instead that "there is, in truth, as much construction in the affective as in the cognitive domain." [13, p. 319]

Kohlberg, in addressing the problem of relating moral stages to larger motivational or ego-developmental theories, states:

In summary, a broad psychological cognitive-developmental theory of moralization is an ego-developmental theory. Furthermore, in understanding moral functioning, one must place the individual's moral stage within the broader context of his ego level. To see moral stages as simple reflections of the ego level, however, is to lose the ability to theoretically define an empirically defined order in the specific moral domain of the human personality. [6, p. 53]

Kohlberg is concerned that a proper distinction be maintained between his stages and other psychological stages, such as those proposed by Loevinger and Wessler (11). However, although it detracts from the uniqueness of Kohlberg's stages, the correspondence between Kohlberg's stages of moral reasoning and those reported from the general literature discussed in child psychology textbooks is perhaps an overlooked strength. Almost all child psychology texts and reference books (e.g., 12) point out that young children are highly sensitive to external rewards and punishments. This universal observation parallels neatly Kohlberg's stages one and two, or the preconventional levels. And the reasons why a conventional morality, Kohlberg's stages three and four, do not appear until somewhat later seems obvious when we consider various findings in developmental psychology. Younger children are egocentric in the preconventional levels and have limited verbal abilities; they are less able to think of others. They will therefore tend to focus on and respond primarily to external rewards and punishments. In fact, other children are viewed as objects to be manipulated rather than as associates. Moreover, besides being unable to appreciate another person's perspective, children at this level of conventional morality are heavily dependent on communication in which one can see and understand messages of rejection and/or approval. These childhood maturational limitations join with factors in the social environment, such as the expectations of caretakers, to produce a conventional morality. For example, caretakers would not point out to a young child what his peers might think of him when they know that the child is unaware of others' opinions and is incapable or insensitive to their rejection or approval. Accordingly, the rationale offered to the very young child by adult caretakers is usually devoid of appeals to conventionality or conformity and tends to emphasize the external consequences such as rewards and punishments.

Kohlberg's concept of postconventional thinking and Piaget's description of autonomous thinking—as well as the opinions of most scholars studying adolescent behavior—also closely correspond. Usually noted during adolescence is an increased interest in moral issues, political activity, economic and social injustice, as well as a general increase in prosocial knowledge and attitudes. Both care-takers and institutions seem to expect the more fully developed adolescent to be more responsible and aware of social and moral concerns; this, along with an accumulated knowledge of social skills, tends to increase the adolescent's expectations of himself. These contributing factors also raise the probability that in normal discourse the adolescent will hear more stage five and six reasoning from associated caretakers and peers than would younger children. These factors probably combine to produce the age trend noted by Kohlberg and others. The fact that not all adolescents reach a postconventional morality is understandable, given the fact that certain social environments may lack stage five and six types of reasoning, and the adolescent would not be expected to reason at such a level without sufficient exposure or opportunity to use it. Kohlberg has recently identified social environments in which certain levels of reasoning are absent (8).

Thus, the age-stage notions of Piaget and Kohlberg are in general agreement with broadly based psychological findings of human development. If we accept their pre-adult stages as accurate, then we can see that the content components model indeed supplements and elaborates the description given by both Piaget and Kohlberg of adult moral thinking.

Emphasis on Content Components

In using this strictly content-based model, we may assume that adequate structure or ability, as opposed to content, is already present, i.e., that the individual possesses sufficient cognitive abilities to handle the wide range of moral thinking, if adequate learning conditions have been provided within the culture. There may be differences in the complexity of different modes of moral thinking, but these differences are not used as a basis for labeling one type of thinking as more mature or better than another. The test is not intended to type or place people into categories but rather to measure their preference for different components of moral reasoning. Each person can be seen to exhibit a unique constellation of components. These various components combine and with other psychological characteristics produce a person's individual character. Our appreciation of the complexity of these components enhances our understanding of the variety and breadth of human individuality.

This model has several strengths. Because it borrows from moral philosophy in postulating ethical categories, it can rely on a fairly complete system of moral thinking. The philosophically based components provide concreteness as well as comprehensiveness in identifying types of moral reasoning—a combination that has been virtually nonexistent in the past.

The model also affords simplicity. By omitting the stage notion, we avoid questions of age regressions, overlapping categories, and the like. Also, the model presented here does not imply desirability in connection with any of the traits, allowing one to avoid biased, preferential judgment of one type of reasoning as being more mature than the others. If one actually is more mature than the others, this may be discovered by other means, but it is not inferred from our test. One should turn to other criteria (e.g., Kohlberg's) for judging moral maturity.

It should be noted that the basic tenets of cognitive-developmentalism seem warranted, i.e., that moral development is the result of interaction between the organism and his environment, and that this development entails to some extent a qualitative as well as a quantitative restructuring of cognitive processes. It is also clear that this development follows Piaget's stage sequence, from heteronomous morality to autonomous morality. It may also follow Kohlberg's stage sequence as he has more recently described it, although it is too early to be certain of this. However, it is also apparent that once autonomy is achieved, once one is subject to his own law rather than to an authority's, one may still hold or return to concepts that have traditionally been considered immature or heteronomous, or one may develop new combinations of thought which have elements of more than one of the components. Insofar as content has, in reality, been separated from structure, this should pose no problem. It should now be obvious that certain content elements, normally thought to be immature, can occur in the context of a mature structure and thus be maturely adhered to. Kohlberg's current model can handle this state of affairs; now it should be possible to avoid confusion between moral content and structure, as when certain content elements come, in practice, to define the structural dimension.

In summary, this is a simpler, more comprehensive, and more explicit model for describing the content of moral thinking than has heretofore been proposed. It is not a description of the development of moral thought and it is not equally applicable to all ages; it applies primarily to persons in the postconventional, autonomous, or formal operations stages of development. Moreover, in this model no components are considered better or worse than others. If evaluation of the components is desired, we suggest that evaluations be made by a rational analysis similar to that used by philosophers or by such other approaches as looking for empirical outcomes and correlates. The only kind of maturity discussed in the framework of this model is the movement from an external focus on material sanctions and consequences to an internal motivational system. Regulation of behavior according to internally based cognitive monitors, using any of the moral content elements (e.g., utilitarianism, rule-deontology), would thus be considered an internally based, mature action.

The simplicity of this model is also exhibited in the fact that it utilizes no special theory of moral thinking or moral behavior. The general models of behavior described in contemporary psychological literature are sufficient to handle any pecularity suggested in the components of moral thought. We have built upon the basic tenets of cognitive-developmental theory, but since our primary concern is with adult thinking, the developmental considerations are not critical. However, the cognitive-developmental theory, as well as the empirical research it has generated, are certainly appropriate for use in conjunction with the model and they clearly provide the most adequate data base currently available.

Social Learning Theory

Social learning theory is another major theoretical position besides cognitive-developmentalism that is helpful in explaining how people acquire knowledge and ideas. Judging by recent statements of the theory, in particular those by Albert Bandura, social learning theory is sufficiently cognitive that the disagreement between it and cognitive-developmental theory is primarily over the postulation of a formal stage sequence by cognitive developmentalists. While avoiding this postulate, contemporary social learning theorists offer their own account of human growth, and it is particularly helpful in explaining the acquisition of the cognitive, self-regulating components. Bandura, reflecting contemporary social learning theory, calls attention to the importance of cognitive variables as determiners of behavior:

With growing evidence that cognition has causal influence on behavior, the arguments against the influence of internal determinants began to lose their force. . . .

A theory that denies that thoughts can regulate actions does not lend itself readily to the explanation of complex human behavior. [3, p. 10]

Again, he says:

Another distinguishing feature of social learning theory is the prominent role it assigns to self-regulatory capacities. By arranging environmental inducements, generating cognitive supports, and producing consequences for their own actions, people are able to exercise some measure of control over their own behavior. To be sure, the self-regulatory functions are created and occasionally supported by external influences. Having external origins, however, does not refute the fact that, once established, self-influence partly determines which act one performs.

A comprehensive theory of behavior must explain how patterns of behavior are acquired and how their expression is continuously regulated by the interplay of self-generated and external sources of influence. From a social learning perspective, human nature is characterized as a vast potentiality that can be fashioned by direct and vicarious experience into a variety of forms within biological limits. [3, p. 13]

The trends in both cognitive-developmental theory and social learning theory indicate that the two views are moving toward each other and the differences, though they still exist, may not be as many as various antagonists or champions of each theory have at times suggested. Certainly social learning theorists are sensitive to individual differences and employ the concept of cognitions within their theory. Cognitive-developmentalists, on the other hand, are certainly willing to acknowledge the massive research data identifying the external influences on learning processes. Thus, it is becoming increasingly apparent that the acquisition of behavior involves the interaction of both developmental and environmental influences. On this, at least, the two theories seem to agree.

Moral Thought and Behavior

The research cited in previous chapters supports these conclusions, indicating that moral reasoning develops from many contributing factors. It has been shown that modeling, reinforcement, peer interaction, confrontation of dilemmas, development of skills (such as cognitive intellectual functioning or role taking) are all partial determinants. Thus, the problem of relating behavior to moral reasoning might be approached differently and more successfully if we approach it in terms of components. It is likely, given the complexity of moral thought, that typologies and stages hinder rather than help precise behavioral prediction because subjects are classified into only one or two levels. Our prediction of behavior will likely be more accurate when psychologists more readily combine consideration of reasoning dimensions with these other social and cultural influences rather than relying on single indices alone. It is clear that the ability to predict behavior accurately will entail the consideration of the many interactive effects of the predictors (1, 2, 4, 17). The content components model may be particularly useful in this regard, as the components may be treated as separate variables providing different interactions among themselves and with other variables. This allows a much broader data base than the measuring typologies can provide.

An important conclusion reached in chapter nine and reiterated above is that an internally based motivational system is the most desirable. This is important with regard to the relationship of moral thought to behavior, because it may be expected that unless one obtained an internally based motivational system little or no relationship would exist between behavior and thought—behavior would be determined primarily by external reinforcing or punishing contingencies. Similarly, the relationship between behavior and thought would be reduced in the case of individuals whose motivational system is socially controlled or conventionally oriented. Even among adults the extent to which orientation is toward either material or social sanctions would influence the amount of correspondence between internal thought and behavior. It is interesting to speculate, therefore, that growth from an external to an internal motivational orientation may be the most important key to understanding moral behavior as well as moral thought.

Application of the Theory by Parents and Educators

On the basis of our research and ideas, we can offer some guidelines for application by parents and teachers. First, we advocate movement away from external orientations. Parents would be advised to rely less often on techniques of reward and punishment. The development of internal monitors of behavior through the reasoning or induction methods outlined in previous chapters would be better. In addition, however, acquainting children with the various components of moral thought would be desirable. A child's exposure to the various components of moral reasoning would have the same advantages that learning any cognitive skills has. Those who possess more skills are in a better position to deal intelligently with the problems that face them.

Such an approach also implies a curriculum for moral educators. Traditionally, moral education programs have been weakened by their inability to resolve the dilemma posed by the conflict between relativism and indoctrination. The educator who is morally relativistic has seemed to lack values or commitment and is sometimes accused of not being moral. On the other hand, moral educators who adopt specific value frameworks and introduce these in the classroom are accused of indoctrinating the students. Arguments could be raised that even teaching Kohlberg's stages (particularly those of the early model) implies a preference for types of thought found in stages five and six, say, over stages three and four. Thus even the Kohlbergian model may be criticized as a means of subtle indoctrination. The psychological-philosophical components model, because it does not advocate the superiority of any of the specific components, clearly helps the instructor avoid indoctrination. On the other hand, the model is not so relativistic as to be meaningless; it advocates acquiring skills to understand and use components of moral thinking, recognizing that no one particular component is necessarily best. Moreover, the model advocates acquiring skills and moving toward an internally based motivational system, providing a very plausible way for moral educators to avoid absolutism. In addition, the research presented in chapters seven and eight suggests that indirect approaches are more effective in influencing more mature or autonomous moral reasoning. Furthermore, they are relatively free of criticisms of indoctrination.

Aside from its utility for parents and moral educators, the components model may be valuable simply because it identifies a full range of components that make up moral content. The following chapters provide examples of moral reasoning which the reader can use to facilitate his own recognition of the various components of moral reasoning and thus determine for himself the usefulness of the psychological-philosophical components model.

NOTE

1. This is why Kohlberg's recent discussion of content (6), though it represents a step in the right direction is inadequate. It is directed toward one's particular judgments rather than toward one's normative assumptions.

11 / Recognizing Moral Content: Student Responses and Examples from Literature

In this chapter we present and discuss several examples of moral reasoning offered by university students in response to ethical dilemmas, material that should assist the reader to recognize the various types of moral content and formulate his own responses to these and similar dilemmas. Examples of moral reasoning selected from various literary works are provided as an additional resource.

University students in two sections of a marriage course were given a two-week presentation on moral reasoning; the basic rationale of the exercise was that moral autonomy can develop only as a consequence of serious confrontation with moral assumptions in an atmosphere of mutual respect and equality. The presentation consisted, first, of formulation and active discussion of several moral dilemmas. Second, students were taught the terminology and framework of normative ethics, which were necessary for the effective conceptualization and expression of moral ideas.

There was no formal attempt to construct this experience as a research study. We intended to gauge the results of the two-week section more informally and subjectively. At the end of the two weeks, a one-hour essay exam was given in which the students responded to two moral dilemmas. In their responses to each dilemma, the students were required to (*a*) state a decision, (*b*) explain the decision, (*c*) identify the basic ethical assumptions underlying the explanation, and (*d*) justify those assumptions. The following two dilemmas were used in the exam:

Dilemma 1

On October 12, 1939, [Mr.] Repouille . . . deliberately put his thirteen-year-old son to death. His reason for this tragic deed was that the child had suffered certain injuries at birth that rendered him an idiot and left all of his limbs grotesquely malformed. He was blind, mute, and deformed; he had to be fed; he had no control over his bowels or his bladder; and he had spent his entire life in a small crib.

Repouille had four other children to whom he was a loving and dutiful father. He concluded that he would not be able to give them the support that they needed and were entitled to if the deformed child were permitted to live. He therefore used chloroform to dispatch him. [7, p. 19]

Dilemma 2

In Europe, a woman was near death from a rare kind of cancer. There was one drug that the doctors thought might save her. It was a form of radium that a druggist in the same town had recently discovered. The drug was expensive to make, but the druggist was charging ten times what the drug cost him to make. He paid $200 for the radium and charged $2,000 for a small dose of the drug. The sick woman's husband, Heinz, went to everyone he knew to borrow the money, but he could only get together about $1,000, which was half of what it cost. He told the druggist that his wife was dying and asked him to sell it less expensively or to let him pay later. But the druggist said, "No, I discovered the drug, and I'm going to make money from it." So Heinz got desperate and broke into the man's store to steal the drug for his wife. Should Heinz have done that?

Before further reading, consider how you would respond to these dilemmas.

Several different levels of quality and types of reasoning were exhibited among the students' responses to these moral situations. Some of the excerpts reproduced here were chosen for their quality and others primarily for their interest as specimens of moral thought. For instance, one student responded to the first dilemma in this way:

Decision: Mr. Repouille should not have killed his son.
Explanation: Moral values are different to different individuals. In this case, I
    disagree with Mr. Repouille. His son did not cause any physical harm to
    anyone else or to himself. Even total vegetables have some realization of
    what goes on around them. Even if the boy could not understand spoken
    words, he would be able to comprehend nonverbal actions and the tone of
    voice. The boy was a human being, entitled to life.

Assumptions: I take somewhat of a deontological attitude toward mercy killings. I think killing someone who is not harmful to society is wrong. A criminal knows that if he kills someone the punishment is his own death. He is not sentenced to die by his peers; he actually is committing suicide. He knew that law. A man who jumps off a bridge knows that the laws of nature say he will be killed.

Mr. Repouille has five children, some older and some younger than thirteen. Instead of looking at the boy as a burden and a time consumer, Mr. Repouille should get off his egoism-teleological high horse and get down to a utilitarian set of values. His other children could learn a lot about life and compassion by sharing the burden of taking care of their brother. A lesson can be learned from any situation. Taught in the right way, the other children would realize that their brother needed them and was a part of their family.

I think a nonhedonistic approach could also be used. By killing the thirteen-year-old, the family would probably feel relieved in the short run. But in the long run, I think they would feel guilty about his death.

Justification: Man's moral values are not inherent. They develop through a learning process which includes personal experience, vicarious experience, and perhaps faith in religious principles.

I see taking a life in this situation as wrong. The principles of the gospel tell us that we will be tried and tested while on this earth, but that these trials are learning experiences for our welfare and that we will not be tested beyond our means. I see this young boy as a test for his family.

This student's response is clear and quite self-explanatory. She has accurately seen her reasoning as deontological (a mixed form); with her view of life as a test, she constructs a partially utilitarian argument that the boy ought to live, at least for the learning experience he provides the family. A second woman agrees in substance:

Mr. Repouille was wrong in giving his son the drug that killed him. In this life we are all given different trials and problems to cope with. Mr. Repouille should have looked at his situation with the attitude of making the best of it. He should have realized that it could have been his test in life or at least one of many. A problem like his, if treated in the right way, could have brought the family closer together. Killing a member of the family, in no matter what condition, could be a blow to the individual members of the family. Mr. Repouille did not set the right example for his children, because killing is wrong.

My assumptions are that (1) killing is wrong—even mercy killing (which would be deontological in nature) and (2) his situation is a trial and, with that in mind, he should endure to the end (which is teleological in nature)—the end being to remain faithful to the end or endure his hardship all through life if called to, no matter if the means are hard or unpleasant.

A third student reacted rather angrily to this dilemma. Her reasoning passes abruptly from a deontological base to a rule-utilitarian one, and she gives no hint that she is aware of this shift. This lack of awareness raises a question about the development of her thought. Is breaking the law wrong simply because it is wrong, or because it will lead to chaos?

I believe Mr. Repouille was very wrong in his decision. The first and most concrete reason his decision was wrong was that it is illegal to kill someone. The legality of the action is trivial, though, when you compare it to the religious and moral obligation involved as a parent. The boy was a human being and no matter what state he was in, no one has the right to take away someone else's life. And, as a parent, Mr. Repouille is obligated to that child (since he is the co-creator) to play the role of the father and care for his son as he does the other children.

My assumptions are: (1) that it is wrong to break the law, (2) that it is wrong to inflict on others' free agency, and (3) that in bringing a child into the world, the parents took on that responsibility for an unlimited period, whether it be eighteen years or sixty years.

Laws were instilled to avoid one's infliction on the rights of others. If there were no laws there would be utter chaos. If everyone did away with something or someone who inconvenienced him, our society would soon destroy itself. So I believe it is imperative that we sustain the law in all things in order to have harmony in society.

In response to the Heinz dilemma, another student wrote this thoughtful response:

If I were in Heinz's place I am positive I would go ahead and steal the drug to save my wife's life.

My decision to steal the drug would definitely be an act of mercy for my wife. The amount of suffering she would be subjected to through her illness would not be worth my preserving my personal moral beliefs about stealing. If I had exhausted every means available to come up with the outrageous amount of money the druggist is asking, then stealing would be my final, but distasteful, alternative. Some of my assumptions are: (1) that it is wrong to let people suffer; (2) that stealing is less of a wrong than to permit suffering; and (3) not to a great extent, but partially, that since the druggist is being so unbelievably unreasonable, I would not be justified in stealing from him, but I wouldn't feel quite as rotten about it either.

My general approach is teleological, very *end*-oriented. It is also very hedonistic in that my purpose would be to prevent suffering, therefore promoting pleasure. My reasons are partly egoistic in that I couldn't live with myself if I let my wife suffer, and also I wouldn't want the pain of losing someone I love. But mainly I think my decision would be utilitarian, not wanting my wife to suffer, and thinking of her pleasure and well-being.

As far as justifying my assumptions goes, I cannot claim my line of reasoning to fall into the category of universal truths, but trying to get in touch with what I really feel would be the most correct action in this situation, knowing that I am stealing at high personal risk (getting caught and being thrown in prison at worst). My justification is simply intuitive. Having used my reasoning powers to their fullest extent, I"feel" that my decision is right and, most important, moral.

In this answer, the student has carefully analyzed her thinking and has recognized the combination, for instance, of egoism with utilitarianism in her thought. She has also clearly recognized the source of her moral assumptions. We would consider her response indicative of a significant degree of moral maturity.

The most surprising responses came from two students who agreed that Repouille was right in killing his son but that Heinz would be wrong to steal the drug. By conventional standards, these are probably the direct inverses of what is generally considered right. Their reasoning is interesting; both adopt a type of teleological thought in answering the Repouille dilemma and primarily a deontological type of thought in answering the Heinz situation. Their responses to both are presented here:

My decision about Mr. Repouille's action is that he was right and justified in what he did. On the assumption that the end justifies the means, from a teleological point of view, it was best for the whole family that the boy die. He already was as if he were dead. The boy was no use to himself or to life and it would not be productive to spend so much time with something that couldn't develop, while neglecting the ones that needed the time and attention so that they could develop and grow. I believe that what Mr. Repouille did was right because all of the time that he spent with something that was just existing, he now could spend helping his other children. If he hadn't done this, their lives might have been ruined in the end. So it's better to have one die and to save the souls of the others, especially since the one is of no value to society or humanity anyway, while the others are alive and normal and will contribute to or affect society and humanity.

My decision on the case with Mr. Heinz and the drug for his wife is that he should not steal the drug. I base my assumption on a deontological point of view, that it is just wrong to steal. It's dishonest and wrong, and usually when someone does something wrong it catches up with him in the end. If he steals the drug, he probably would get caught or he would administer the drug to his wife in a harmful way, not helping the situation at all.

All I can say is that I just feel and know that it would be wrong to steal. If he does have to steal, it would probably lead to other crimes like lying, forging, or even murdering.

I think Mr. Repouille was right in taking the life of his thirteen-year-old child. I am assuming that the child is a complete vegetable, meaning that he cannot think, is bedridden like a tiny baby, and there is no chance of the child ever recovering. Even today "vegetables" seldom, if ever, recover. By committing this act of painlessly destroying a life, he (the father) is freeing himself and especially his children of a great burden. The children would be burdened in their normal development, physically, socially, and character-wise, if they were deprived the privilege of having a mother and a father. It would be like raising orphans because of one time-consuming element.

The assumptions I am making are teleological; the end does justify the means. Basically it is utilitarian and hedonistic—pleasure for numbers—even though I'm sure it was not a pleasure to take the life of his son.

On the other hand, no way is Heinz's stealing justifiable. His wife is dying of cancer, and he needs the drug to keep her alive, and with a thousand dollars more he could buy the drug. So he steals and gets the drug, and his wife is saved. But I assume that there are no children involved. By that man stealing he is losing his own soul. He is risking a big chance of being caught and either being fined a large sum of money he probably couldn't pay, or even being put in jail. Then, is his wife better off being alone and alive? I don't think so. I would believe that there would be some way that he could get $1,000 legally, through a loan of some type, mortgaging, if necessary, or even selling the house. Heinz should be more concerned about his own welfare than that of the drug manufacturer who is making the profit. There are many cases in our society when the producer makes huge amounts of profit, and everyone cannot just go out and steal what they don't earn. It would upset the entire economy. (Many do try it though.)

So if the issue is the wife's life or stealing, let the wife go. She would have a better chance of making it in heaven with her husband if he did not steal.

So, my assumption is deontological, the end does not justify the means.

The "end" is not affecting numerous others as in the previous case, and dying is not the final end.

The first student's responses seem to lack careful thought and analysis. She answers the dilemmas, but her reasoning does not appear to be carefully constructed; her attempt at a teleological argument in the Heinz dilemma (e.g., it will catch up with him, it will

probably lead to other crimes) is confusing. Is hers a mixed deontology, combining deontological and teleological thought, or merely
an attempt at an argument more likely than pure deontology to
persuade a listener? She does not, however, justify whatever assumptions she does make. Her responses are not well reasoned and
the certainty of them, despite their lack of careful thought, indicates
that her moral concepts have been "handed down" and that she has
accepted them rather heteronomously. We would not think her moral
thought is very mature. This seems to be true of the second student as
well. Her quick change from teleology to deontology—with little
explanation—leaves one suspicious that these are merely post hoc
devices designed to rationalize her prejudices, rather than carefully
considered normative assumptions. If that is the case, then her moral
thought would not be considered autonomous or mature either.

The above examples and discussion should have prompted the
reader to his own moral inquiry and helped him to acquire skill in
recognizing and analyzing moral arguments. For instance, it should
be reasonably clear that the first two examples are forms of mixed
rule-deontology. The remaining examples illustrate both utilitarianism and deontology, depending on the dilemma in question.

Some of the best examples of moral thinking—specifically, of what
we have called moral content—are to be found in the world's great
literary works. In the following section we present the cases of
characters in various literary works who are faced with moral issues
and who thus exemplify the types of moral thought that have been
described—egoism, utilitarianism, and so forth. These examples will
give the reader further opportunity to become acquainted with the
categories of moral philosophy and to see their usefulness in describing moral content. The background information needed to
understand and appreciate each character's example of moral reasoning will be provided before the passages are quoted.

EXAMPLES FROM LITERATURE

The Case of Huckleberry Finn

One literary critic has said that *The Adventures of Huckleberry Finn* is
one of the most moral books ever written (6). The entire story unfolds
as an epic presenting a moral theme. Because of the novel's emphasis

upon various issues involving moral reasoning, it becomes much more than an adventure story of a twelve-year-old boy.

Huck had been living with the religious and moralizing Miss Watson, but Huck's father insists that he return home. To escape his father's drunkenness and violence, Huck makes it appear that he is dead, and then he runs away. He soon meets Jim, Miss Watson's runaway slave, and the two join in their flight. However, Huck, a white Southern boy in pre-Civil War America, suffers great moral torment because he likes Jim as a person, but he realizes that it is wrong to help a runaway slave. The following passages illustrate Huck's dilemma:

Jim talked out loud all the time while I was talking to myself. He was saying how the first thing he would do when he got to a free State he would go to saving up money and never spend a single cent, and when he got enough he would buy his wife, which was owned on a farm close to where Miss Watson lived; and then they would work to buy the two children, and if their master wouldn't sell them, they'd get an Ab'litionist to go and steal them.

It most froze me to hear such talk. He wouldn't ever dared to talk such talk in his life before. Just see what a difference it made in him the minute he judged he was about free. It was according to the old saying, "give a nigger an inch and he'll take an ell." Thinks I, this is what comes of my not thinking. Here was this nigger which I had as good as helped to run away, coming right out flat-footed and saying he would steal his children—children that belonged to a man I didn't even know; a man that hadn't ever done me no harm.

I was sorry to hear Jim say that, it was such a lowering of him. [13, pp. 123–24]

And then think of *me*! It would get all around, that Huck Finn helped a nigger to get his freedom; and if I was ever to see anybody from that town again, I'd be ready to get down and lick his boots for shame. That's just the way: a person does a low-down thing, and then he don't want to take no consequences of it. Thinks as long as he can hide it, it ain't no disgrace. That was my fix exactly. The more I studied about this, the more my conscience went to grinding me, and the more wicked and low-down and ornery I got to feeling. [13, p. 269–70]

"That's so, my boy—good-by, good-by. If you see any runaway niggers you get help and nab them, and you can make some money by it."

"Good-by, sir," says I, "I won't let no runaway niggers by me if I can help it."

They went off and I got aboard the raft, feeling bad and low, because I knowed very well I had done wrong, and I see it warn't no use for me to try to learn to do right; a body that don't get *started* right when he's little ain't got no show—when the pinch comes there ain't nothing to back him up and keep him to his work, and so he gets beat. Then I thought a minute, and says to myself, hold on,—s'pose you'd a done right and give Jim up; would you felt better than what you do now? No, says I, I'd feel bad—I'd feel just the same way I do now. Well, then, says I, what's the use you learning to do right, when it's troublesome to do right and ain't no trouble to do wrong, and the wages is just the same? I was stuck. I couldn't answer that. So I reckoned I wouldn't bother no more about it, but after this always do whichever come handiest at the time. [13, pp. 127–28]

In these passages, Huck appears to be struggling with two "consciences." One is the morality of all pre- (and post-?) Civil War America that tells him blacks are inferior and are not human beings at all. Within this moral framework, he shudders at the thought of actually setting a slave free, and even more at the possibility that this slave would actually presume to steal his own children. This side of Huck's personality accepts everything that the Miss Watsons have told him. But the other conscience he struggles with tells him that he would not feel any better even if he did "right" and turned Jim in. This conscience recognizes that Jim is more than a slave; he is a human being with dignity and rights. Huck realizes that he would feel guilty if he returned Jim to a condition offering any less than that.

One conscience reflects the heteronomous value, which is imposed often by one's culture, that one race is superior to another and should be treated accordingly. The other conscience displays the emergence of another value, more autonomously held, that all human life is to be respected and treated with dignity, regardless of race. It is conceivable that Twain symbolized all of America in Huck—the struggle of national racial prejudice fighting against the more equalitarian concept of mutual respect and equality. Huck's growing pains are symbolic of the growing pains of a whole nation, away from heteronomously acquired national prejudices toward the emergence of more autonomously held equalitarian values. Huck's internal struggle is an essential part of the maturing process and illustrates the difficulty one faces in abandoning a heteronomous (class or national) morality while moving toward a self-directed, autonomous, mode of moral thought.

The Case of
Hester Prynne, Reverend Dimmesdale,
and Roger Chillingworth

Like *Huckleberry Finn*, *The Scarlet Letter* also deals with many moral issues. The novel poignantly portrays the moral strength of Hester Prynne as she individually suffers the shame of her adultery. Living in a strict Puritan culture, she struggles bravely under the stigma, imposed upon her by the community, of her sin, while protecting her partner in the sin, the Reverend Arthur Dimmesdale. In the following excerpt, Roger Chillingworth, Hester's former husband, subtly but directly confronts Reverend Arthur Dimmesdale on his refusal to publicly share Hester's shame. The reverend speaks first:

"Why should a wretched man, guilty, we will say, of murder, prefer to keep the dead corpse buried in his own heart, rather than fling it forth at once, and let the universe take care of it!"

"Yet some men bury their secret thus," observed the calm physician.

"True; there are such men," answered Mr. Dimmesdale. "But, not to suggest more obvious reasons, it may be that they are kept silent by the very constitution of their nature. Or,—can we not suppose it?—guilty as they may be, retaining, nevertheless, a zeal for God's glory and man's welfare, they shrink from displaying themselves black and filthy in the view of men; because, thenceforward, no good can be achieved by them; no evil of the past be redeemed by better service. So, to their own unutterable torment, they go about among their fellow-creatures, looking pure as new-fallen snow while their hearts are all speckled and spotted with iniquity of which they cannot rid themselves."

"These men deceive themselves," said Roger Chillingworth, with somewhat more emphasis than usual, and making a slight gesture with his forefinger. "They fear to take up the shame that rightfully belongs to them. Their love for man, their zeal for God's service,—these holy impulses may or may not coexist in their hearts and with the evil inmates to which their guilt has unbarred the door, if they seek to glorify God, let them not lift heavenward their unclean hands! If they would serve their fellowmen, let them do it by making manifest the power and reality of conscience, in constraining them to penitential self-abasement! Wouldst thou have me to believe, O wise and pious friend, that a false show can be better—can be more for God's glory, or man's welfare—than God's own truth? Trust me, such men deceive themselves!" [4, pp. 159–60]

Hester's plea to Arthur Dimmesdale to forgive her for having lied to protect him is touching and exhibits her great moral torment.

"O Arthur," cried she, "forgive me! In all things else, I have striven to be true! Truth was the one virtue which I might have held fast, and did hold fast, through all extremity; save when thy good,—thy life,—thy fame,—were put in question! Then I consent to a deception. But a lie is never good, even though death threaten on the other side!" [4, p. 236]

Dimmesdale's basically utilitarian argument that he has hidden his sin in "zeal for God's glory and man's welfare" may in fact be a disguised egoism, a fear of shame. This is Chillingworth's accusation and it may be as applicable to actual life situations as it is to this literary one. It is true that we often translate our egoistic motivations into more "acceptable" utilitarian ones. Chillingworth claims that those, such as Dimmesdale, who do this (e.g., sincerely try to please God through deception) are deceiving themselves. It may be that the process of developing moral maturity is simultaneous with overcoming such self-deception.

The Case of "Joe Davis's boy" and the California Land Owners

In *The Grapes of Wrath*, John Steinbeck tells the story of poor sharecroppers who are forced from their lands in Oklahoma. Because their outdated methods of farming cannot keep pace with the technology of improved farm machinery, they are forced to leave. In desperation, these people migrate to California where they have heard there are thousands of grape-picking jobs available. When they arrive, however, they discover so few jobs and so many workers that the jobs go for a fraction of their normal value. The narrator here describes the pitiful conditions of the workers and of the greed and cruelty of the land owners. In the first excerpt below, Joe Davis's boy explains his reasons for destroying sharecroppers' homes in order to force them to leave. In the second excerpt, the narrator describes, and comments on, the greed and corruption the workers experienced in California:

"Why, you're Joe Davis' boy?"

"Sure," the driver said.

"Well, what you doing this kind of work for—against your own people?"

"Three dollars a day, I got damn sick of creeping for my dinner—and not getting it. I got a wife and kids. We got to eat. Three dollars a day, and it comes every day."

"That's right," the tenant said. "But for your three dollars a day fifteen or twenty families can't eat at all. Nearly a hundred people have to go out and wander on the roads for your three dollars a day. Is that right?"

And the driver said, "Can't think of that. Got to think of my own kids. Three dollars a day, and it comes every day. Times are changing, mister, don't you know? Can't make living on the land unless you've got two, five, ten thousand acres and a tractor. Crop land isn't for little guys like us anymore. You don't kick up a howl because you can't make Fords, or because you're not the telephone company. Well, crops are like that now. Nothing to do about it. You try to get three dollars a day someplace. That's the only way." . . .

The driver munched the branded pie and threw the crust away. "Times are changed, don't you know? Thinking about stuff like that don't feed the kids. Get your three dollars a day, feed your kids. You got no call to worry about anybody's kids but your own. You get a reputation for talking like that, and you'll never get three dollars a day. Big shots won't give you three dollars a day if you worry about anything but your three dollars a day."

"Nearly a hundred people on the road for your three dollars. Where will we go?"

"And that reminds me," the driver said, "you better get out soon. I'm going through the dooryard after dinner."

"You filled in the well this morning."

"I know. Had to keep the line straight. But I'm going through the dooryard after dinner. Got to keep the lines straight. And—well, you know Joe Davis, my old man, so I'll tell you this. I got orders wherever there's a family not moved out—if I have an accident—you know, get too close and cave the house in a little—well, I might get a couple of dollars. And my youngest kid never had no shoes yet." [11, pp. 50, 51]

The works of the roots of the vines, of the trees, must be destroyed to keep up the price, and this is the saddest, bitterest thing of all. Carloads of oranges dumped on the ground. The people came for miles to take the fruit, but this could not be. Why would they buy oranges at twenty cents a dozen if they could drive out and pick them up? And more with hoses squirt kerosene on the oranges, and they are angry at the crime, angry at the people who have come to take the fruit. A million hungry people, needing the fruit—and kerosene sprayed over the golden mountains.

And the smell of rot fills the country.

Burn coffee for fuel in the ships. Burn corn to keep warm, it makes a hot fire. Dump potatoes in the rivers and place guards along the banks to keep the hungry people from fishing them out. Slaughter the pigs and bury them, and let the putrescence drip down into the earth.

There is a crime here that goes beyond denunciation. There is a sorrow here that weeping cannot symbolize. There is a failure here that topples all our success. The fertile earth, the straight tree rows, the sturdy trunks, and the ripe fruit. And children dying of pellagra must die because a profit cannot be taken from an orange. And coroners must fill in the certificates— died of malnutrition—because the food must rot, must be forced to rot.

The people come with nets to fish for potatoes in the river, and the guards hold them back; they come in rattling cars to get the dumped oranges, but the kerosene is sprayed. And they stand still and watch the potatoes float by, listen to the screaming pigs being killed in a ditch and covered with quicklime, watch the mountains of oranges slop down to a putrefying ooze; and in the eyes of the people there is failure; and in the eyes of the hungry there is wrath. In the souls of the people the grapes of wrath are filling and growing heavy, growing heavy for the vintage. [11, pp. 476–77]

The Grapes of Wrath is also a novel with a primarily moral theme. In the second excerpt, the narrator deplores the egoistic reasoning of the landowners and their obsession with profits while thousands of people suffer from starvation, but does he also deplore the reasoning of Joe Davis's boy in the first excerpt? Possibly, in examples such as the first one, Steinbeck is merely illustrating the type of situation that an obsessive profit motive at the top creates for people at the bottom. It turns people against each other, requiring some to make a living at the expense of others. This may have been what Steinbeck intended, but it still does not release the burden of morality that the people at the bottom must carry. The reader should ask himself what he would do in the same situation. Would he be willing to "send a hundred people on the road" in order to care for his own family?

The Case of "The Student"

The following excerpt from Dostoyevsky's *Crime and Punishment* presents a striking example of teleological, particularly utilitarian, moral thinking. The example is self-contained and needs no introduction.

"I could kill that damned old woman and make off with her money, I assure you, without the faintest conscience-prick," the student added with warmth. The officer laughed again while Raskolnikov shuddered. How strange it was!

"Listen, I want to ask you a serious question," the student said hotly. "I was joking of course, but look here; on one side we have a stupid, senseless, worthless, spiteful, ailing, horrid old woman, not simply useless but doing actual mischief, who has not an idea what she is living for herself, and who will die in a day or two in any case. You understand? You understand?"

"Yes, yes, I understand," answered the officer, watching his excited companion attentively.

"Well, listen then. On the other side, fresh young lives thrown away for want of help and by thousands, on every side! A hundred thousand good deeds could be done and helped, on that old woman's money which will be buried in a monastery! Hundreds, thousands perhaps, might be set on the right path; dozens of families saved from destitution, from ruin, from vice, and with the help of it devote oneself to the service of humanity and the good of all. What do you think, would not one tiny crime be wiped out by thousands of good deeds? For one life, thousands would be saved from corruption and decay. One death, and a hundred lives in exchange—it's simple arithmetic! Besides, what value has the life of that sickly, stupid, ill-natured woman in the balance of existence! No more than the life of a louse, of a black beetle, less in fact because the old woman is doing harm. She is wearing out the lives of others; the other day she bit Lizaveta's finger out of spite; it almost had to be amputated."

"Of course she does not deserve to live," remarked the officer, "but there it is, it's nature."

"Oh, well, brother, but we have to correct and direct nature, and, but for that, we should drown in an ocean of prejudice. But for that, there would never have been a single great man. They talk of duty, conscience—I don't want to say anything against duty and conscience;—but the point is what do we mean by them." [3, pp. 66–67]

The end-versus-the-means argument (or teleology versus deontology) is as well presented in this excerpt as it is almost anywhere else in literature. The speaker's thinking is clearly teleological and utilitarian, and it illustrates the extremes that are possible in attempts at maximizing the good in the world. The speaker is quite excited, however, and it is not clear that he has in fact considered all the alternatives. As discussed in chapter two, an act, to be right, must not only result in greater good than some other act would, but it must result in greater good than *any* other possible act would. It is not clear that the speaker has considered this, though, and thus even many utilitarians would take issue with his argument as it is presented here.

The Case of Raskolnikov

The following excerpt, also from Dostoyevsky's *Crime and Punishment*, presents an example of teleological thinking. In this case,

Raskolnikov, the novel's main character, is being questioned about an article he had previously written. Here he takes the opportunity to clarify the main points of that article.

"In [Raskolnikov's] article all men are divided into 'ordinary' and 'extraordinary.' Ordinary men have to live in submission, have no right to transgress the law, because, don't you see, they are ordinary. But extraordinary men have a right to commit any crime and to transgress the law in any way, just because they are extraordinary. That was your idea, if I am not mistaken?"

"What do you mean? That can't be right?" Razumihim muttered in bewilderment.

Raskolnikov smiled again. He saw the point at once, and knew where they wanted to drive him. He decided to take up the challenge.

"That wasn't quite my contention," he began simply and modestly. "Yet I admit that you have stated it almost correctly; perhaps, if you like, perfectly so." (It almost gave him pleasure to admit this.) "The only difference is that I don't contend that extraordinary people are always bound to commit breaches of morals, as you call it. In fact, I doubt whether such an argument could be published. I simply hinted that an 'extraordinary' man has the right . . . that is not an official right, but an inner right to decide in his own conscience to overstep . . . certain obstacles, and only in case it is essential for the practical fulfillment of his idea (sometimes, perhaps, of benefit to the whole of humanity). You say that my article isn't definite; I am ready to make it as clear as I can. Perhaps I am right in thinking you want me to; very well. I maintain that if the discoveries of Kepler and Newton could not have been made known except by sacrificing the lives of one, a dozen, a hundred, or more men, Newton would have had the right, would indeed have been in duty bound . . . to *eliminate* the dozen or the hundred men for the sake of making his discoveries known to the whole of humanity. But it does not follow from that that Newton had a right to murder people right and left and to steal every day in the market. Then, I remember, I maintain in my article that all . . . well, legislators and leaders of men, such as Lycurgus, Solon, Mahomet, Napoleon, and so on, were all without exception criminals, from the very fact that, making a new law, they transgressed the ancient one, handed down from their ancestors and held sacred by the people, and they did not stop short at bloodshed either, if that bloodshed—often of innocent persons fighting bravely in defence of ancient law—were of use to their cause. It's remarkable, in fact, that the majority, indeed, of these benefactors and leaders of humanity were guilty of terrible carnage. In short, I maintain that all great men or even men a little out of the common, that is to say capable of giving some new word, must from their very nature be criminals—more or less, of course. Otherwise it's hard for them to get out of the common rut; and to remain in the common rut is what they can't submit to, from their very nature again, and to my mind they ought not, indeed, to submit to it. [3, pp. 254–55]

Here, as in the previous example, the issue is primarily one of the end versus the means. In this case, though, Raskolnikov seems to have considered his position carefully—circumstances *could* arise where the very best act that could be performed would be to kill those, however many, who stood in the way of some new word or idea. In examining this argument, special care should be given to Raskolnikov's concept of the good. This can be compared with the student's concept in the previous example and help clarify the differences between these two essentially utilitarian arguments.

The Case of Jean Valjean

The following short excerpt from Hugo's *Les Miserables* raises not only the question of one's duty to his family, but also that of how a given society administers justice. The story, for our purposes, needs no introduction.

There was a very severe winter; Jean had no work, the family had no bread; literally, no bread and seven children.

One Sunday night, Maubert Isabeau, the baker on the Place de l'Eglise, in Faverolles, was just going to bed when he heard a violent blow against the barred window of his shop. He got down in time to see an arm thrust through the aperture made by the blow of a fist on the glass. The arm seized a loaf of bread and took it out. Isabeau rushed out; the thief used his legs valiantly; Isabeau pursued him and caught him. The thief had thrown away the bread, but his arm was still bleeding. It was Jean Valjean. . . .

Jean Valjean was found guilty: The terms of the code were explicit; in our civilization there are fearful hours; such are those when the criminal law pronounces shipwreck upon a man. What a mournful moment is that in which society withdraws itself and gives up a thinking being for ever. Jean Valjean was sentenced to five years in the galleys. . . .

While they were with heavy hammer-strokes behind his head riveting the bolt of his iron collar, he was weeping. The tears choked his words, and he only succeeded in saying from time to time: "I was a pruner at Faverolles." Then, sobbing as he was, he raised his right hand and lowered it seven times, as if he was touching seven heads of unequal height, and at this gesture one could guess that whatever he had done, had been to feed and clothe seven little children. [5, pp. 84–85]

The reader has probably already formed at least a partial answer to the dilemma of Heinz and the drug; is this situation the same? A more important question, perhaps, is that of the role of society in handling such crimes. The narrator obviously considers the greater crime in this case to be the punishment society has meted out to a rather harmless individual. What implications does this have for moral reasoning?

The Case of Fantine

The following excerpt from Hugo's *Les Miserables* deals with the story of a mother, Fantine, and her devotion to the welfare of her young daughter. The passage is quoted extensively to fully illustrate this devotion and to raise the question of the extent to which one should go to insure the welfare of loved ones.

One day she received from the Thenardiers a letter in these words: "Cosette is sick of an epidemic disease—a miliary fever they call it. The drugs necessary are dear. It is ruining us, and we can no longer pay for them. Unless you send us 40 francs within a week the little one will die."

She burst out laughing and said to her old neighbor: "Oh, they are nice! Forty francs—think of that! That is 2 napoleons! Where do they think I can get them? Are they fools, these boors?"

She went, however, to the staircase, near a dormer window, and read the letter again.

Then she went downstairs and out of doors, running and jumping, still laughing.

Somebody who met her said to her: "What is the matter with you that you are so gay?"

She answered: "A stupid joke that some country people have just written me. They ask me for 40 francs, the boors!"

As she passed through the square, she saw many people gathered about an odd-looking carriage, on the top of which stood a man in red clothes declaiming. He was a juggler and a traveling dentist, and was offering to the public complete sets of teeth, opiates, powders, and elixirs.

Fantine joined the crowd and began to laugh with the rest at this harangue, in which were mingled slang for the rabble and jargon for the better sort. The puller of teeth saw this beautiful girl laughing, and suddenly called out: "You have pretty teeth, you girl who are laughing there. If you will sell me your incisors I will give you a gold napoleon for each of them."

"What is that? What are my incisors?" asked Fantine.

"The incisors," resumed the professor of dentistry, "are the front teeth, the two upper ones."

"How horrible!" cried Fantine.

"Two napoleons!" grumbled a toothless old hag who stood by. "How lucky she is!"

Fantine fled away and stopped her ears not to hear the shrill voice of the man, who called after her: "Consider, my beauty! Two napoleons! How much good they will do you! If you have the courage for it come this evening to the inn of the *Tillac d'Argent*; you will find me there."

Fantine returned home. She was raving and told the story to her good neighbor Marguerite: "Do you understand that? Isn't he an abominable man; why do they let such people go about the country? Pull out my two front teeth—why, I should be horrible! . . . I would rather throw myself from the fifth story, head first, to the pavement! He told me that he would be this evening at the *Tillac d'Argent*."

"And what was it he offered you?" asked Marguerite.

"Two napoleons."

"That is 40 francs."

"Yes," said Fantine; "that makes 40 francs."

She became thoughtful and went about her work. In a quarter of an hour she left her sewing and went to the stairs to read again the Thenardiers letter.

On her return she said to Marguerite, who was at work near her:

"What does this mean—a miliary fever? Do you know?"

"Yes," answered the old woman. "It is a disease."

"Then it needs a good many drugs?"

"Yes; terrible drugs."

"How does it come upon you?"

"It is a disease that comes in a moment."

"Does it attack children?"

"Children especially."

"Do people die of it?"

"Very often," said Marguerite.

Fantine withdrew and went once more to read over the letter on the stairs.

In the evening, she went out and took the direction of the Rue de Paris where the inns are.

The next morning when Marguerite went into Fantine's chamber before daybreak—for they always worked together and so made one candle do for the two—she found Fantine seated upon her couch, pale and icy. She had not been in bed. Her cap had fallen upon her knees. The candle had burned all night and was almost consumed.

Marguerite stopped upon the threshold, petrified by this wild disorder, and exclaimed: "Good Lord! the candle is all burned out. Something has happened."

Then she looked at Fantine. . . .

Fantine had grown ten years older since evening.

"Bless us!" said Marguerite, "what is the matter with you, Fantine?"

"Nothing," said Fantine. "Quite the contrary. My child will not die with that frightful sickness for lack of aid. I am satisfied."

So saying, she showed the old woman 2 napoleons that glistened on the table.

"Oh! good God!" said Marguerite. "Why there is a fortune! Where did you get these louis d'or?"

"I got them," answered Fantine.

At the same time she smiled. The candle lit up her face. It was a sickening smile, for the corners of her mouth were stained with blood, and a dark cavity revealed itself there.

The two teeth were gone.

She sent the 40 francs to Montfermeil.

And this was a ruse of the Thenardiers to get money. Cosette was not sick. . . .

She sewed seventeen hours a day; but a prison contractor, who was working prisoners at a loss, suddenly cut down the price, and this reduced the day's wages of free labourers to 9 sous. Seventeen hours of work, and 9 sous a day! Her creditors were more pitiless than ever. The second-hand dealer, who had taken back nearly all his furniture, was constantly saying to her:

"When will you pay me, wench?"

Good God! What did they want her to do? She felt herself hunted down, and something of the wild beast began to develop within her. About the same time Thenardier wrote to her that really he had waited with too much generosity and that he must have 100 francs immediately, or else little Cosette, just convalescing after her severe sickness, would be turned out of doors into the cold and upon the highway, and that she would become what she could, and would perish if she must. "A hundred francs," thought Fantine. "But where is there a place where one can earn 100 sous a day?"

"Come!" said she, "I will sell what is left."

The unfortunate creature became a woman of the town. [5, pp. 187–89, 190]

Western cultures traditionally have been opposed to prostitution, and although it appears that this tradition is fading partially, a large population still considers prostitution immoral. For these people, the story of Fantine raises a serious question: Is prostitution ever justified, even to save the life of a loved one? It would be unfair to resort to the argument that Cosette was not really sick and that Fantine could have discovered this. In Fantine's mind her child was sick and her life was threatened; the dilemma takes place in her mind. For those people particularly concerned with the morality of sex-related issues, this is a serious dilemma indeed.

The Case of Shylock

Shakespeare's *Merchant of Venice* takes place in Italy and revolves around the themes of Christian versus Jew and mercy versus justice. Jews at this time were bitterly hated by the Christians because of their practice of usury. In this play, a Christian merchant named Antonio finds it necessary to borrow from one such Jew, Shylock. The terms of the bond agreed to by Antonio and Shylock are that if Antonio does not return the required sum on the proper date, Shylock would be entitled to a pound of Antonio's flesh taken nearest his heart. Because of various mishaps, Antonio is not able to pay the sum on the agreed date, and so Shylock legally demands his pound of flesh. The following excerpt, taken from act four, takes place as Portia, disguised as a judge, sits in judgment over the dispute. She begins by arguing for mercy:

> PORTIA. The quality of mercy is not strained,
> It droppeth as the gentle rain from heaven
> Upon the place beneath. It is twice blest;
> It blesseth him that gives and him that takes.
> 'Tis mightiest in the mightiest. It becomes
> The throned monarch better than his crown.
> His scepter shows the force of temporal power,
> The attribute to awe and majesty
> Wherein doth sit the dread and fear of kings.
> But mercy is above this sceptered sway,
> It is enthroned in the hearts of kings,
> It is an attribute to God himself,
> And earthly power doth then show likest God's
> When mercy seasons justice. Therefore, Jew,
> Though justice be thy plea, consider this,
> That in the course of justice none of us
> Should see salvation. We do pray for mercy,
> And that same prayer doth teach us all to render
> The deeds of mercy. I have spoke thus much
> To mitigate the justice of thy plea,
> Which if thou follow, this strict court of Venice
> Must needs give sentence 'gainst the merchant there.
> SHYLOCK. My deeds upon my head! I crave the law,

The penalty and forfeit of my bond.
   PORTIA. Is he not able to discharge the money?
   BASSANIO. Yes, here I tender it for him in the court,
Yea, twice the sum. If that will not suffice,
I will be bound to pay it ten times o'er
On forfeit of my hands, my head, my heart.
If this will not suffice, it must appear
That malice bears down truth. And I beseech you
Wrest once the law to your authority.
To do a great right, do a little wrong,
And curb this cruel devil of his will.
   PORTIA. It must not be. There is no power in Venice
Can alter a decree established.
'Twill be recorded for a precedent,
And many an error, by the same example,
Will rush into the state. It cannot be.
   SHYLOCK. A Daniel come to judgment! Yea, a Daniel
O wise young judge, how I do honor thee!
   PORTIA. I pray you let me look upon the bond.
   SHYLOCK. Here 'tis, most reverend Doctor, here it is.
   PORTIA. Shylock, there's thrice thy money offered thee.
   SHYLOCK. An oath, an oath, I have an oath in Heaven,
Shall I lay perjury upon my soul?
No, not for Venice.
   PORTIA. Why, this bond is forfeit,
And lawfully by this the Jew may claim
A pound of flesh, to be by him cut off
Nearest the merchant's heart. Be merciful.
Take thrice the money, bid me tear the bond.
   SHYLOCK. When it is paid according to the tenor?
It doth appear you are a worthy judge,
You know the law, your exposition
Hath been most sound. I charge you by the law,
Whereof you are a well-deserving pillar,
Proceed to judgment. By my soul I swear
There is no power in the tongue of man
To alter me. I stay here on my bond.
                        [9, IV. 1. 184–242]

   Of course, later in the trial, Portia points out that the contract makes no allowance for the spilling of blood, whereupon she directs Shylock to take his pound of flesh, but warns him that if he spills one drop of blood, he will properly be punished for his crime.

The issue, at least as Shylock sees it, is that of justice versus mercy, merely a difference in moral values. But is that the real issue? Justice would be served by Bassanio's offer of payment ten times over, but Shylock rejects the offer. Is his concern with justice or with revenge against the Christians?

The Case of Creon

The play *Antigone* opens with the deaths of Antigone's two brothers. One had been ruling Thebes and the other had risen in rebellion against him. Now with both of them dead, Creon, the new ruler of Thebes, declares that the one brother should receive an honorable burial while the other should receive none at all. Antigone, however, feels enjoined by the laws of heaven to bury her brother properly. Defying Creon's decree, she buries him even though the penalty for such disobedience is death. Creon feels that he must punish Antigone, and his reasoning for carrying out the penalty follows:

> If I allow disorder in my house
> I'd surely have to licence it abroad.
> A man who deals in fairness with his own,
> he can make manifest justice in the state.
> But he who crosses law, or forces it,
> or hopes to bring the rulers under him,
> shall never have a word of praise from me.
> The man the state has put in place must have
> obedient hearing to his least command
> when it is right, and even when it's not.
> He who accepts this teaching I can trust,
> ruler, or ruled, to function in his place,
> to stand his ground even in the storm of spears,
> a mate to trust in battle at one's side.
> There is no greater wrong than disobedience.
> This ruins cities, this tears down our homes,
> this breaks the battle-front in panic-rout.
> If men live decently it is because
> discipline saves their very lives for them.
> So I must guard the men who yield to order,
> not let myself be beaten by a woman.
> Better, if it must happen, that a man

should overset me.
I won't be called weaker than womankind.
                    [10, ll.659–80]

What is to be thought of Creon's statement that the state-appointed ruler must be obeyed in all things, both right and wrong? His argument is ostensibly rule-utilitarian: disobedience is the ruin of cities and the defeat of armies, whereas men's obedience "saves their very lives for them." Regardless of this point, Creon's reason may more fundamentally be one of pride rather than rule-utilitarianism. Consider his final statement. Is he just too proud to allow a woman to disobey him? His utilitarian argument may be a guise for this pride. Consider the final lines of the play.

> Our happiness depends
> on wisdom all the way.
> The gods must have their due.
> Great words by men of pride
> bring greater blows upon them
> So wisdom comes to the old.
>   [10, ll.1346–52]

Given the point made in these final lines, it may be that, rather than his ostensible rule-utilitarianism, it is Creon's egoism that is the focus of the play.

The Case of Sydney Carton

In *A Tale of Two Cities*, set against the background of the French Revolution, Charles Dickens describes life and conditions in London and Paris. Against this background, the story of Sydney Carton, Charles Darnay, and Lucie Darnay unfolds. The plot revolves around the love triangle of these three—Charles and Lucie are married and completely devoted to each other, but Sydney is also in love with Lucie. Eventually, Charles is convicted in France of being "an enemy of the Republic" and is sentenced to death by guillotine. However, Sydney, who bears a close resemblance to Charles, replaces Charles in prison and goes to the guillotine in his place. The following passage presents Sydney's thoughts as he waits at the foot of the guillotine, just before his execution:

"I see the lives for which I lay down my life, peaceful, useful, prosperous and happy, in that England which I shall see no more. I see Her with a child upon her bosom, who bears my name. I see her father, aged and bent, but otherwise restored, and faithful to all men in his healing office, and at peace. I see the good old man, so long their friend, in ten years' time enriching them with all he has, and passing tranquilly to his reward.

"I see that I hold a sanctuary in their hearts, and in the hearts of their descendants, generations hence. I see her, an old woman, weeping for me on the anniversary of this day. I see her and her husband, their course done, lying side by side in their last earthly bed, and I know that each was not more honoured and held sacred in the other's soul, than I was in the souls of both.

"I see that child who lay upon her bosom and who bore my name, a man winning his way up in that path of life which once was mine. I see him winning it so well, that my name is made illustrious there by the light of his. I see the blots I threw upon it, faded away. I see him, foremost of just judges and honoured men, bringing a boy of my name, with a forehead that I know and golden hair, to this place—then fair to look upon, with not a trace of this day's disfigurement—and I hear him tell the child my story, with a tender and a faltering voice.

"It is a far, far better thing that I do, than I have ever done; it is a far, far better rest that I go to than I have ever known." [2, p. 437]

Does Carton perform this heroic feat for the praise and honor he will receive? It may be that he acts because of a concern for Charles and Lucie and that in this passage he merely recognizes that he also gains a portion of dignity in the process. Would he have sacrificed himself for the honor and dignity alone, or are they merely by-products? Western cultures have traditionally considered suicide to be wrong; was Sydney's act essentially one of suicide?

These examples of moral reasoning have been taken from literary works in which morality is an obvious, but nevertheless implicit, issue. Many pieces of literature, however, are less subtle and address moral concerns quite didactically. The remaining examples in this chapter are taken from literary works in which the author is explicit and overtly moralistic in his approach.

Advice from Buddha

There are two extremes, O Bhikkhus, which the man who has given up the world ought not to follow—the habitual practice, on the one hand, of self-indulgence which is unworthy, vain and fit only for the worldly-minded—and the habitual practice, on the other hand, of self-mortification, which is painful, useless and unprofitable. . . .

"A middle path, O Bhikkhus, avoiding the two extremes, has been discovered by the Tathagata—a path which opens the eyes, and bestows understanding, which leads to peace of mind, to the higher wisdom, to full enlightenment, to Nirvana!

"What is the middle path, O Bhikkhus, avoiding these two extremes, discovered by the Tathagata—that path which opens the eyes, and bestows understanding, which leads to peace of mind, to the higher wisdom, to full enlightenment, to Nirvana?

"Let me teach you, O Bhikkhus, the middle path, which keeps aloof from both extremes. By suffering, the emaciated devotee produces confusion and sickly thoughts in his mind. Mortification is not conducive even to worldly knowledge; how much less to a triumph over the senses!

"He who fills his lamp with water will not dispel the darkness, and he who tries to light a fire with rotten wood will fail. And how can anyone be free from self by leading a wretched life, if he does not succeed in quenching the fires of lust, if he still hankers after either worldly or heavenly pleasures. But he in whom self has become extinct is free from lust; he will desire neither worldly nor heavenly pleasures, and the satisfaction of his natural wants will not defile him. However, let him be moderate, let him eat and drink according to the needs of the body.

"Sensuality is enervating; the self-indulgent man is a slave to his passions, and pleasure-seeking is degrading and vulgar.

"But to satisfy the necessities of life is not evil. To keep the body in good health is a duty, for otherwise we shall not be able to trim the lamp of wisdom, and keep our mind strong and clear. Water surrounds the lotus-flower, but does not wet its petals.

"This is the middle path, O Bhikkhus, that keeps aloof from both extremes [and leads to Nirvana]." [1, pp. 49, 50–51]

Advice from Machiavelli

It is unquestionably very praiseworthy in princes to be faithful to their engagements; but among those of the present day that have been distinguished for great exploits, few indeed have been remarkable for this virtue, or have scrupled to deceive others who may have relied on their good faith.

It should, therefore, be known that there are two ways of deciding any contest: the one by laws, the other by force. The first is peculiar to men, the second to beasts; but when laws are not sufficiently powerful, it is necessary to recur to force. A prince ought, therefore, to understand how to use both these means.

From the fox, therefore, a prince will learn dexterity in avoiding snares; and from the lion, how to employ his strength to keep the wolves in awe. But they that entirely rely upon the lion's strength, will not always meet with success: in other words, a prudent prince cannot and ought not to keep his word, except when he can do it without injury to himself, or when the circumstances under which he contracted the engagement still exist.

I should be cautious in inculcating such a precept if all men were good; but as the generality of mankind are wicked, and ever ready to break their word, a prince should not pique himself on keeping his more scrupulously, especially as it is always easy to justify a breach of faith on his part. I could give numerous proofs of this, and show numberless engagements and treaties that have been violated by the treachery of princes, and that those who enacted the part of the fox have always succeeded best in their affairs. But it is necessary to disguise the appearance of craft, and thoroughly to understand the art of feigning and dissembling; for men generally are so simple and so weak that he who wishes to deceive easily finds dupes.

One example, taken from the history of our own times, will be sufficient. Pope Alexander VI played during his whole life a game of deception; and though his faithless conduct was extremely well known, his artifices always proved successful. Oaths and protestations cost him nothing; never did a prince so often break his word or pay less regard to his engagements. This was because he so well understood this chapter in the art of government.

It is not necessary, however, for a prince to possess all the good qualities I have enumerated, but it is indispensable that he should appear to have them. I will even venture to affirm, that it is sometimes dangerous to use them, though it is always useful to appear to possess them. A prince should earnestly endeavor to gain the reputation of kindness, clemency, piety, justice, and fidelity to his engagements. He should possess all these good qualities, but still retain such power over himself as to display their opposites whenever it may be expedient. [8, pp. 72, 73–74]

Machiavellian reasoning in *The Prince* is familiar to most people. The term *Machiavellianism* is common in psychological research and is generally familiar to the lay public as well. Basically it is a teleological philosophy and is thus end-oriented. However, it is important to note the end Machiavelli was concerned with promoting—is it egoistic or utilitarian?

Advice from Thoreau

Must the citizen ever for a moment, or in the least degree, resign his conscience to the legislator? Why has every man a conscience, then? I think that we should be men first, and subjects afterward. It is not desirable to cultivate a respect for the law, so much as for the right. The only obligation which I have a right to assume, is to do at any time what I think right. . . .

Unjust laws exist: shall we be content to obey them, or shall we endeavor to amend them, and obey them until we have succeeded, or shall we transgress them at once? Men generally, under such a government as this, think that they ought to wait until they have persuaded the majority to alter them. They think that, if they should resist, the remedy would be worse than the evil. But it is the fault of the government itself that the remedy *is* worse than the evil. *It* makes it worse. Why is it not more apt to anticipate and provide for reform? Why does it not cherish its wise minority? Why does it cry and resist before it is hurt? Why does it not encourage its citizens to be on the alert to point out its faults, and *do* better than it would have them? Why does it always crucify Christ, and excommunicate Copernicus and Luther, and pronounce Washington and Franklin rebels? . . .

I do not hesitate to say, that those who call themselves Abolitionists should at once effectually withdraw their support, both in person and property, from the government of Massachusetts, and not wait till they constitute a majority of one, before they suffer the right to prevail through them. I think that it is enough if they have God on their side, without waiting for that other one. Moreover, any man more right than his neighbors constitutes a majority of one already. [12, pp. 125, 133–34, 135]

Mahatma Gandhi in India, Martin Luther King, Jr., in the United States, and others are modern leaders of movements for social justice who espouse principles like Thoreau's in *Civil Disobedience*. Compare Thoreau's reasoning with Creon's. Is there a third alternative?

12/Recognizing Moral Content: Examples from Law

In this chapter, we turn to examples from the law to present additional moral dilemmas that will facilitate the reader's development of skills in moral reasoning and analysis. Here the reader will not encounter isolated situations in which moral decisions must be made, as in the previous chapter, but, rather, conflicting legal opinions which are, to one extent or another, based upon principles of morality. The conflicting opinions expressed in these passages will not only introduce the reader to fundamental moral issues but also will help him develop his skills in recognizing and analyzing moral arguments. But first we must see how law is related to morality and then briefly treat the role of morals in law enforcement.

THE MORAL FOUNDATION OF AMERICAN LAW

The relationship between morality and American law is apparent. Berman (2), among others, is quick to point this out, providing at least two evidences for it. First, the United States Constitution provides for protection of various rights, apparently on the basis of either natural law or natural rights (the point has been much debated). For example, Berman comments:

The Constitution itself specifically enacts, as positive law, certain broad principles of moral justice. Thus, the Constitution states that no person may be deprived of life, liberty, or property without "due process of law"—a phrase which means to an American what the phrase "natural law" has meant traditionally, namely, equality, consistency, impartiality, justice,

235

fairness. The Constitution also guarantees certain broad freedoms such as freedom of speech and of religion, and certain broad rights such as the right not to be subjected to unreasonable searches and seizures, the right to an impartial trial, and the right of all citizens to equal protection of the laws. By requiring that all laws must conform to these moral principles, the Constitution has encouraged American judges to submit to the test of conscience not only legislation, but all legal rules and all governmental acts, including their own judicial decisions. [2, pp. 224–25]

Because the Constitution seems to be tied so closely to morality, and because the court system is intended to uphold the Constitution, it appears that the courts themselves are greatly concerned with moral issues.

Second, since World War II there has been a partial reemergence of natural "higher" law theory in America. Apparently, according to Berman, it was realized that if a positivist (essentially neutral) legal system is adopted, there is no illegality in war crimes such as those committed by some citizens of the German nation. If legality is merely a function of the will of the state, then those Germans who followed commands in executing extermination orders are free of blame, for they were merely obeying the laws of the land. The realization of this consequence has led many legalists to adopt a position based more fully than before on natural law (2, p. 233).

In addition, the legislation that courts must interpret and enforce is often moral in nature as well. Many criminal and civil laws have their origin in moral principles, ancient or modern. Statutes are based on the assumption that some things are right and some things are wrong; the foundation for that obviously is a moral one. Even if a judge adopts a morally neutral stance, he reflects the conscience of the people in his judgments and in that way, if no other, his decisions are moral ones. In short, it appears that morality is the basic foundation of law.[1]

THE ENFORCEMENT OF MORALS

Given that legal rules and decisions are ultimately founded on morality, the question arises: To what extent does morality become enforceable by law? If all law is ultimately moral, should all morals be law? This issue is too broad to be covered adequately here, but it is obviously an important concern and should receive some attention before more particular issues such as freedom of expression and the rights of the accused are discussed. Therefore, two conflicting positions on this issue of using laws to enforce morality will be presented. Lord Devlin, in responding to legalization of homosexuality in Britain, gave the following answer to the question of whether laws should enforce morals:

But an established morality is as necessary as good government to the welfare of society. Societies disintegrate from within more frequently than they are broken up by external pressures. There is disintegration when no common morality is observed and history shows that the loosening of moral bonds is often the first stage of disintegration, so that society is justified in taking the same steps to preserve its moral code as it does to preserve its government and other essential institutions. The suppression of vice is as much the law's business as the suppression of subversive activities; it is no more possible to define a sphere of private morality than it is to define one of private subversive activity. It is wrong to talk of private morality or of the law not being concerned with immorality as such or to try to set rigid bounds to the part which the law may play in the suppression of vice. There are not theoretical limits to the power of the State to legislate against treason and sedition, and likewise I think there can be no theoretical limits to legislation against immorality. You may argue that if a man's sins affect only himself it cannot be the concern of society. If he chooses to get drunk every night in the privacy of his own home, is any one except himself the worse for it? But suppose a quarter or a half of the population got drunk every night, what sort of society would it be? You cannot set a theoretical limit to legislate against drunkenness. [5, pp. 13–14]

Essentially, Devlin's position is that society has a right and an obligation to protect itself. It can do this by determining those acts which, if performed by a substantial number, would be harmful to society and then entirely restricting those acts. Because the acts would be harmful if substantial numbers participated in them, and because a substantial number is indeterminate, society must protect itself by outlawing the acts even on a small scale.

In answer to this position, Burton Leiser writes:

[Drinking] is society's business, he says, because society would not long survive if large numbers of people got drunk every night in the privacy of their homes. Of course not. But until society is in imminent danger because of such widespread private drunkenness, does it have the right to interfere with the private behavior of individual citizens? Because some activity might lead to disaster if it were carried out on a large scale, it does not follow that that activity ought to be outlawed if it is carried out on a small and relatively harmless scale. When vast numbers of people use detergents, there is danger of eutrophication of lakes, and such use can therefore properly be outlawed. But if only a few people had been using detergents, there would be no such washing habits. The rights of privacy and of freedom of action deserve to be protected, and should be interfered with only when private behavior ceases to be private and becomes a menace to the public or to some part of the public. [6, pp. 29–30]

Both men appear to be taking utilitarian positions, but Devlin's is a rule orientation while Leiser's seems to be more of an act orientation. In terms of legislation and law enforcement they differ greatly. Leiser would wait until a clear danger existed before acting, whereas Devlin would attempt to insure that the danger never arose. This obviously is an important difference and lies at the heart of much legal debate. For this reason, consideration of this issue is helpful in examining the legal arguments that follow.

In turning to more particular aspects of law and morality, we will examine opinions about the rights of the accused and freedom of expression. The discussion of various Supreme Court cases and the presentation of relevant excerpts from the justices' opinions, along with an occasional quotation of a legal scholar other than a Supreme Court justice, will present conflicting legal and moral opinions relating to each of the two issues we have chosen. As these cases are presented, the reader should remember that some decisions may not necessarily reflect the justices' personal views on morality, but simply their understanding of the people's will or "spirit."

THE RIGHTS OF THE ACCUSED

Fourth Amendment
The right of the people to be secure in their persons, houses, papers, and effects, against unreasonable searches and seizures, shall not be violated, and no Warrants shall issue, but upon probable cause, supported by Oath or affirmation, and particularly describing the place to be searched, and the persons or things to be seized.

Fifth Amendment
No person shall be held to answer for a capital, or otherwise infamous crime, unless on a presentment or indictment of a Grand Jury, except in cases arising in the land or naval forces, or in the Militia, when in actual service in time of War or public danger; nor shall any person be subject for the same offence to be twice put in jeopardy of life or limb; nor shall be compelled in any criminal case to be a witness against himself, nor be

deprived of life, liberty, or property, without due process of law; nor shall private property be taken for public use, without just compensation.

Sixth Amendment

In all criminal prosecutions, the accused shall enjoy the right to a speedy and public trial, by an impartial jury of the State and district wherein the crime shall have been committed, which district shall have been previously ascertained by law, and to be informed of the nature and cause of the accusation; to be confronted with the witnesses against him; to have compulsory process for obtaining witnesses in his favor, and to have the Assistance of Counsel for his defense.

The rights of the accused in criminal cases have been a subject of intense interest and importance in constitutional law, especially within the last thirty years. In that period such landmark cases as *Mapp* v. *Ohio, Escobedo* v. *Illinois,* and *Miranda* v. *Arizona* have occurred—all of which have been significant and far-reaching in the rights they have extended to those accused of criminal offense. For each of the cases that will be discussed, legal opinion has been divided: Have we gone too far in protecting the criminal's rights—so far that justice itself is seriously obstructed? Or have we merely chosen finally to enforce the rights that an accused person has always been guaranteed by the Constitution? In the following pages some specific instances of these questions will be presented.

Mapp v. *Ohio* (1961)

On 23 May 1957 the apartment of a Miss Mapp in Cleveland, Ohio, was broken into by police officers and searched for a person wanted for questioning in a recent bombing. The police had no search warrant and they did not find the individual for whom they were looking. However, in the course of their search, the police uncovered several obscene books and pictures belonging to Miss Mapp in violation of law. Although police action represented unlawful search and seizure, the obscene material was introduced as evidence at Miss Mapp's trial. She was convicted of possession of lewd and obscene material on this evidence. Question: Can material obtained illegally be introduced as evidence into a criminal trial or should it be excluded from trial proceedings? In an earlier case, *Wolf* v. *Colorado,* it had been decided that for state offenses and state trials, such evidence could be used. Should that decision be overturned? The Supreme Court decided that it should and accordingly reversed the conviction of Miss Mapp on the grounds that evidence seized unlawfully is not admissable in court because it is a violation of the individual's right to privacy. Writing for the Court, Justice Clark said:

There are those who say, as did Justice (then Judge) Cardozo, that under constitutional exclusionary doctrine "[t]he criminal is to go free because the constable has blundered." In some cases this will undoubtedly be the result. But, as was said in *Elkins*, "there is another consideration—the imperative of judicial integrity." The criminal goes free, if he must, but it is the law that sets him free. Nothing can destroy a government more quickly than its failure to observe its own laws, or worse, its disregard of the charter of its own existence. As Mr. Justice Brandeis, dissenting, said in *Olmstead v. United States*, (1928): "Our government is the potent, the omnipresent teacher. For good or for ill, it teaches the whole people by its example. . . . If the government becomes a lawbreaker, it breeds contempt for law; it invites every man to become a law unto himself; it invites anarchy." . . .

Having once recognized that the right to privacy embodied in the Fourth Amendment is enforceable against the States, and that the right to be secure against rude invasions of privacy by state officers is, therefore, constitutional in origin, we can no longer permit that right to remain an empty promise. Because it is enforceable in the same manner and to like effect as other basic rights secured by the Due Process Clause, we can no longer permit it to be revocable at the whim of any police officer who, in the name of law enforcement itself, chooses to suspend its enjoyment. Our decision, founded on reason and truth, gives to the individual no more than that which the Constitution guarantees him, to the police officer no less than that to which honest law enforcement is entitled, and, to the courts, that judicial integrity so necessary in the true administration of justice. [8, vol. 367, pp. 659, 660]

Olmstead v. *United States* (1928)

In an earlier case concerning the rights of the accused, the Supreme Court maintained that wiretapping is not a violation of the unlawful search-and-seizure clause of the Fourth Amendment. Chief Justice Taft wrote:

The Amendment itself shows that the search is to be of material things— the person, the house, his papers or his effects. The description of the warrant necessary to make the proceeding lawful, is that it must specify the place to be searched and the person or *things* to be seized. . . . The evidence was secured by the use of the sense of hearing and that only. There was no entry of the houses or offices of the defendants. . . . The intervening wires are not part of his house or office any more than are the highways along which they are stretched. [8, vol. 277, pp. 464–65]

Justice Holmes dissented from the Court, observing: "We have to choose and for my part I think it a less evil that some criminals should escape than that the Government should play an ignoble part" (8, vol. 277, p. 470). Justice Brandeis also dissented, declaring rather prophetically:

Clauses guaranteeing to the individual protection against specific abuses of power must have a similar capacity of adaptation to a changing world. . . . The progress of science in furnishing the Government with means of espionage is not likely to stop with wire-tapping. Ways may someday be developed by which the Government, without removing papers from secret drawers, can reproduce them in court, and by which it will be enabled to expose to a jury the most intimate occurrences of the home. . . . Can it be that the Constitution affords no protection against such invasions of individual security? [8, vol. 277, pp. 472–74]

In his decision, Chief Justice Taft seems to be utilizing the letter of the law in order to justify something else. What is his concern? His reasoning seems to be largely teleological. What about that of Justices Brandeis and Holmes? What is the ignoble act to which Holmes referred? To Brandeis, a more future-oriented rule-utilitarianism outcome is the basic issue.

Hoffa v. United States (1966)

A later case concerned with privacy and unlawful search and seizure involved the attempts of James Hoffa to bribe jury members during the so-called Test Fleet trial. Much of the evidence that led to Hoffa's conviction for bribery was obtained by a government informer, an individual named Partin, to whom Hoffa made a number of incriminating statements. Writing for the Court in upholding the conviction, Justice Stewart said:

What the Fourth Amendment protects is the security a man relies upon when he places himself or his property within a constitutionally protected area, be it his home or his office, his hotel room or his automobile. . . . In the present case, however, it is evident that no interest legitimately protected by the Fourth Amendment is involved. . . . Partin was in the suite by invitation, and every conversation which he heard was either directed to him or knowingly carried on in his presence. The petitioner, in a word, was not relying on the security of the hotel room; he was relying upon his misplaced confidence that Partin would not reveal his wrong-doing. . . . Neither this Court nor any member of it has ever expressed the view that the Fourth Amendment protects a wrongdoer's misplaced belief that a person to whom he voluntarily confides his wrongdoing will not reveal it. [8, vol. 385, pp. 301–302]

However, in a later case (*Osborn* v. *United States*), Justice Douglas made it clear that he would have voted to reverse the Hoffa decision had it been established that Partin was "planted" in Hoffa's suite to obtain incriminating evidence. Justice Douglas wrote:

[A] person may take the risk that a friend will turn on him and report to the police. But that is far different from the Government's "planting" a friend in a person's entourage so that he can secure incriminating evidence. In the one case, the Government has merely been the willing recipient of information supplied by a fickle friend. In the other, the Government has actively encouraged and participated in a breach of privacy by sending in an undercover agent. . . . the Government unlawfully enters a man's home when its agent crawls through a window, breaks down a door, enters surreptitiously, or, as alleged here, gets in by trickery and fraud. [8, vol. 385, p. 347]

Douglas had made his philosophy clear in an earlier case of eavesdropping (*Silverman* v. *United States*). In that case, the Court had applied the unlawful search-and-seizure clause to officials' use of an electronic device because, due to the depth of its penetration into a heat duct, the device was considered to be trespassing. Justice Douglas concurred that unlawful search and seizure had occurred, but for a different reason:

The depth of the penetration of the electronic device—even the degree of its remoteness from the inside of the house—is not the measure of the injury. . . . Our concern should not be with the trivialities of the local law of trespass, as the opinion of the Court indicates. But neither should the command of the Fourth Amendment be limited by nice distinctions turning on the kind of electronic equipment employed. Rather our sole concern should be with whether the privacy of the home was invaded. [8, vol. 365, p. 513]

In these cases of eavesdropping, it appears that Justices Holmes, Brandeis, and Douglas are all of the same general persuasion: Each holds the right of individual privacy above government attempts to obtain evidence. Is theirs a natural right, essentially rule-deontological, philosophy (even if, in the positivist sense they are only reflecting the will of the state), or is it a natural law, act-utilitarian, philosophy? The Court, in these cases, seems more willing to "ease up" on the right to privacy in order to obtain evidence and facilitate the course of justice, which appears to be a form of act-utilitarianism.

Escobedo v. *Illinois* (1964)

On 30 January 1960, Danny Escobedo was arrested for the murder of his brother and held at a Chicago police station for questioning. During the interrogation Escobedo was denied access to his attorney and, through extensive questioning, a confession was finally obtained. The Supreme Court of Illinois determined that the confession was voluntary and the conviction of the lower courts was upheld. The Supreme Court of the United States, however, reversed the conviction, ruling that Escobedo's right to assistance of counsel had been violated by not allowing him to seek advice from his attorney. Up until this case, the right to counsel had been considered applicable only to proceedings following indictment and not to police interrogation; this decision significantly altered that concept and has had a far-reaching effect on police proceedings. Justice Goldberg delivered the opinion of the Court.

The interrogation here was conducted before petitioner was formally indicted. But in the context of this case, that fact should make no difference. When petitioner requested, and was denied, an opportunity to consult with his lawyer, the investigation had ceased to be a general investigation of "an unsolved crime." Petitioner had become the accused, and the purpose of the interrogation was to "get him" to confess his guilt despite his constitutional right not to do so. At the time of his arrest and throughout the course of the interrogation, the police told petitioner that they had convincing evidence that he had fired the fatal shots. Without informing him of his absolute right to remain silent in the face of this accusation, the police urged him to make a statement. . . . The "guiding hand of counsel" was essential to advise petitioner of his rights in this delicate situation. This was the "stage when legal aid and advice" were most critical to petitioner. . . . It would exalt form over substance to make the right to counsel, under these circumstances, depend on whether at the time of the interrogation, the authorities had secured a formal indictment. Petitioner had, for all practical purposes, already been charged with murder.

It is argued that if the right to counsel is afforded prior to indictment, the number of confessions obtained by the police will diminish significantly, because most confessions are obtained during the period between arrest and indictment, and "any lawyer worth his salt will tell the suspect in no uncertain terms to make no statement to police under any circumstances." This argument, of course, cuts two ways. The fact that many confessions are obtained during this period points up its critical nature as a "stage when legal aid and advice" are surely needed. The right to counsel would indeed be hollow if it began at a period when few confessions were obtained. There is necessarily a direct relationship between the importance of a stage to the police in their quest for a confession and the criticalness of that stage to the accused in his need for legal advice. Our Constitution, unlike some others, strikes the balance in favor of the right of the accused to be advised by his lawyer of his privilege against self-incrimination.

We have learned the lesson of history, ancient and modern, that a system of criminal law enforcement which comes to depend on the "confession" will, in the long run, be less reliable and more subject to abuses than a system which depends on extrinsic evidence independently secured through skillful investigation. . . . We have also learned the companion lesson of history that no system of criminal justice can, or should, survive if it comes to depend for its continued effectiveness on the citizens' abdication through unawareness of their constitutional rights. No system worth preserving should have to *fear* that if an accused is permitted to consult with a lawyer, he will become aware of, and exercise, these rights. If the exercise of constitutional rights will thwart the effectiveness of a system of law enforcement, then there is something very wrong with that system.

Nothing we have said today affects the powers of the police to investigate "an unsolved crime" . . . by gathering information from witnesses and by other "proper investigative efforts." We hold only that when the process shifts from investigatory to accusatory—when its focus is on the accused and its purpose is to elicit a confession—our adversary system begins to operate, and, under the circumstances here, the accused must be permitted to consult with his lawyer. [8, vol. 378, pp. 485–86, 488–90, 492]

Justice Stewart dissented from the opinion of the Court. Somewhat caustically he wrote:

The confession which the Court today holds inadmissible was a voluntary one. It was given during the course of a perfectly legitimate police investigation of an unsolved murder. The Court says that what happened during this investigation "affected" the trial. I had always supposed that the whole purpose of a police investigation of a murder was to "affect" the trial of the murderer, and that it would be only an incompetent, unsuccessful, or corrupt investigation which would not do so. The Court further says that the

Illinois police officers did not advise the petitioner of his "constitutional rights" before he confessed to the murder. This Court has never held that the Constitution requires the police to give any "advice" under circumstances such as these. [8, vol. 378, p. 494]

Justice White also wrote a strong dissent.

The right to counsel now not only entitles the accused to counsel's advice and aid in preparing for trial but stands as an impenetrable barrier to any interrogation once the accused has become a suspect. From that very moment apparently his right to counsel attaches, a rule wholly unworkable and impossible to administer unless police cars are equipped with public defenders and undercover agents and police informants have defense counsel at their side. . . . Under this new approach one might just as well argue that a potential defendant is constitutionally entitled to a lawyer before, not after, he commits a crime, since it is then that crucial incriminating evidence is put within the reach of the government by the would-be accused.

The Court chooses to . . . rely on the virtues and morality of a system of criminal law enforcement which does not depend on the "confession." No such judgment is to be found in the Constitution. . . . The only "inquisitions" the Constitution forbids are those which compel incrimination. Escobedo's statements were not compelled and the Court does not hold that they were.

This new American judge's rule, which is to be applied in both federal and state courts, is perhaps thought to be a necessary safeguard against the possibility of extorted confessions. To this extent it reflects a deep-seated distrust of law enforcement officers everywhere, unsupported by relevant data or current material based upon our own experience. Obviously law enforcement officers can make mistakes and exceed their authority, as today's decision shows that even judges can do, but I have somewhat more faith than the Court evidently has in the ability and desire of prosecutors and of the power of the appellate courts to discern and correct such violations of the law.

I do not suggest for a moment that law enforcement will be destroyed by the rule announced today. The need for peace and order is too insistent for that. But it will be crippled and its task made a great deal more difficult, all in my opinion, for unsound, unstated reasons, which can find no home in any of the provisions of the Constitution. [8, vol. 378, pp. 496–97, 498–99]

It can be seen that in this case, as well as in the others, the dispute is largely between the process of order and insuring justice, apparently teleological (utilitarian) concerns, and individual rights, evidently based on deontological issues. Again, as was seen much earlier, this is a fundamental polarity in moral thought.

Miranda v. *Arizona* (1966)

On 13 March 1963, Ernesto Miranda was arrested at his home for kidnapping and rape and was taken to a Phoenix, Arizona, police station for questioning. While there he was identified by the victim and subsequently interrogated by police officers for two hours. During that time he signed a statement confessing to the crimes. At the top of the signed confession was a paragraph stating the entirely voluntary nature of the confession and the fact that the confession was made with Miranda's full understanding of his legal rights. Furthermore, during the interrogation Miranda made no request for counsel, to which he legally would have been entitled (*Escobedo* v. *Illinois*). Miranda's confession was ruled admissible by the Supreme Court of Arizona and he was found guilty. The United States Supreme Court, however, overturned the conviction, ruling that, because Miranda had not been advised of his right to counsel and his right not to incriminate himself had been ineffectively protected, his confession was inadmissable. Chief Justice Warren delivered the opinion of the court.

We start here, as we did in Escobedo, with the premise that our holding is not an innovation in our jurisprudence, but is an application of principles long recognized and applied in other settings. We have undertaken a thorough re-examination of the Escobedo decision and the principles it announced, and we reaffirm it. That case was but an explication of basic rights that are enshrined in our Constitution—that "No person . . . shall be compelled in any criminal case to be a witness against himself," and that "the accused shall . . . have the Assistance of Counsel"—rights which were put in jeopardy in that case through official overbearing. These precious rights were fixed in our Constitution only after centuries of persecution and struggle. And in the words of Chief Justice Marshall, they were secured "for ages to come and . . . designed to approach immortality as nearly as human institutions can approach it." [8, vol. 384, p. 442]

In speaking of the need for proper safeguards against self-incrimination during interrogation, the Chief Justice wrote:

It is obvious that such an interrogation environment is created for no purpose other than to subjugate the individual to the will of his examiner. This atmosphere carries its own badge of intimidation. To be sure, this is not physical intimidation, but it is equally destructive of human dignity. The current practice of incommunicado interrogation is at odds with one of our

Nation's most cherished principles—that the individual may not be compelled to incriminate himself. Unless adequate protective devices are employed to dispel the compulsion inherent in custodial surroundings, no statement obtained from the defendant can truly be the product of his free choice.

Today, then, there can be no doubt that the Fifth Amendment privilege is available outside of criminal court proceedings and serves to protect persons in all settings in which their freedom of action is curtailed in any significant way from being compelled to incriminate themselves. We have concluded that without proper safeguards the process of in-custody interrogation of persons suspected or accused of crime contains inherently compelling pressures which work to undermine the individual's will to resist and to compel him to speak where he would not otherwise do so freely. In order to combat these pressures and to permit a full opportunity to exercise the privilege against self-incrimination, the accused must be adequately and effectively apprised of his rights and the exercise of those rights must be fully honored. [8, vol. 384, pp. 457–58, 467]

It was in the Court's decision in this case that the fourfold warning to be given to any person in custody was developed: He has the right to remain silent, that anything the individual says may be used against him, that he has the right to the presence of an attorney during questioning, and that, if indigent, an attorney will be appointed to him without charge. In his dissenting opinion, Justice Harlan reacted to these rules on a utilitarian basis:

What the Court largely ignores is that the rules impair, if they will not eventually serve wholly to frustrate, an instrument of law enforcement that has long and quite reasonably been thought worth the price paid for it. There can be little doubt that the Court's new code would markedly decrease the number of confessions. To warn the suspect that he may remain silent and remind him that his confession may be used in court are minor obstructions. To require also an express waiver by the suspect and an end to questioning whenever he demurs must heavily handicap questioning. And to suggest or provide counsel for the suspect simply invites the end of the interrogation.

How much harm this decision will inflict on law enforcement cannot fairly be predicted with accuracy. . . . We do know that some crimes cannot be solved without confessions, that ample expert testimony attests to their importance in crime control, and that the Court is taking a real risk with society's welfare in imposing its new regime on the country. The social costs of crime are too great to call the new rules anything but a hazardous experimentation.

Miranda's oral and written confessions are now held inadmissable under the Court's new rules. One is entitled to feel astonished that the Constitution can be read to produce this result. These confessions were obtained during brief, daytime questioning conducted by two officers and unmarked by any of the traditional indicia of coercion. They assured a conviction for a brutal and unsettling crime, for which the police had and quite possibly could obtain little evidence other than the victim's identifications, evidence which is frequently unreliable. There was, in sum, a legitimate purpose, no perceptible unfairness, and certainly little risk of injustice in the interrogation. Yet the resulting confessions, and the responsible course of police practice they represent, are to be sacrificed to the Court's own finespun conception of fairness which I seriously doubt is shared by many thinking citizens in this country. [8, vol. 384, pp. 516–17, 518–19]

Justice White also dissented from the majority opinion:

Criticism of the Court's opinion cannot . . . stop with a demonstration that the factual and textual bases for the rule it propounds are, at best, less than compelling. Equally relevant is an assessment of the rule's consequences measured against community values. The Court's duty to assess the consequences of its action is not satisfied by the utterance of the truth that a value of our system of criminal justice is "to respect the inviolability of the human personality" and to require government to produce the evidence against the accused by its own independent labors. More than the human dignity of the accused is involved; the human personality of others in the society must also be preserved. Thus the values reflected by the privilege are not the sole desideratum; society's interest in the general security is of equal weight.

The most basic function of any government is to provide for the security of the individual and of his property. These ends of society are served by the criminal laws which for the most part are aimed at the prevention of crime. Without the reasonably effective performance of the task of preventing private violence and retaliation, it is idle to talk about human dignity and civilized values. [8, vol. 384, pp. 537, 539]

Justice White continues, somewhat bitterly:

I have no desire whatsoever to share the responsibility for [the] impact on the present criminal process.

In some unknown number of cases the Court's rule will return a killer, a rapist or other criminal to the streets and to the environment which produced him, to repeat the crime whenever it pleases him. As a consequence, there will not be a gain, but a loss, in human dignity. The real concern is not the unfortunate consequences of this new decision on the criminal law as an abstract, disembodied series of authoritative proscriptions, but the impact on those who rely on the public authority for protection and who without it can only engage in violent self-help with guns, knives and the help of their neighbors similarly inclined. There is, of course, a saving factor: the next victims are uncertain, unnamed and unrepresented in this case. [8, vol. 384, pp. 542–43]

The point at issue in this case is similar to that in all those above: What are the rights of the accused in relation to the process of justice and social welfare? Some justices adopt what apparently is a natural-right, rule-deontological position with regard to self-incrimination and the right to privacy, while others adopt a more act-utilitarian view.

FREEDOM OF EXPRESSION

First Amendment
Congress shall make no law respecting an establishment of religion, or prohibiting the free exercise thereof; or abridging the freedom of speech, or of the press; or the right of the people peaceably to assemble, and to petition the Government for a redress of grievances.

The scope of the First Amendment has been a source of debate among legal scholars for many years. The issue generally revolves around whether freedom of speech is an absolute—a deontological rule—or merely a principle, or an interest, to be balanced against other interests. The notion of balancing implies an act-utilitarian base rather than a deontological one. We give examples of both types of reasoning so that the reader can choose between them or, if possible, formulate a third possibility.

Schenck v. *United States* (1919)

While the United States was engaged with Germany in World War I, a group of American dissenters published a pamphlet encouraging eligible men not to submit to the draft. The defendants were convicted for causing insubordination and for obstructing enlistment in the Armed Forces of the United States. The Supreme Court upheld the conviction. It was in this decision that Justice Holmes formulated the famous doctrine of a clear and present danger:

We admit that in many places and in ordinary times the defendants in saying all that was said in the circular would have been within their constitutional rights. But the character of every act depends upon the circumstances in which it is done. The most stringent protection of free speech would not protect a man in falsely shouting fire in a theatre and causing a panic. It does not even protect a man from an injunction against uttering words that may have all the effect of force. The question in every case is whether the words used are used in such circumstances and are of such a nature as to create a clear and present danger that they will bring about the substantive evils that Congress has a right to prevent. It is a question of proximity and degree. When a nation is at war many things that might be said in time of peace are such a hindrance to its effort that their utterance will not be endured so long as men fight and that no Court could regard them as protected by any constitutional right. [8, vol. 249, p. 52]

Gitlow v. New York (1925)

The defendant in *Gitlow* v. *New York* was a member of the Left Wing Section of the Socialist party in New York. He was also a member of the section's National Council and as such was party to the printing and distributing of a "Left Wing Manifesto," which urged overthrow of the democratic state by revolution. He was brought to trial for "criminal anarchy" and convicted in New York State. The Supreme Court upheld the conviction. Writing the majority opinion, Justice Sanford argued:

The State cannot reasonably be required to measure the danger from every such utterance in the nice balance of a jeweler's scale. A single revolutionary spark may kindle a fire that, smoldering for a time, may burst into a sweeping and destructive conflagration. It cannot be said that the State is acting arbitrarily or unreasonably when in the exercise of its judgment as to the measures necessary to protect the public peace and safety, it seeks to extinguish the spark without waiting until it has enkindled the flame or blazed into the conflagration. It cannot reasonably be required to defer the adoption of measures for its own peace and safety until the revolutionary utterances lead to actual disturbances of the public peace or imminent and immediate danger of its own destruction; but it may, in the exercise of its judgment, suppress the threatened danger in its incipiency. [8, vol. 268, p. 669]

Justice Holmes dissented from the Court's decision. In this passage his legal positivism is manifest:

It is said that this manifesto was more than a theory, that it was an incitement. Every idea is an incitement. It offers itself for belief and if believed it is acted on unless some other belief outweighs it or some failure of energy stifles the movement at its birth. The only difference between the expression of an opinion and an incitement in the narrower sense is the speaker's enthusiasm for the result. Eloquence may set fire to reason. But whatever may be thought of the redundant discourse before us it had no chance of starting a present conflagration. If in the long run the beliefs expressed in proletarian dictatorship are destined to be accepted by the dominant forces of the community, the only meaning of free speech is that they should be given their chance and have their way. [8, vol. 268, p. 673]

In two decisions by Justice Holmes we have seen him propose the clear-and-present-danger test—a balancing concept—and, nevertheless, argue that if the people ever opt for a proletarian dictatorship, the only meaning of free speech is that they should have it. Against what standard is Justice Holmes measuring "clear and present danger"—an inherent concept of justice or the will of the people?

Numerous legal scholars have also written on the First Amendment. Carl Auerbach, for instance, has argued that absolutism contains an inherent contradiction. Against Holmes, he maintains that a democracy has every right to suppress totalitarian movement within its borders, irrespective of clear and present danger.

. . . if the theory that there are no political orthodoxies is taken to mean that we must also be skeptical about the value of freedom and therefore tolerate freedom's enemies, it will tend to produce, in practice, the very absolutism it was designed to avoid—as experience with modern totalitarianism demonstrates. When, therefore, Mill says that "we can never be sure that the opinion we are endeavoring to stifle is a false opinion," he could not consistently have been referring to the opinion that freedom of opinion itself should be suppressed. There is a passage in *On Liberty* which, I think, supports this inference and has significance for our contemporary problem. Asking whether the law should enforce an agreement under which an individual sells himself, voluntarily, as a slave, Mill says no and argues: "The reason for not interfering, unless for the sake of others, with a person's voluntary acts, is consideration for his liberty. . . . but by selling himself for a slave, he abdicates his liberty; he foregoes any future use of it, beyond that single act. He therefore defeats, in his own case, the very purpose which is the justification of allowing him to dispose of himself. . . . The principle of freedom cannot require that he should be free not to be free. It is not freedom, to be allowed to alienate his freedom."

So, in suppressing totalitarian movements a democratic society is not acting to protect the status quo, but the very same interests which freedom of speech itself seeks to secure—the possibility of peaceful progress under freedom. That suppression may sometimes have to be the means of securing and enlarging freedom is a paradox which is not unknown in other areas of the law of modern democratic states. The basic "postulate," therefore, which should "limit and control" the First Amendment is that it is part of the framework for a constitutional democracy and should, therefore, not be used to curb the power of Congress to exclude from the political struggle those groups which, if victorious, would crush democracy and impose totalitarianism. Whether in any particular case and at any particular time, Congress should suppress a totalitarian movement should be regarded as a matter of wisdom for its sole determination. But a democracy should claim the moral and constitutional right to suppress these movements whenever it deems it advisable to do so. [1, pp. 188–89]

To this point, two basic theories of balancing freedom of speech have been advanced: that of Auerbach and the Supreme Court in *Gitlow* v. *New York*, and that of Justice Holmes. The first proposes the suppression of all speech intended, essentially, to overthrow free speech, while the second maintains that freedom of speech guarantees the right of the people ultimately to overthrow freedom of speech itself. Only imminent danger can abridge the right of speech; if the people ultimately do not desire free speech then loss of that freedom is not dangerous because it is, in fact, what the people want. In that case there is no clear and present danger and, therefore, no basis for the Court to act.

It remains, however, to illustrate an absolute theory of the First Amendment. Perhaps the most interesting of the absolute arguments is that of Alexander Meiklejohn:

. . . no one who reads with care the text of the First Amendment can fail to be startled by its absoluteness. The phrase, "Congress shall make no law . . . abridging the freedom of speech," is unqualified. It admits of no exceptions. To say that no laws of a given type shall be made means that no laws of that type shall, under any circumstances, be made. That prohibition holds good in war as in peace, in danger as in security. The men who adopted the Bill of Rights were not ignorant of the necessities of war or of national danger. It would, in fact, be nearer to the truth to say that it was exactly those necessities which they had in mind as they planned to defend freedom of discussion against them.

No one can doubt that, in any well-governed society, the legislature has both the right and the duty to prohibit certain forms of speech. Libellous assertions may be, and must be, forbidden and punished. So too must slander. Words which incite men to crime are themselves criminal and must be dealt with as such. [T]reason may be expressed by speech or writing. And, in those cases, decisive repressive action by the government is imperative for the sake of the general welfare. All these necessities that speech be limited are recognized and provided for under the Constitution. They were not unknown to the writers of the First Amendment. That amendment, then, we make take it for granted, *does not forbid the abridging of speech*. But, at the same time, *it does forbid the abridging of the freedom of speech*. It is to the solving of that paradox, that apparent self-contradiction, that we are summoned if, as free men, we wish to know what the right of freedom of speech is.

. . . the vital point, as stated negatively, is that no suggestion of policy shall be denied a hearing because it is on one side of the issue rather than another. And this means that though citizens may, on other grounds, be barred from speaking, they may not be barred because their views are thought to be false or dangerous. No plan of action shall be outlawed because someone in control thinks it unwise, unfair, un-American. No speaker may be declared "out of order" because we disagree with what he intends to say.

If, then, on any occasion in the United States it is allowable to say that the Constitution is a good document it is equally allowable, in that situation, to say that the Constitution is a bad document. If a public building may be used in which to say, in time of war, that the war is justified, then the same building may be used in which to say that it is not justified. If it be publicly argued that conscription for armed service is moral and necessary, it may likewise be publicly argued that it is immoral and unnecessary. If it may be said that American political institutions are superior to those of England or Russia or Germany, it may, with equal freedom, be said that those of England or Russia or Germany are superior to ours. These conflicting views may be expressed, must be expressed, not because they are valid, but because they are relevant. If they are responsibly entertained by anyone, we, the voters, need to hear them. When a question of policy is "before the house," free men choose to meet it not with their eyes shut, but with their eyes open. To be afraid of ideas, any idea, is to be unfit for self-government. Any such suppression of ideas about the common good, the First Amendment condemns with its absolute disapproval. The freedom of ideas shall not be abridged.

In [1919], and in the years which have ensued, the court, following the lead of Justice Oliver Wendell Holmes, has persistently ruled that the freedom of speech of the American community may constitutionally be abridged by legislative action. That ruling annuls the most significant purpose of the First Amendment. It destroys the intellectual basis of our plan of self-government. The court has interpreted the dictum that Congress shall not abridge the freedom of speech by defining the conditions under which such abridging is allowable. Congress, we are now told, is forbidden to destroy our freedom except when it finds it advisable to do so.

In the judgment of the Constitution, some preventions are more evil than are the evils from which they would save us. And the First Amendment is a case in point. If that amendment means anything, it means that certain substantive evils which, in principle, Congress has a right to prevent, must be endured if the only way of avoiding them is by the abridging of that freedom of speech upon which the entire structure of our free institutions rests. [7, pp. 20, 21, 26–27, 27–28, 30, 44]

Here Meiklejohn offers a type of mixed deontological argument. He seems to argue first by principle—it is simply wrong, under any circumstances, to abridge freedom of speech or of ideas. At any time if one idea may be put forth, freedom requires the right of a conflicting, even harmful, idea to also be put forth. The clear-and-present-danger test, based on act-utilitarian principles, is discarded as being incongruent with this principle. Second, he closes with the proposal that freedom of speech is the foundation of the entire structure of our free institutions—this implies a teleological, rule-utilitarian principle. Meiklejohn seems to be arguing (a) that the very act of abridging freedom of speech is itself wrong, and (b) even if it were not, the right to speech is the foundation of our free society and our society will be maintained only if we always make decisions in its favor.

We have dealt here with three theories of the First Amendment's scope and power. The differences seem to be largely moral ones. The Court, in *Gitlow* v. *New York*, was largely teleological and utilitarian in its decision. Holmes's position is also teleological and utilitarian, but on a much narrower scale and with the added provision that it is the people who should decide the teleological end, not the Court. Finally, there is a mixed element in the argument of Meiklejohn, making it, apparently, a form of mixed rule-deontology.

Roth v. United States, Alberts v. California (1957)

Roth, a New York publisher, was convicted of mailing obscene and lewd material in violation of federal obscenity laws. Alberts, a California mail-order seller, was convicted of possession of obscene books for sale in violation of California obscenity laws. Both convictions were upheld by the Supreme Court. It was ruled that obscenity does not come under the protection of the First Amendment. Writing for the Court, Justice Brennan stated:

> The dispositive question is whether obscenity is utterance within the area of protected speech and press. Although this is the first time the question has been squarely presented to this Court, either under the First Amendment or under the Fourteenth Amendment, expressions found in numerous opinions indicate that this Court has always assumed that obscenity is not protected by the freedoms of speech and press. [8, vol. 354, p. 481]

In an important concurring opinion, relying on a different type of reasoning, Chief Justice Warren observed:

> The line dividing the salacious or pornographic from literature or science is not straight and unwavering. Present laws depend largely upon the effect that the materials may have upon those who receive them. It is manifest that the same object may have a different impact, varying according to the part of the community it reached. But there is more to these cases. It is not the book that is on trial; it is a person. The conduct of the defendant is the central issue, not the obscenity of a book or picture. The nature of the materials is, of course, relevant as an attribute of the defendant's conduct, but the materials are thus placed in context from which they draw color and character. A wholly different result might be reached in a different setting.
>
> [The defendants] were plainly engaged in the commercial exploitation of the morbid and shameful craving for materials with prurient effect. I believe that the State and Federal Governments can constitutionally punish such conduct. That is all that these cases present to us, and that is all we need to decide. [8, vol. 354, pp. 495, 496]

In concurring with the Alberts decision, Justice Harlan made this observation with respect to the effects of pornography:

> . . . even assuming that pornography cannot be deemed ever to cause, in an immediate sense, criminal sexual conduct, other interests within the proper cognizance of the States may be protected by the prohibition placed on such materials. The State can reasonably draw the inference that over a long period of time the indiscriminate dissemination of materials, the essential character of which is to degrade sex, will have an eroding effect on moral standards. And the State has a legitimate interest in protecting the privacy of the home against invasion of unsolicited obscenity. [8, vol. 354, p. 502]

In a dissenting opinion, Justice Douglas argued:

The test of obscenity the Court endorses today gives the censor free range over a vast domain. To allow the State to step in and punish mere speech or publication that the judge or the jury thinks has an *undesirable* impact on thoughts but that is not shown to be a part of unlawful action is drastically to curtail the First Amendment. As recently stated by two of our outstanding authorities on obscenity, "The danger of influencing a change in the current moral standards of the community, or of shocking or offending readers, or of stimulating sex thoughts or desires apart from objective conduct, can never justify the losses to society that result from interference with literary freedom."

[If] the First Amendment guarantee of freedom of speech and press is to mean anything in this field, it must allow protests even against the moral code that the standard of the day sets for the community. The legality of a publication in this country should never be allowed to turn either on the purity of thought which it instills in the mind of the reader or on the degree to which it offends the community conscience. By either test the role of the censor is exalted, and society's values in literary freedom are sacrificed.

I would give the broad sweep of the First Amendment full support. I have the same confidence in the ability of our people to reject noxious literature as I have in their capacity to sort out the true from the false in theology, economics, politics, or any other field. [8, vol. 354, pp. 509–10, 513, 514]

In response to the charge that pornography has no clear behavioral effects, one legal scholar, Alexander Bickel, has argued in this manner:

The question about obscenity is not whether books get girls pregnant, or sexy or violent movies turn men to crime. To view it in this way is to try to shoehorn the obscenity problem into the clear-and-present-danger analysis, and the fit is a bad one. Books, let us assume, do not get girls pregnant; at any rate, there are plenty of other efficient causes of pregnancy, as of crime. We may assume further that it is right to protect privacy, and that we have no business therefore, punishing anyone for amusing himself obscenely in his home. But the question is, should there be a right to obtain obscene books and pictures in the market, or to foregather in public places—discreet, but accessible to all—with others who share a taste for the obscene? To grant this right is to affect the world about the rest of us, and to impinge on other privacies and other interests, as those concerned with the theater in New York have found, apparently to their surprise. Perhaps each of us can, if he wishes, effectively avert the eye and stop the ear. Still, what is commonly read and seen and heard and done intrudes upon us all, wanted or not, for it constitutes our environment. [3, pp. 72–73]

The issue in these opinions on obscenity appears to be the same as with the cases previously mentioned: To what extent, if any, can the right to freedom of speech be abridged? Is it an absolute right or value (as implied by Douglas) or is it an interest to be balanced against other interests and consequences? Do we adopt a rule-deontological or rule-utilitarian principle, or, seemingly with the majority of the Court, an *act* orientation, and if so, how then do we decide in particular cases?

In conjunction with this issue of obscenity, it is important to note that the Court has maintained that *ideas* commonly considered obscene are protected by the First Amendment. In a case in which New York State denied license to show the film "Lady Chatterly's Lover" because it presented adultery in a favorable light, the Court ruled that the First Amendment had been violated (*Kingsley International Pictures Corp.* v. *Regents*). In delivering the opinion of the court, Justice Stewart observed:

> What New York has done, therefore, is to prevent the exhibition of a motion picture because that picture advocates an idea—that adultery under certain circumstances may be proper behavior. Yet the First Amendment's basic guarantee is of freedom to advocate ideas. The State, quite simply, has thus struck at the very heart of constitutionally protected liberty.
>
> It is contended that the State's action was justified because the motion picture attractively portrays a relationship which is contrary to the moral standards, the religious precepts, and the legal code of its citizenry. This argument misconceives what it is that the Constitution protects. Its guarantee is not confined to the expression of ideas that are conventional or shared by a majority. It protects advocacy of the opinion that adultery may sometimes be proper, no less than advocacy of socialism or the single tax. And in the realm of ideas it protects expression which is eloquent no less than that which is unconvincing. [8, col. 360, p. 688–89]

Since the Roth case, the Supreme Court has consistently maintained that obscenity is not protected by the First Amendment's guarantee of freedom of speech. A major legal question since that time, therefore, has been, Exactly what constitutes obscenity—how is it to be defined? The more fundamental issue, however, is not what the precise definition of obscenity should be, but that it should be defined at all. This is the moral question raised by the First Amendment. Is the right of the individual to freedom of expression an absolute right or value that no consequence (other than criminality) can abridge? Or is it to be carefully balanced against social consequences, or even religious principles of moral decency? All of these questions revolve around basic moral issues, making the matter extremely complicated and volatile.

By now, however, the reader should be in an improved position to discuss such issues. The exercises of the last two chapters should not only have assisted the reader in recognizing types of moral reasoning, or moral content, but should have helped toward some clarification of his own moral thought as well. If so, then the primary purposes of this book have been achieved.

NOTE

1. This discussion is oversimplified, of course. There are several different philosophies of American law (e.g., legal positivism, sociological jurisprudence, historical jurisprudence, legal realism, etc.), and each views the relationship of law and morality differently. Nevertheless, whether a judge makes overtly moral decisions or whether he acts merely on the will (legislation) or "spirit" of the people, his decision is often based fundamentally on moral concerns. The difference is that in one case the judge defines morality and in the other case the "people" do. See Berman (2) and Bodenheimer (4) for a fuller discussion of American philosophies of law.

Appendix

Format. The basic format used by Rest in his objective test of moral reasoning (which was designed to reveal Kohlbergian structural elements in the subject's thinking) was followed in the construction of this test. There are some major changes in the content of the test (i.e., new dilemmas) and some rather minor wording changes (i.e., rewording of "importance" headings for rating purposes). First, a dilemma is presented followed by a question as to what one should do and a series of statements outlining a reason for the action. The subject is asked to indicate his choice and reasoning preference.

Dilemma construction. Since the most widely cross-cutting issue in moral philosophy is that of the end versus the means (or, roughly, teleology versus deontology) the rationale in constructing dilemmas for the test was to provide a clear end-versus-means dilemma in each story. Issues tapped were: stealing versus saving a life (the familiar Heinz story, in this test called "The Drug"); turning in a good man versus breaking the law ("The Deserter"); mercy killing (avoidance of pain) versus killing ("The Dying Loved One"); providing for one's family versus lying ("The Taxes"); and saving two lives versus killing ("The Mine Shaft"). During a small pilot study, the dilemmas were written and rewritten until each was considered a difficult dilemma by most subjects (college students). We found in the pilot study that subjects responded differently when the dilemma concerned someone else than when it directly concerned the subject himself. Specifically, most subjects said that decisions were more difficult when they were directly implicated rather than when they were merely deciding what someone else should do. Accordingly, because this difficulty was considered evidence of greater moral involvement, the dilemmas were so worded as to place the subject himself in the moral situation. This technique represents a departure from that used by Rest and seems, at least for the purposes of this test, to be an improvement.

259

Item construction.   The reasoning statements (issue items) that are rated and then ranked according to their relative importance for each dilemma were written to reflect the various types of moral reasoning as categorized in moral philosophy. For example, the item "If everyone stole society would be so chaotic that there could be no happiness or peace of mind for anyone" represents nonhedonistic rule-utilitarianism. It is nonhedonistic in its emphasis on happiness and peace of mind and rule-utilitarian in its emphasis on utilitarian rules. For each story there is an issue item representing each of the following types of reasoning:

> hedonistic egoism
> nonhedonistic egoism
> hedonistic rule-utilitarianism
> nonhedonistic rule-utilitarianism
> hedonistic act-utilitarianism
> nonhedonistic act-utilitarianism
> rule-deontology
> act-deontology

As the subject rates the items according to their importance he is rating these types of reasoning. This provides an index over five dilemmas about the subject's preferred type(s) of moral reasoning or content.

It should be noted that the act deontologist who acts purely on intuition or who existentially "invents," may, on a given dilemma, say either that something is "just right" or that it is "just wrong"— there is no way to tell which "feel" he might have. Thus, for each of the dilemmas, both "right" and "wrong" act-deontology items are included, making a total of nine ethical statements from which to choose for each dilemma.

Also, it should be noted that the deontological items (both rule and act) represent pure forms of deontology. Mixed forms of deontology are inferred from total test scores—how the individual combines these deontological types of reasoning with others.

Also, the test includes only two categories of the good. For the sake of simplicity *nonhedonism* is intended to include both qualitative hedonism and nonhedonism, while *hedonism* refers exclusively to quantitative hedonism. The added simplicity this provides compensates for the degree of detail that is lost as a result.

Finally, among the items for each dilemma is either an irrelevant statement (e.g., "Sometimes you've had to go downtown yourself") or a meaningless statement (e.g., "What if everyone proved the substantiality of taxation to be more transient than the cessation of essence?"). These provide some control for random marking and bring to ten the total number of issue items to be rated for each dilemma.

Data collection. Tests were administered to undergraduate students enrolled in a marriage course at Brigham Young University. The test was administered again four weeks later with no intervening treatment or discussion. Invalid tests were determined and discarded following the rule, suggested by Rest for his test: look at a subject's check-mark ratings of his first and second ranks, and discard the whole test if there are inconsistencies on more than two dilemmas. This procedure was followed for both pre- and posttests, and the subject's entire protocol was discarded if either test violated this rule of thumb. Analyzable protocols numbered forty-two (female=27, male=15). Mean age of subjects was 22.4.

Results. Results of the test-retest stability analysis were as follows:

Hedonistic egoism	.32
Nonhedonistic egoism	.85
Hedonistic rule-utilitarianism	.75
Nonhedonistic rule-utilitarianism	.80
Hedonistic act-utilitarianism	.75
Nonhedonistic act-utilitarianism	.73
Rule-deontology	.60
Act-deontology	.75
	$\overline{X} = .69$

Since there were so few subjects who responded to the category of hedonistic egoism there is particular concern over the accuracy of its reliability coefficient of only .32. Without this category, the mean coefficient for the other seven categories is .75. This mean reveals more closely the reliability of the entire instrument.

As mentioned in chapter ten, and discussed more fully below, it is possible to collapse over various dimensions to create new scores for each subject. For example, preference for utilitarianism can be obtained by combining nonhedonistic utilitarianism, egoistic utilitarianism, and act- and rule-utilitarianism scores. The reliability coefficients of these combined scores are:

Egoism	.64
Rule-utilitarianism	.89
Act-utilitarianism	.84
Hedonism	.64
Nonhedonism	.65
Rule-oriented	.83
Act-oriented	.83
Utilitarianism	.82
Deontology	.68
	$\overline{X} = .76$

The above test-retest reliability coefficients were considered amply sufficient. The accuracy of the reasoning responses (items) was checked by agreement between the authors and then between the authors and a moral philosopher. Total agreement was the criterion. Later, six undergraduate students were asked to learn the categories of moral philosophy and then assign each item to the appropriate category. A 90 percent inter-rater agreement was obtained.

Currently, a great deal of additional data on the test is being sought, including its correlation with the structural elements measured in Rest's Defining Issues Test, as well as its correlation with other personality tests. Other correlational and demographic data are being sought as well. Preliminary evidence, however, already suggests that this test may be very useful to researchers interested in exploring the content dimensions of moral reasoning.

INSTRUCTIONS FOR SCORING THE
MORAL CONTENT TEST

1. A scoring grid resembling the one presented below should be available for each subject's test.

	Hedonistic Egoism	Nonhedonistic Egoism	Hedonistic R-U	Nonhedonistic R-U	Hedonistic A-U	Nonhedonistic A-U	Rule-Deontology	Act-Deontology
Drug								
Deserter								
Relative								
Taxes								
Mine								

2. The following is a scoring key for each of the dilemmas. Thus, for "The Drug," statement 1 represents hedonistic egoism, statement 2 is a meaningless item, and so on.

The Drug
1. Hedonistic egoism
2. Meaningless
3. Rule-deontology
4. Nonhedonistic R-U
5. Nonhedonistic A-U
6. Nonhedonistic egoism
7. Act-deontology
8. Hedonistic R-U
9. Hedonistic A-U
10. Act-deontology

The Deserter
1. Meaningless
2. Act-deontology
3. Nonhedonistic egoism
4. Hedonistic R-U
5. Hedonistic A-U
6. Act-deontology
7. Hedonistic egoism
8. Nonhedonistic R-U
9. Nonhedonistic A-U
10. Rule-deontology

Dying Relative
1. Rule-deontology
2. Hedonistic A-U
3. Hedonistic R-U
4. Meaningless
5. Act-deontology
6. Hedonistic egoism
7. Nonhedonistic R-U
8. Nonhedonistic A-U
9. Act-deontology
10. Nonhedonistic egoism

The Taxes
1. Nonhedonistic R-U
2. Hedonistic A-U
3. Nonhedonistic egoism
4. Hedonistic egoism
5. Act-deontology
6. Hedonistic R-U
7. Meaningless
8. Rule-deontology
9. Act-deontology
10. Nonhedonistic A-U

The Mine
1. Act-deontology
2. Hedonistic A-U
3. Hedonistic egoism
4. Hedonistic R-U
5. Nonhedonistic A-U
6. Act-deontology
7. Nonhedonistic R-U
8. Rule-deontology
9. Meaningless
10. Nonhedonistic egoism

3. At the bottom of each page of rated statements, the subject has also ranked the four statements he considers most important. The rankings are in order from *Most important* to *Fourth most important*. Values for these rankings are as follows:

Most important:	4 points
Second most important:	3 points
Third most important:	2 points
Fourth most important:	1 point

4. As you read the rankings for each dilemma, fill in the scores (4, 3, 2, and 1) for the preferred types of reasoning in the appropriate boxes on the scoring grid. For example, suppose a subject's rankings look like this for the drug dilemma:

Most important:	10
Second most important:	3
Third most important:	8
Fourth most important:	4

Then, looking at the scoring key, it can be seen that statement 10 represents act-deontology. Thus, in the scoring grid, the act-deontology box for the drug dilemma is given 4 points. Similarly, it can be seen that the second most important statement, 3, represents rule-deontology. Thus, the rule-deontology box for the drug dilemma is given 3 points, and so on: the hedonistic rule-utilitarianism box (for statement 8) is given 2 points, and the nonhedonistic rule-utilitarianism box (for statement 4) is given 1 point. This scoring can be seen in the following sample grid.

	Hedo-nistic Egoism	Nonhedo-nistic Egoism	Hedo-nistic R-U	Nonhedo-nistic R-U	Hedo-nistic A-U	Nonhedo-nistic A-U	Rule-Deon-tology	Act-Deon-tology
Drug			2	1			3	4
Deserter								
Relative								
Taxes								
Mine								

5. After this procedure has been followed for all five dilemmas of a subject's test, the grid will be complete. Now, simply add the scores for each of the types of reasoning. The following example is taken from an actual grid.

	Hedo-nistic Egoism	Nonhedo-nistic Egoism	Hedo-nistic R-U	Nonhedo-nistic R-U	Hedo-nistic A-U	Nonhedo-nistic A-U	Rule-Deon-tology	Act-Deon-tology
Drug			2	1			3	4
Deserter			2		1		4	3
Relative			2	1			4	3
Taxes			1	2			3	4
Mine			1	2			4	3
	0	0	8	6	1	0	18	17

6. The raw totals seen above are appropriate for comparing those eight specific categories with one another. For instance, it can be seen that rule- and act-deontology received far higher scores than any other of the ethical categories. The two rule-utilitarianism categories also received fairly high scores. At a glance, then, such a grid of raw scores allows a meaningful comparison of the relative weight of these eight specific components in the individual's moral thought.

However, if you desire to collapse categories and find, for instance, the total egoism score or the total hedonism score or the total utilitarianism score, etc., then the raw score must be converted to a percentage score. This is done by dividing the total raw score by the total *possible* score of those combined categories.

For instance, there are two deontology columns. If you want to obtain the total deontology score, disregarding rule and act orientations, the total possible score must first be figured. Thus, the highest possible score will be reached if all 4s and 3s fall into those two categories. This would result in five 4s and five 3s, making a total of 35 possible points. To get a percentage score, the raw score must be divided by this total possible score of 35. In the above example the raw score is also 35, yielding a percentage score of 100.

Conversely, utilitarianism includes four columns. The total possible score is thus obtained if all 4, 3, 2, and 1 scores fall into these four columns. This would make a total of 50 possible points. Thus, the raw score for these combined columns must be divided by 50 to get the percentage score. In the above example the raw score for these columns is 15, yielding a percentage score of 30.

The following list specifies the procedure necessary to obtain percentage score for all of the collapsed categories.

Egoism: Add columns 1 and 2, divide by 35.
Hedonism: Add columns 1, 3, and 5, divide by 45.
Nonhedonism: Add columns 2, 4, and 6, divide by 45.
Rule-utilitarianism: Add columns 3 and 4, divide by 35.
Act-utilitarianism: Add columns 5 and 6, divide by 35.
Utilitarianism: Add columns 3, 4, 5, and 6, divide by 50.
Deontology: Add columns 7 and 8, divide by 35.
Rule orientation: Add columns 3, 4, and 7, divide by 45.
Act orientation: Add columns 5, 6, and 8, divide by 45.

Thus, these are the percentage score for the collapsed categories in the above example:

Egoism:	0
Hedonism:	20
Nonhedonism:	13
Rule-utilitarianism:	40
Act-utilitarianism:	03
Utilitarianism:	30
Deontology:	100
Rule orientation:	71
Act orientation:	40

Thus, it can be seen that this individual is highly deontological and highly rule oriented as well. The moderately high score on act orientation is due almost exclusively to the influence of deontology. Similarly, the utilitarianism used is almost exclusively of the rule variety. Thus, his moral reasoning is highly deontological and rule oriented, and this provides a fairly global picture of his approach to moral issues. Obtaining this global picture can often show clear trends in moral thought that are not immediately apparent when comparing only the raw scores of the eight specific categories. For this reason it is usually advisable to compute both types of data, specific and global.

CAUTIONS IN SCORING THE TEST

1. As mentioned earlier, the test presently includes only two categories of the good. *Nonhedonism* is intended to include both qualitative hedonism and nonhedonism, while *hedonism* refers exclusively to quantitative hedonism. This is an important factor for interpreting test scores.

2. Also as mentioned earlier, it will also be noticed that for each dilemma, two act-deontological statements (i.e., "It is just right" and "It is just wrong") are provided. This is because it is impossible to predict how some intuitive act-deontologists will respond in a given situation. Both alternatives, therefore, must be provided.

If an individual ranks both act-deontological statements, however, give points only to the one which is ranked higher. Ignore the second one; do not assign it any points.

3. If a subject's rankings do not consistently correspond with his check-mark ratings, discard the test. As a rule of thumb, generally following Rest's suggestion, look at the subject's check-mark ratings

of his first and second ranks, and discard the test if there are inconsistencies on three or more of the dilemmas.

4. Discard the test if two dilemmas have more than seven items rated at the same level of importance (e.g., "To Some Extent important").

5. If an individual fails to rank all four statements, simply assign the appropriate points to those he did rank.

References

INTRODUCTION

1. Sellars, W. Science and ethics. A revised version of a paper read to the Phoebe Griffin Noyes Library Association, Old Lyme, Conn. 26 January 1960.

CHAPTER ONE

1. Aristotle. *Nicomachean ethics*. In McKeon, R., ed., *The basic works of Aristotle*. New York: Random House, 1941.
2. Bailey, C. *Epicurus: The extant remains*. Oxford: Clarendon Press, 1926.
3. Bentham, J. An introduction to the principles of morals and legislation (1879). In Bowring, J., ed., *The works of Jeremy Bentham*. Vol. 1. New York: Russell & Russell, 1962.
4. Dewey, J. *Human nature and conduct*. New York: Modern Library, 1930.
5. Frankena, W. K. *Ethics*. 2nd ed. Englewood Cliffs, N.J.: Prentice-Hall, 1973.
6. Garner, R. T., and Rosen, B. *Moral philosophy: A systematic introduction to normative ethics and meta-ethics*. New York: Macmillan, 1967.
7. Hobbes, T. *Leviathan*. London: Routledge & Sons, 1885.
8. Hospers, J. *Human conduct: Problems of ethics*. New York: Harcourt Brace Jovanovich, 1972.
9. Kant, I. *Lectures on ethics*. Trans. Louis Infeld. New York: Harper & Row, 1963.
10. Mill, J. S. "Mill's journal." In Schneewind, J. B., ed., *Mill's ethical writings*. New York: Collier, 1965.
11. Mill, J. S. *Utilitarianism*, ed. Gorovitz, S. New York: Bobbs-Merrill, 1971.
12. Nietzsche, F. *The antichrist*. In Kaufmann, W., ed., *The portable Nietzsche*. New York: Viking, 1954.
13. Paterson, R. W. K. *The nihilistic egoist: Max Stirner*. London: Oxford University Press, 1971.
14. Plato. *The republic*. In Loomis, L. R., ed., *Plato: Five great dialogues*. Trans. B. Jowett. New York: Walter J. Black, 1942.
15. Prichard, H. A. Duty and interest. In Sellars, W. and Hospers, J., eds., *Readings in ethical theory*. 2nd ed. New York: Appleton-Century-Crofts, 1970, 690–703.
16. Ross, W. D. *The right and the good*. Oxford: Clarendon Press, 1930.
17. Sahakian, W. S. *Ethics: An introduction to theories and problems*. New York: Barnes & Noble, 1974.
18. Stirner, M. *The ego and his own*. Trans. S. T. Byington, ed. Carroll, J. rev. ed. London: Jonathan Cape, 1971.
19. Taylor, A. E. *Plato: The man and his work*. 7th ed. London: Methuen, 1960. (First published, 1926.)

269

CHAPTER TWO

1. Bentham, J. An introduction to the principles of morals and legislation (1879). In Bowring, J., ed., *The Works of Jeremy Bentham*. Vol. 1. New York: Russell & Russell, 1962.
2. Frankena, W. K. *Ethics*. 2nd ed. Englewood Cliffs, N.J.: Prentice-Hall, 1973.
3. Garner, R. T., and Rosen, B. *Moral philosophy: A systematic introduction to normative ethics and meta-ethics*. New York: Macmillan, 1967.
4. Hospers, J. *Human conduct: Problems of ethics*. New York: Harcourt Brace Jovanovich, 1972.
5. Mill, J. S. *Utilitarianism, liberty, and representative government*. New York: E. P. Dutton, 1951.
6. Rashdall, H. *The theory of good and evil*. Vol. 1. London: Oxford University Press, 1924.
7. Rawls, J. Two concepts of rules. *Philosophical Review* (1955) 64: 3–32.
8. Taylor, P. W., ed. *Problems of moral philosophy: An introduction to ethics*. 2nd ed. Encino, Cal.: Dickenson, 1972.

CHAPTER THREE

1. Carritt, E. F. *The theory of morals*. London: Oxford University Press, 1928.
2. Cudworth, R. *A treatise concerning eternal and immutable morality*. London, 1731.
3. Garner, R. T., and Rosen, B. *Moral philosophy: A systematic introduction to normative ethics and meta-ethics*. New York: Macmillan, 1967.
4. Kant, I. Fundamental principles of the metaphysic of morals. In Taylor, P. W., ed., *Problems of moral philosophy: An introduction to ethics*. 2nd ed. Encino, Cal.: Dickenson, 1972.
5. Kant, I. *Lectures on ethics*. Trans. Louis Infeld. New York: Harper & Row, 1963.
6. Ross, W. D. *Foundations of ethics*. Oxford: Clarendon Press, 1939.
7. Ross, W. D. *The right and the good*. Oxford: Clarendon Press, 1930.
8. Sartre, J.-P. *Existentialism*. Trans. Bernard Frechtman. New York: Philosophical Library, 1947.

CHAPTER FOUR

1. Ayer, A. J. *Language, truth and logic*. New York: Dover, 1946.
2. Brandt, R. B. *Ethical theory*. Englewood Cliffs, N.J.: Prentice-Hall, 1959.
3. Ewing, A. C. *The definition of good*. New York: Macmillan, 1947.
4. Firth, R. Ethical absolutism and the ideal observer. *Philosophy and Phenomenological Research* (1952) 12: 317–45. In W. Sellars and J. Hospers, eds., *Readings in Ethical Theory*. 2nd ed. New York: Appleton-Century-Crofts, 1970, 200–21.
5. Frankena, W. K. *Ethics*. 2nd ed. Englewood Cliffs, N.J.: Prentice-Hall, 1973.
6. Hare, R. M. *Freedom and reason*. Oxford: Clarendon Press, 1963.
7. Hare, R. M. *The language of morals*. Oxford: Clarendon Press, 1963.
8. Hume, D. *A treatise of human nature*. Ed. L. A. Selby-Bigge. 3 vols. Oxford: Clarendon Press, 1896; reprinted 1958.
9. Kant, I. *Critique of pure reason*. Trans. J. M. D. Meiklejohn. *Great books of the western*

world. Vol. 42. Chicago: Encyclopaedia Britannica, 1952.

10. Kant, I. *Lectures on ethics*. Trans. Louis Infeld. London: Methuen, and New York: Harper & Brothers 1930.
11. Moore, G. E. *Ethics*. New York: Oxford University Press, 1965.
12. Moore, G. E. *Principia ethica*. Cambridge: Cambridge University Press, 1959.
13. Nowell-Smith, P. H. *Ethics*. London: Penguin, 1954.
14. Perry, R. B. *Realms of value*. Cambridge, Mass.: Harvard University Press, 1954.
15. Popper, K. R. *Conjectures and refutations: The growth of scientific knowledge*. 3rd ed. London: Routledge & Kegan Paul, 1969.
16. Popper, K. R. *The logic of scientific discovery*. New York: Basic, 1959.
17. Prichard, H. A. *Moral obligation*. New York: Oxford University Press, 1950.
18. Ross, W. D. *Foundations of ethics*. Oxford: Clarendon Press, 1939.
19. Ross, W. D. *The right and the good*. Oxford: Clarendon Press, 1930.
20. Sellars, W. Science and ethics. A revised version of a paper read to the Phoebe Griffin Noyes Library Association, Old Lyme, Conn., 26 January 1960.
21. Sharp, F. C. *Ethics*. New York: Appleton-Century-Crofts, 1928.
22. Sidgwick, H. *The methods of ethics*. London: Macmillan, 1913.
23. Stevenson, C. L. *Ethics and language*. New Haven, Conn.: Yale University Press, 1944.
24. Stevenson, C. L. *Facts and values*. New Haven, Conn.: Yale University Press, 1963.
25. Westermarck. E. *Ethical relativity*. New York: Harcourt, Brace & World, 1932.
26. Westermarck, E. *The origin and development of the moral ideas*. 2 vols. New York: Macmillan, 1906.

CHAPTER FIVE

1. Alston, W. P. Comments on Kohlberg's 'From Is to Ought.' In Michel, T., ed., *Cognitive development and epistemology*. New York: Academic, 1971, 269–84.
2. Aronfreed, J. Moral development from the standpoint of a general psychological theory. In Lickona, T., ed., *Moral development and behavior: Theory, research, and social issues*. New York: Holt, 1976, 54–70.
3. Bandura, A. *Social learning theory*. New York: General Learning, 1971.
4. Bandura, A. *Social learning theory*. Englewood Cliffs, N.J.: Prentice-Hall, 1977.
5. Bateson, G. *Steps to an ecology of mind*. New York: Ballantine, 1972.
6. Bentham, J. *The works of Jeremy Bentham*. Ed. J. Bowring. New York: Russell & Russell, 1962.
7. Berkowitz, L. *Development of motives and values in a child*. New York: Basic, 1964.
8. Hilgard, E., and Atkinson, R. *Introduction to psychology*. 6th ed. New York: Harcourt Brace Jovanovich, 1975.
9. Hoffman, M. Conscience, personality, and socialization techniques. *Human Development* (1970) 13: 90–126.
10. Kant, I. *Lectures on ethics*. Trans. Louis Infeld. New York: Harper & Row, 1963.
11. Kohlberg, L. The child as a moral philosopher. No. 21 in *Readings in developmental psychology today*. Del Mar, Cal.: CRM Books, 1970, 109–15.
12. Kohlberg, L. Continuities in childhood and adult moral development revisited. In Baltes, P., and Shaie, K. W., eds., *Life-span developmental psychology: Personality and socialization*. New York: Academic, 1973.

13. Kohlberg, L. Development of moral character and moral ideology. In Hoffman, H., and Hoffman, L., eds., *Review of child development research*. Vol. 1. New York: Russell Sage foundation, 1964.

14. Kohlberg, L. Education for justice: A modern statement of the Platonic view. Ernest Burton lecture on moral education, Harvard University, 23 April 1968.

15. Kohlberg, L. From is to ought: How to commit the naturalistic fallacy and get away with it in the study of moral development. In Mischel, T., ed., *Cognitive development and epistemology*. New York: Academic, 1971, 151–235.

16. Kohlberg, L. Moral development and identification. In *The 62nd yearbook of the national society for the study of education*. Chicago: University of Chicago Press, 1963.

17. Kohlberg, L. Moral stages and moralization. In Lickona, T., ed., *Moral development and behavior: Theory, research, and social issues*. New York: Holt, Rinehart & Winston, 1976, 31–53.

18. Kohlberg, L. Stage and sequence: The cognitive-developmental approach to socialization. In Goslin, D., ed., *Handbook of socialization theory and research*. Chicago: Rand McNally, 1969.

19. Kohlberg, L. Stages and aging in moral development: Some speculations. *Gerontologist* (1973) 13: 497–502.

20. Kurtines, W., and Greif, E. B. The development of moral thought: Review and evaluation of Kohlberg's approach. *Psychological Bulletin* (1974) 81: 453–70.

21. Mancuso, J., and Sarbin, T. A paradigmatic analysis of psychological issues at the interface of jurisprudence and moral conduct. In Lickona, T., ed., *Moral development and behavior: Theory, research, and social issues*. New York: Holt, Rinehart & Winston, 1976, 326–41.

22. Miller, D., and Swanson, F. *Inner conflict and defenses*. New York: Holt, Rinehart & Winston, 1960.

23. Mischel, W., and Mischel, H. N. A cognitive social-learning approach to morality and self-regulation. In Lickona, T., ed., *Moral development and behavior: Theory, research, and social issues*. New York: Holt, Rinehart & Winston, 1976, 84–107.

24. Paterson, R. W. K. *The nihilistic egoist: Max Stirner*. London: Oxford University Press, 1971.

25. Piaget, J. *The moral judgment of the child*. New York: Free Press, 1965.

26. Piaget, J. *The origins of intelligence in children*. New York: International Universities Press, 1952.

27. Piaget, J. *Psychology of intelligence*. New York: Harcourt, Brace, 1950.

28. Rest, J. R., Cooper, D., Coder, R., Masanz, J., and Anderson D. Judging the important issues in moral dilemmas–An objective measure of development. *Developmental Psychology* (1974) 10: 491–501.

29. Sidgwick, H. *The methods of ethics*. London: Macmillan, 1913.

30. Spinoza, B. *Ethics*. Trans. W. Hale White. London: Oxford University Press, 1927.

31. Stevenson, C. L. *Ethics and language*. New Haven, Conn.: Yale University Press, 1944.

32. Stevenson, C. L. *Facts and values*. New Haven, Conn.: Yale University Press, 1963.

33. Stirner, M. *The ego and his own*. Rev. ed. Trans. Steven T. Byington, ed. John Carrol. London: Jonathan Cape, 1971.

34. Taylor, J. G. *The behavioral basis of perception*. New Haven, Conn.: Yale University Press, 1962.

35. Westermarck, E. *Ethical relativity*. New York: Harcourt, Brace & World, 1932.

36. Westermarck, E. *The origin and development of the moral ideas*. 2 vols. New York: Macmillan, 1906.

CHAPTER SIX

1. Albrecht, S. L., and Carpenter, K. E. Attitudes as predictors of behavior versus behavior intentions: A convergence of research traditions. *Sociometry* (1976) 39: 1–10.

2. Aronfreed, J. The concept of internalization. In Goslin, D.A., ed., *Handbook of socialization theory and research*. Chicago: Rand McNally, 1969.

3. Bandura, A. *Social Learning Theory*. Englewood Cliffs, N.J.: Prentice-Hall, 1977.

4. Bandura, A., and Huston, A. Identification as a process of incidental learning. *Journal of Abnormal and Social Psychology* (1961) 63:311–18.

5. Bandura, A., and McDonald, F. J. The influence of social reinforcement and the behavior of models in shaping children's moral judgment. *Journal of Abnormal and Social Psychology* (1963) 67: 274–81.

6. Bandura, A., and Walters, R. *Social learning and personality development*. New York: Holt, Rinehart, & Winston, 1963.

7. Beloff, H., and Patron, X. Bronfenbrenner's moral dilemmas in Britain: Children, their peers and their parents. *International Journal of Psychology* (1970) 5: 27–32.

8. Benedict, R. *The chrysanthemum and the sword*. Boston: Houghton Mifflin, 1946.

9. Boehm, L. D. The development of conscience: A comparison of American children of different mental and socioeconomic levels. *Child Development* (1962) 33: 575–90.

10. Britton, J. H., Britton, J. O., and Fisher, C. F. Perceptions of children's moral and emotional behavior: A comparison of Finnish and American children. *Human Development* (1969) 12:55–63.

11. Bronfenbrenner, U. Reactions to social pressure from adults versus peers among Soviet day school and boarding school pupils in the perspective of an American sample. *Journal of Personality and Social Psychology* (1970) 57: 179–89.

12. Bronfenbrenner, U. Reactions to social pressure from peers versus adults among Soviet and American school children. *International Journal of Psychology* (1967) 2: 199–207.

13. Bronfenbrenner, U. The role of age, sex, class, and culture in studies of moral development. *Religious Education* (1962) 57: 3–17.

14. Bronfenbrenner, U. Some familial antecedents of responsibility and leadership in adolescents. Petrullo, N. L., and Bass, B., eds., *Leadership and interpersonal behavior*. New York: Holt, Rinehart, & Winston, 1961, 239–72.

15. Bronfenbrenner, U. Soviet methods of character education. *American Psychologist* (1962) 17: 550–64.

16. Campagna, A. F., and Harter, S. Moral judgment in sociopathic and normal children. *Journal of Personality and Social Psychology* (1975) 31: 199–205.

17. Chesser, E. *The sexual, marital, and family relationships of the English woman*. London: Hutchison Medical Publishers, 1956.

18. Cheyne, J. A. Punishment and "reasoning" in the development of self-control. Paper presented at the Society for Research in Child Development, Santa Monica, Cal., 1969.

19. Cheyne, J. A. Some parameters of punishment affecting resistance to deviation and generalization of a prohibition. *Child Development* (1971) 42: 1249–61.

20. Coogan, J. E. Religion: A preventive of delinquency. *Federal Probation* (1954) 18: 25–29. Cited in Hirschi, T., and Stark, R. Hellfire and delinquency. *Social Problems* (1969) 17: 202–13.

21. Crowley, P. M. Effects of training upon objectivity of moral judgment in grade school children. *Journal of Personality and Social Psychology* (1968) 8: 228–32.

22. Dedman, J. The relationship between religious attitude and attitude towards premarital sex relations. *Marriage & Family Living* (1959) 21: 171–76.

23. Devereux, E. C., Jr., Bronfenbrenner, U., and Rogers, R. R. Child rearing in England and the United States: A cross-cultural comparison. *Journal of Marriage & the Family* (1969) 31: 257–70.

24. Devereux, E. C., Jr., Bronfenbrenner, U., and Suci, G. J. Patterns of parent behavior in the United States and West Germany: A cross-national comparison. *International Social Science Journal* (UNESCO) (1962) 14: 488–506.

25. Durkin, D. Children's concepts of justice: A comparison with the Piaget data. *Child Development* (1959) 30: 59–67.

26. Erickson, E. H. *Childhood and society.* New York: Norton, 1950.

27. Fishkin, J., Keniston, K., and MacKinnon, C. Moral reasoning and political ideology. *Journal of Personality and Social Psychology* (1973) 27: 109–19.

28. Fodor, E. M. Delinquency and susceptibility to social influence among adolescents as a function of level of moral development. *Journal of Social Psychology* (1972) 86: 257–60.

29. Fodor, E. M. Resistance to social influence among adolescents as a function of level of moral development. *Journal of Social Psychology* (1971) 85: 121–26.

30. Freud, A. *The ego and the mechanisms of defense.* New York: International Universities Press, 1946.

31. Garbarino, J., and Bronfenbrenner, U. The socialization of moral judgment and behavior in cross-cultural perspective. In Lickona, T., ed., *Moral development and behavior: Theory, research, and social issues.* New York: Holt, Rinehart & Winston (1975): 70–83.

32. Gorsuch, R. L., and Aleshire, D. Christian faith and ethnic prejudice: A review and interpretation of research. *Journal for the Scientific Study of Religion* (1974) 13: 281–307.

33. Gorsuch, R. L., and Barnes, M. L. Stages of ethical reasoning and moral norms of Carib youths. *Journal of Cross-Cultural Psychology* (1973): 283–301.

34. Gorsuch, R. L., and Smith, R. A. Changes in college students' evaluations of moral behavior: 1969 vs. 1939, 1949, 1958. *Journal of Personality and Social Psychology* (1972) 24: 381–91.

35. Grim, P., Kohlberg, L., and White S. Some relationships between conscience and attentional processes. *Journal of Personality and Social Psychology* (1968) 8: 239–53.

36. Grinder, R. E. Relations between behavioral and cognitive dimension of conscience in middle childhood. *Child Development* (1964) 35: 881–91.

37. Grinder, R. E., and McMichael, R. E. Cultural influence on conscience development: Resistance to temptation and guilt among Samoans and American Caucasians. *Journal of Abnormal and Social Psychology* (1963) 66: 503–7.

38. Haan, N. M., Smith, M. B., and Block J. Moral reasoning of young adults: Political-social behavior, family background, and personality correlates. *Journal of Personality and Social Psychology* (1968) 10: 183–201.

39. Hardeman, M. Children's moral reasoning. *Journal of Genetic Psychology* (1972) 120: 49–59.
40. Hartshorne, H., and May, M. A. *Studies in the nature of character. Vol. I: studies in deceit.* New York: Macmillan, 1928.
41. Henshel, A. The relationship between values and behavior: A developmental hypothesis. *Child Development* (1971) 42: 1997–2007.
42. Hirschi, T., and Stark, R. Hellfire and delinquency. *Social Problems* (1969) 17: 202–13.
43. Hoffman, M. L. Moral development. In P. H. Musson, ed. *Carmichael's manual of child psychology.* 3rd ed. Vol. 2. New York: Wiley, 1970, 261–359.
44. Hogan, R. A dimension in moral judgement. *Journal of Consulting and Clinical Psychology* (1970) 35: 205–12.
45. Hogan, R. Moral conduct and moral character: A psychological perspective. *Psychological Bulletin* (1973) 79: 217–31.
46. Hogan, R. Moral development and the structure of personality. In DePalma, D. J., and Foley, J. M., *Moral development: Current theory and research.* New York: Erlbaum and Associates, 1975.
47. Holstein, C. B. Moral judgment change in early adolescence and middle age: A longitudinal study. Paper presented at the Society for Research in Child Development, Philadelphia, 1973.
48. Ives, Rev. D. S. *New York Times,* 5 January 1865. Quoted in Garrison, Karl C. *Psychology of adolescence.* Englewood Cliffs, N. J.: Prentice-Hall, 1965, 174.
49. Jensen, L. C. *What's right? What's wrong?* Washington, D.C.: Public Affairs Press, 1975.
50. Jensen, L. C., and Hafen, G. E. The effect of training children to consider intentions when making moral judgments. *Journal of Genetic Psychology* (1973) 122: 223–44.
51. Jensen, L. C., and Hughston, K. The effect of training children to make moral judgments that are independent of sanctions. *Journal of Developmental Psychology* (1971) 5: 367.
52. Jensen, L. C., and Rytting, A. Changing children's beliefs about punishment. *British Journal of Social and Clinical Psychology* (1975) 14: 91–92.
53. Jensen, L. C., and Rytting, M. The effects of information and relatedness on children's belief in immanent justice. *Journal of Developmental Psychology* (1972) 7: 93–97.
54. Jensen, L. C., and Saadatmand, B. A cross-cultural investigation of the influence of parents, culture, and age on the moral reasoning of children. Paper presented at of the Society for Research in Child Development, Philadelphia, 1973.
55. Jensen, L. C., Vance, B., and Cropper, L. The effects of training children to cope with reciprocity. Unpublished manuscript. Brigham Young University, 1972.
56. Johnson, R. C., Dokecki, L., and Mowrer, O. H. *Conscience, contract and social reality.* New York: Holt, Rinehart & Winston, 1972.
57. Keasey, C. B. Implicators of cognitive development for moral reasoning. In DePalma, D. J., and Foley, J. M., eds., *Moral development: Current theory and research.* New York: Lawrence Erlbaum Associates, 1975, 39–56.
58. Keasey, C. B. The lack of sex differences in the moral judgments of preadolescence. *Journal of Social Psychology* (1972) 86: 157–58.

59. Keasey, C. B. Social participation as a factor in the moral development of pre-adolescents. *Developmental Psychology* (1971) 5: 216–20.
60. Klinger, E., Albaum, A., and Hetherington, M. Factors influencing severity of moral judgment. *Journal of Social Psychology* (1964) 63: 319–26.
61. Klinger, M.R.B. Moral values across cultures. *Personnel and Guidance Journal* (1962) 41: 139–43.
62. Kohlberg, L. Development of moral character and ideology. In Hoffman, M. L., and Hoffman, L. W., eds., *Review of child development research*, Vol. 1. New York: Social Science Research Council, 1964.
63. Kohlberg, L. Education for justice: A modern statement of the Platonic view. In Sizer, N. F., and Sizer, T. P., eds., *Moral education: Five lectures*. Cambridge, Mass.: Harvard University Press, 1970, 58–83.
64. Kohlberg, L. Relationships between the development of moral judgment and moral conduct. Paper presented at the Society for Research in Child Development, Minneapolis, 26 March 1965.
65. Kohlberg, L. Stage and sequence: The cognitive-developmental approach to socialization. In Goslin, D. A., ed., *Handbook of socialization theory and research*. Chicago: Rand McNally, 1969, 347–480.
66. Kohlberg, L., and Kramer, R. Continuities and discontinuities in childhood and adult moral development. *Human Development* (1969) 12: 93–120.
67. Krebs, R. L. Teacher perceptions of children's moral behavior. *Psychology in the Schools* (1969) 6: 394–95.
68. Kurtines, W., and Greif, E. B. The development of moral thought: Review and evaluation of Kohlberg's approach. *Psychological Bulletin* (1974) 81: 453–70.
69. LaPiere, R. Attitudes vs. action. *Social Forces* (1934) 13: 230–37.
70. LaVoie, J. C. A developmental study of reasoning and its effects on resistance to deviation in children of high and low maturity of moral judgment. Paper presented at the Society for Research in Child Development, Philadelphia, 1973.
71. LaVoie, J. C. The effects of an aversive stimulus, a rationale, and sex of child on punishment effectiveness and generalization. *Child Development* (1973) 44: 505–10.
72. Lazarowritze, R., Stephan, W. G., and Friedman, S. T. Effects of moral justification and moral reasoning on altruism. *Developmental Psychology* (1976) 4: 353–54.
73. Leming, J. S. Moral reasoning, sense of control, and social-political activism among adolescents. *Adolescence* (1974) 9: 507–28.
74. Lickona, T. Piaget misunderstood: A critique of the criticism of his theory of moral development. *Merrill-Palmer Quarterly of Behavior and Development* (1969) 15: 337–50.
75. Light, H. K. Attitudes of rural and urban adolescent girls toward selected concepts. *Family Coordinator*, July 1970, 225–27.
76. London, P., Schulman, R. E., and Black, M. S. Religion, guilt, and ethical standards. *Journal of Social Psychology* (1964) 63: 145–59.
77. Mead, M. Social change and cultural surrogates. In Kluckhohn, C., and Murray, H. A., eds., *Personality in nature, society, and culture*. 2nd ed. New York: Knopf, 1955, 651–62.
78. Medinnus, G. R. Behavioral and cognitive measures of conscience development. *Journal of Genetic Psychology* (1966) 109: 147–50.
79. Middleton, R., and Putney, S. Religion, normative standards and behavior. *Sociometry* (1962) 25: 141–52.

80. Mischel, W. A social learning view of sex differences in behavior. In Maccoby, E. E., ed., *The development of sex differences*. Stanford, Cal.: Stanford University Press, 1966, 56–81.

81. Mischel, W., and Mischel, H. N. A cognitive social-learning approach to morality and self-regulation. In Lickona, T., ed., *Moral development and behavior: Theory, research, and social issues*. New York: Holt, Rinehart & Winston, 1976, 84–107.

82. Moir, D. J. Egocentrism and the emergence of conventional morality in preadolescent girls. *Child Development* (1974) 45: 299–304.

83. Muir, D. E., and Weinstein, E. A. The social debt: An investigation of lower-class and middle-class norms of social obligation. *American Sociological Review* (1962) 27: 532–39.

84. Ossowska, M., *Social determinants of moral ideas*. Philadelphia: University of Pennsylvania Press, 1970.

85. Nakasato, Y., and Aoyama, Y. Some relations between children's resistance to temptation and their moral judgment. *Reports of the National Research Institute of Police Science research on prevention of crime and delinquency* (1972) 13: 62–70.

86. Nelsen, E. A., Grinder, R. E., and Biaggio, A. M. Relationships among behavioral, cognitive-developmental, and self support measures of morality and personality. *Multivariate Behavioral Research* (1969) 4: 483–500.

87. Nelsen, E. A., Grinder, R. E., and Challas, J. H. Resistance to temptation and moral judgment: Behavioral correlates of Kohlberg's measure of moral development. Mimeographed paper, University of Wisconsin, 1968.

88. Piaget, J. *The moral judgment of the child*. New York: Harcourt, Brace & World, 1932.

89. Podd, M. H. Ego identity status and morality: The relationship between two developmental constructs. *Developmental Psychology* (1969) 37: 225–52.

90. Rest, J. Recent research on an objective test in moral judgment: How the important issues of a moral dilemma are defined. In DePalma, D. J., and Foley, J. M., eds., *Moral development: Current theory and research*. New York: Wiley, 1975, 75–94.

91. Rest, J. New approaches in the assessment of moral judgment. In Lickona, T., ed., *Moral development and behavior*. New York: Holt, 1976, 198–218.

92. Rest, J. R., Cooper, D. Coder, R., Masanz, J., and Anderson, D. Judging the important issues in moral dilemmas—an objective measure of development. *Developmental Psychology* (1974) 10: 491–501.

93. Rodgers, R. R., Bronfenbrenner, U., and Devereux, E. C., Jr. Standards of social behavior among school children in four cultures. *International Journal of Psychology* (1968) 3: 31–41.

94. Rokeach, M. *Beliefs, attitudes and values*. San Francisco: Jossey-Bass, 1968.

95. Rokeach, M. Faith, hope and bigotry. *Psychology Today* (1970) 3: 33–37.

96. Rokeach, M. *The nature of human values*. New York: Free Press, 1975.

97. Rokeach, M. Religious values and social compassion. *Review of Religious Research* (1969) 11: 3–23.

98. Rokeach, M. Value systems in religion. *Review of Religious Research* (1969) 11: 24–39.

99. Rubin, K. H., and Schneider, F. W. The relationship between moral judgment, egocentrism, and altruistic behavior. *Child Development* (1973) 44: 661–65.

100. Saltzstein, H. D., Diamond, R. M., and Belenky, M. Moral judgment level and conformity behavior. *Developmental Psychology* (1972) 7: 327–36.

101. Schneider, F. W., and Shaw, M. E. Sanctioning behavior in Negro and in white populations. *Journal of Social Psychology* (1970) 81: 63–72.

102. Schwartz, S. Elicitation of moral obligation and self-sacrificing behavior: An experimental study of volunteering to be a bone-marrow donor. *Journal of Personality and Social Psychology* (1970) 15: 283–93.
103. Schwartz, S. H. Moral decision making and behavior. In Maccaulay, J., and Berkowitz, L., eds., *Altruism and helping behavior.* New York: Academic, (1970) 127–43.
104. Schwartz, S. Words, deeds, and the perception of consequences and responsibility in action situations. *Journal of Personality and Social Psychology* (1968) 10: 232–42.
105. Schwartz, S., and Clausen, G. Responsibility, norms and helping in an emergency. *Journal of Personality and Social Psychology* (1970) 16: 299–310.
106. Schwartz, S., Feldman, K., Brown, M., and Heingartner, A. Some personality correlates of conduct in two situations of moral conflict. *Journal of Personality* (1969) 37: 41–58.
107. Staub, E. *The development of prosocial behavior in children.* New York: General Learning, 1975.
108. Staub, E. Effects of persuasion and modeling on delay of gratification. *Developmental Psychology* (1972) 6: 166–77.
109. Staub, E. Helping a person in distress: The influence of implicit and explicit "rules" of conduct on children and adults. *Journal of Personality and Social Psychology* (1971) 17: 137–44.
110. Thompson, G. G., and Gardner, E. F. Adolescents' perceptions of happy-successful living. *Journal of Genetic Psychology* (1969) 115: 107–20.
111. Tomlinson-Keasey, C., and Keasey, C. B. The mediating role of cognitive development in moral judgment. *Child Development* (1974) 45: 291–98.
112. Turiel, E. An experimental test of the sequentiality of developmental stages in the child's moral judgments. *Journal of Personality and Social Psychology* (1966) 3: 611–18.
113. Turiel, E., and Rothman, G. The influence of reasoning on behavior choices at different stages of moral development. *Child Development* (1972) 43: 741–56.
114. Wright, D. *The psychology of moral behavior.* Baltimore: Penguin, 1975.
115. Wright, D., and Cox, E. A study of the relationship between moral judgment and religious belief in a sample of English adolescents. *Journal of Social Psychology* (1967) 135–44.
116. Yankelovich, D. *The new morality.* New York: McGraw-Hill, 1974.

CHAPTER SEVEN

1. Bronfenbrenner, U. The role of age, sex, class and culture in studies of moral development. *Religious Education* (1962) 57 (Research Supplement): 3–17. Cited in Lickona, T., ed., *Moral development and behavior: Theory, research, and social issues.* New York: Holt, Rinehart & Winston, 1976, 71.
2. Hoffman, M. Moral development. In Mussen, P., ed., *Carmichael's manual of child psychology.* New York: Wiley, 1970.
3. Jensen, L. C., and Hafen, G. E. The effect of training children to consider intentions when making moral judgments. *Journal of Genetic Psychology* (1973) 122: 223–44.

4. Jensen, L. C., and Hughston, K. The effect of training children to make moral judgments that are independent of sanctions. *Journal of Developmental Psychology* (1971) 5: 367.

5. Jensen, L. C., and Larm, C. Effects of two training procedures on intentionality in moral judgments among children. *Developmental Psychology* (1970) 2: 310.

6. Jensen, L. C., and Rytting, A. Changing children's beliefs about punishment. *British Journal of Social and Clinical Psychology* (1975) 14: 91–92.

7. Jensen, L. C., and Vance, B. Changing children's beliefs, about immanent justice. In *Effects of training on the ethical reasoning of children*. Report to U.S. Department of Health, Education and Welfare, Office of Education, November 1972.

8. Jensen, L. C., Vance, B., and Cropper, L. The effects of training children to cope with reciprocity. Paper presented at the Society for Research in Child Development, Philadelphia, April 1973.

9. Kelman, H. Compliance, identification, and internalization: Three processes of attitude change. *Journal of Conflict Resolution* (1958) 2: 51–60.

10. Kohlberg, L. Development of moral character and moral ideology. In Hoffman, M. L., and Hoffman, L. W., eds., *Review of Child Development Research*. New York: Russell Sage Foundation, 1964, 383–431.

11. Lickona, T. An experimental test of Piaget's theory of moral development. Paper presented at the Society for Research in Child Development, Philadelphia, April 1973.

12. Peck, R. F., and Havighurst, R. J. *The psychology of character development*. New York: Wiley, 1962.

13. Piaget, J. *The moral judgment of the child*. New York: Harcourt, Brace, 1932.

14. Scott, D. F. *Internalization of norms: A sociological theory of moral commitment*. Englewood Cliffs, N.J.: Prentice-Hall, 1971.

CHAPTER EIGHT

1. Arbuthnot, J. Modification of moral judgment through role playing. *Developmental Psychology* (1975) 11: 319–24.

2. Bandura, A., and Walters, R. *Social learning and personality development*. New York: Holt, Rinehart, & Winston, 1963.

3. Beloff, H., and Temperley, K. The power of the peers: Bronfenbrenner's moral dilemmas in Scotland. *Scottish Educational Studies* (1972) 4: 3–8.

4. Berkowitz, L., and Walker, N. Laws and moral judgments. *Sociometry* (1967) 30: 410–22.

5. Bronfenbrenner, U. The changing Soviet family. In Brown, D. R., ed., *The role and status of women in the Soviet Union*. New York: Teachers College Press, Columbia University, 1968.

6. Bronfenbrenner, U. Response to pressure from peers versus adults among Soviet and American school children. *International Journal of Psychology* (1967) 2: 199–207.

7. Bronfenbrenner, U. Soviet methods of character education: Some implications for research. *American Psychologist* (1962) 17: 550–64.

8. Bronfenbrenner, U. *Two worlds of childhood: U.S.A. and U.S.S.R.* New York: Russell Sage Foundation, 1970.

9. Campagna, A. F., and Harter, S. Moral judgment in sociopathic and normal children. *Journal of Personality and Social Psychology* (1975) 31: 199–205.

10. Cowan, P. A., Langer, J., Heavenrich, J., and Nathanson, M. Social learning and Piaget's cognitive theory of moral development. *Journal of Personality and Social Psychology* (1969) 11: 261–74.

11. Garbarino, J., and Bronfenbrenner, U. The socialization of moral judgment and behavior in cross-cultural perspective. In Lickona, T., ed., *Moral development and behavior: Theory, research, and social issues.* New York: Holt, Rinehart & Winston, 1976, 70–83.

12. Hartup, W. W., and Yonas, A. Developmental psychology. In Mussen, P. H., and Rosenzweig, M. R., eds., *Annual Review of Psychology* (1971) 22: 337–92.

13. Keasey, C. B. Experimentally induced changes in moral opinions and reasoning. *Journal of Personality and Social Psychology* (1973) 26: 30–38.

14. Keasey, C. B. Social participation as a factor in the moral development of preadolescents. *Developmental Psychology* (1971) 5: 216–20.

15. Kohlberg, L. Moral stages and moralization: The cognitive developmental approach. In Lickona, T., ed., *Moral development and behavior: Theory, research, and social issues.* New York: Holt, Rinehart & Winston, 1976, 31–53.

16. Lickona, T. An experimental test of Piaget's theory of moral development. Paper presented at the Society for Research in Child Development, Philadelphia, April 1973.

17. Matefy, R. E., and Acksen, B. A. The effect of role-playing discrepant positions on change in moral judgments and attitudes. *Journal of Genetic Psychology* (1976) 128: 189–200.

18. Merchant, R. L., and Rebelsky, F. Effects of participation in rule formulation on the moral judgment of children. *Genetic Psychology monographs* (1972) 85: 287–304.

19. Moir, D. J. Egocentrism and the emergence of conventional morality in preadolescent girls. *Child Development* (1974) 45: 299–304.

20. Piaget, J. *The moral judgment of the child.* New York: Harcourt, Brace, 1932.

21. Prentice, N. M. The influence of live and symbolic modeling on promoting moral judgment of adolescent delinquents. *Journal of Abnormal Psychology* (1972) 80: 157–61.

22. Selman, R. *First thing: Social reasoning.* New York: Guidance Associates, 1974.

23. Selman, R. *First thing: Values.* New York: Guidance Associates, 1971.

24. Selman, R. L. The relation of role taking to the development of moral judgment in children. *Child Development* (1971) 42: 79–91.

25. Selman, R. L. Social-cognitive understanding: A guide to educational and clinical practice. In Lickona, T., ed., *Moral development and behavior: Theory, research and social issues.* New York: Holt, Rinehart & Winston, 1976, 299–316.

CHAPTER NINE

1. Adler, A. *Social interest: A challenge to mankind.* New York: Capricorn, 1964.

2. Adler, A. *Understanding human nature.* Greenwich: Fawcett, 1954.

3. Adler, A. *What life should mean to you.* New York: Capricorn, 1958.

4. Allred, G. H. *How to strengthen your marriage and family.* Provo, Utah: Brigham Young University Press, 1976.

5. Ansbacher, H. L., and Ansbacher, R. R. *The individual psychology of Alfred Adler.* New York: Basic, 1956.
6. Arbuthnot, J. Modification of moral judgment through role playing. *Developmental Psychology* (1975) 11: 319–24.
7. Asch, S. E. *Social psychology.* Englewood Cliffs, N.J.: Prentice-Hall, 1942.
8. Bateson, G., Jackson, Don D., Haley, J., and Weakland, J. Toward a theory of schizophrenia. *Behavioral Science* (1956) 1: 251–64.
9. Bowen, M. Toward the differentiation of a self in one's own family. In Framo, J. L., ed., *Family interaction: A dialogue between family researchers and family therapists.* New York: Springer, 1972.
10. Bronfenbrenner, U. Some familial antecedents of responsibility and leadership in adolescents. In Petrullo, L., and Bass, B., eds., *Leadership and interpersonal behavior.* New York: Holt, Rinehart & Winston, 1961, 239–72.
11. Brow, A. W., Morrison, J., and Couch, G. B. Influence of affectual family relationships on character development. *Journal of Abnormal and Social Psychology* (1947): 422–28.
12. Cowan, P. A., Langer, J., Heavenrich, J., and Nathanson, M. Social learning and Piaget's cognitive theory of moral development. *Journal of Personality and Social Psychology* (1969) 11: 261–74.
13. Dinkmeyer, D., and McKay, G. D. *Raising a responsible child.* New York: Simon & Schuster, 1973.
14. Dreikurs, R. *Psychology in the classroom.* New York: Harper & Row, 1967.
15. Dreikurs, R., et al. *Adlerian family counseling: A manual for counseling centers.* Eugene, Ore.: University of Oregon Press, 1957.
16. Dreikurs, R., and Grey, L. *A new approach to discipline: Logical consequences.* New York: Hawthorn, 1968.
17. Dreikurs, R., and Soltz, V. *Children: The challenge.* New York: Meredith Press, 1964.
18. Ekstein, R. The schizophrenic adolescent's struggle toward and against separation and individuation. In Feinstein, S.C., and Giovacchini, P. L., eds., *Adolescent Psychiatry.* Vol. 2. New York: Basic, 1973, 5–24.
19. Erikson, E. *Childhood and society.* New York: Norton, 1950.
20. Erikson, E. *Identity: Youth and crisis.* New York: Norton, 1968.
21. Gallatin, J. E. *Adolescence and individuality: A conceptual approach to adolescent psychology.* New York: Harper & Row, 1975.
22. Giovacchini, P. L. The adolescent process and character formation: Clinical aspects—with reference to Dr. Masterson's 'The borderline adolescent.' In Feinstein, S.C., and Giovacchini, P. L., eds., *Adolescent Psychiatry.* Vol. 2. New York: Basic, 1973, 269–284.
23. Haley, J. The family of the schizophrenic: a model system. *The Journal of Nervous and Mental Disease* (1959) 129: 357–74. In Erickson, G. D. and Hogan, T. P., eds., *Family therapy: An introduction to theory and technique.* Monterey, Cal.: Brooks/Cole, 1972.
24. Haley, J. Speech sequences of normal and abnormal families with two children present. *Family Process* (1967) 6: 81–97.
25. Haley, J. *Strategies of psychotherapy.* New York: Grune & Stratton, 1963.
26. Hoffman, M. L. Moral development. In Mussen, P., ed., *Carmichael's manual of child psychology.* Vol. 2. New York: Wiley, 1970, 361–456.

27. Hoffman, M. L., and Saltzstein, H. D. Parent discipline and the child's moral development. *Journal of Personality and Social Psychology* (1967) 5: 45–47.
28. Holstein, C. B. *Parental determinants of the development of moral judgment.* Ph.D. dissertation, University of California, Berkeley, 1968.
29. Keasey, C. B. Experimentally induced changes in moral opinions and reasoning. *Journal of Personality and Social Psychology* (1973) 26: 30–38.
30. Kurtines, W., and Greif, E. B. The development of moral thought: Review and evaluation of Kohlberg's approach. *Psychological Bulletin* (1974) 81: 453–70.
31. Masterson, J. F. The borderline adolescent. In Feinstein, S.C., and Giovacchini, P. L., eds., *Adolescent Psychiatry.* Vol. 2. New York: Basic, 1973, 240–68.
32. Minuchin, S. *Families and family therapy.* Cambridge, Mass.: Harvard University Press, 1974.
33. Peck, R. F., and Havighurst, R. J. *The psychology of character development.* New York: Wiley, 1960.
34. Piaget, J. *The moral judgment of the child.* Harcourt, Brace, 1932.
35. Ralston, N., and Thomas, G. P. *The adolescent: Case studies for analysis.* New York: Chandler, 1974.
36. Rutherford, E., and Mussen, P. Generosity in nursery school boys. *Child Development* (1968) 39: 755–65.
37. Saltzstein, H. D. Social influence and moral development: A perspective on the role of parents and peers. In Lickona, T., ed., *Moral development and behavior: Theory, research, and social issues.* New York: Holt, Rinehart & Winston, 1976, 253–65.
38. Satir, V. *Conjoint family therapy.* Palo Alto, Cal.: Science and Behavior Books, 1967.
39. Sherif, M. A. A study of some social factors in perception. *Archives of Psychology* (1935) no. 187.
40. Shoffeit, P. G. *The moral development of children as a function of parental moral judgments and childrearing.* Ph.D. dissertation: George Peabody College for Teachers, 1971.
41. Tracy, J. J., and Cross, H. J. Antecedents of shift in moral judgment. *Journal of Personality and Social Psychology* (1973) 26: 238–44.
42. Turiel, E. An experimental test of the sequentiality of developmental stages in the child's moral judgments. *Journal of Personality and Social Psychology* (1966) 3: 611–18.
43. Watzlawick, P., Beavin, J. H., and Jackson, D. D. *Pragmatics of human communication.* New York: Norton, 1967.
44. Wynne, L., Ryckoff, I., Day, J., and Hirsch, S. Pseudomutuality in the family life of schizophrenics. *Psychiatry* (1958) 21: 205–20.

CHAPTER TEN

1. Acock, A. C., and DeFleur, M. L. A configuration approach to contingent consistency in the attitude-behavior relationship. *American Sociological Review* (1976) 34: 714–26.
2. Albrecht, S. L., and Carpenter, K. E. Attitudes as predictors of behavior versus behavior intentions: A convergence of research traditions. *Sociometry* (1976) 39: 1–10.
3. Bandura, A. *Social learning theory.* Englewood Cliffs, N.J.: Prentice-Hall, 1977.

4. DeFleur, M. L., and Westie, F. R. Verbal attitudes and overt acts: An experiment on the salience of attitudes. *American Sociological Review* (1958) 33: 667–73.
5. Kohlberg, L. From is to ought: How to commit the naturalistic fallacy and get away with it in the study of moral development. In Mischel, T., ed., *Cognitive development and epistemology.* New York: Academic, 1971, 151–235.
6. Kohlberg, L. Moral stages in moralization. In Lickona, T., ed., *Moral development and behavior: Theory, research, and social issues.* New York: Holt, Rinehart & Winston, 1976, 31–53.
7. Kohlberg, L. Stage and sequence: The cognitive-developmental approach to socialization. In Goslin, D. A., ed., *Handbook of socialization theory and research.* Chicago: Rand McNally, 1969, 347–480.
8. Kohlberg, L., Scharf, P., and Hiskey, J. The justice structure of the prison core: A theory and an intervention. *Prison Journal* (1972) 51, no. 2.
9. Kurtines, W., and Greif, E. B. The development of moral thought: Review and evaluation of Kohlberg's approach. *Psychological Bulletin* (1974) 81: 453–70.
10. Lickona, T. Critical issues in moral development and behavior. In Lickona, T., ed., *Moral Development and behavior: Theory, research, and social issues.* New York: Holt, Rinehart & Winston, 1976, 3–27.
11. Loevinger, J., and Wessler, R. *Measuring ego development.* Vols. 1 & 2. San Francisco: Jossey-Bass, 1970.
12. McCandless, B. R., and Evans, E. D. *Children and youth: Psychological development.* Hinsdale, Ill.: Dryden Press, 1976.
13. Mischel, T. Piaget: Cognitive conflict and the motivation of thought. In Mischel, T., ed., *Cognitive development and epistemology.* New York: Academic, 1971, 311–55.
14. Mischel, W., and Mischel, H. N. A cognitive social-learning approach to morality and self-regulations. In Lickona, T., ed., *Moral development and behavior: Theory, research, and social issues.* New York: Holt, Rinehart & Winston, 1976, 84–107.
15. Rest, J. R. Recent research on an objective test of moral judgment: How the important issues of a moral dilemma are defined. In DePalma, D. J., and Foley, J. M., eds., *Moral development: Current theory and research.* New York: Wiley, 1975, 75–94.
16. Simpson, E. L. Moral development research: A case of scientific cultural bias. *Human Development* (1974) 17: 81–106.
17. Warner, L. G., and DeFleur, M. L. Attitude as an interactional concept: Social constraint and social distance as intervening variables between attitudes and actions. *American Sociological Review* (1969) 34: 153–69.

CHAPTER ELEVEN

1. Buddha. The sermon at Benares. In Carus, P., *The gospel of Buddha.* Chicago: Open Court, 1915, 49–55.
2. Dickens, C. *A tale of two cities.* In *The works of Charles Dickens*, vol. 21, New York: Scribner's, 1899.
3. Dostoyevsky, Y. *Crime and punishment.* Trans. Constance Garnett. New York: Carlton House, n.d.
4. Hawthorne, N. *The scarlet letter.* Boston: Houghton, Mifflin, 1874.
5. Hugo, V. *Les miserables.* vol. 1. Trans. C. E. Wilbour. New York: A. L. Burt, n.d.

6. King, A. H. Literature and testimony. Commissioner's Lecture. Provo, Utah: Brigham Young University, 1972.

7. Leiser, B. M. *Liberty, justice, and morals: Contemporary value conflicts*. New York: Macmillan, 1973.

8. Machiavelli, N. *The prince*. Intro. S. G. W. Benjamin. The National Alumni, 1907.

9. Shakespeare, W. The merchant of Venice. In Harrison, G. B., ed., *Shakespeare: The complete works*. New York: Harcourt, Brace, & World, 1968.

10. Sophocles. Antigone. In Greene, D., and Lattimore, R., eds., *The complete Greek tragedies: Sophocles I*. Chicago: University of Chicago Press, 1954, 157–204.

11. Steinbeck, J. *Grapes of wrath*. New York: Viking, 1939.

12. Thoreau, H. D. Civil disobedience. In Thoreau, H. D., *A yankee in Canada*. Boston: Ticknor and Fields, 1866, 124–51.

13. Twain, M. *Adventures of Hucklebury Finn*. New York: Charles L. Webster, 1885.

CHAPTER TWELVE

1. Auerbach, C. The Communist Control Act of 1954: A proposed legal-political theory of free speech. *University of Chicago Law Review* (1956) 23: 173–220.

2. Berman, H. J. Philosophical aspects of American law. In Berman, H. J. ed., *Talks on American Law*. New York: Vintage, 1961, 221–35.

3. Bickel, A. M. The "uninhibited, robust, wide-open" First Amendment. In Cline, V. B. ed., *Where do you draw the line?* Provo, Utah: Brigham Young University Press, 1974, 63–78.

4. Bodenheimer, E. *Jurisprudence: The philosophy and methods of the law*. Cambridge, Mass.: Harvard University Press, 1962.

5. Devlin, P. *The enforcement of morals*. London: Oxford University Press, 1965.

6. Leiser, B. M. *Liberty, justice, and morals: contemporary value conflicts*. New York: Macmillan, 1973.

7. Meiklejohn, A. *Political freedom*. New York: Harper, 1948, 1960.

8. United States Reports: *Cases Adjudged in the Supreme Court*. Washington, D.C.: United States Government Printing Office.

Index